Sparks & Wiry Cries

songSLAM Songbook, Vol. 1

Curated by Martha Guth & Erika Switzer

Edited by Dennis Tobenski

www.newmusicshelf.com

NEWMUSICSHELF, INC.

Published in the United States of America
by NewMusicShelf, Inc.
34-29 32nd St., 3rd floor, Astoria, NY 11106
www.newmusicshelf.com

First printing 2020

This volume is dedicated to Judy Cope (1958-2019) of the Sorel Organization, who was instrumental in supporting the very first song*SLAM and the mission of* Sparks & Wiry Cries, *as well as the artistic endeavors of its co-founders.*

Contents

Acknowledgments

Thanks to each of our families for their support in this endeavor, to the board and the advisory board of Sparks, to Stephanie Blythe, Tom Cipullo, Margo Garrett, Kenneth Griffiths, Kayo Iwama, Graham Johnson, Deen Larsen, Paul Sperry, and Susan Youens, for their support and wise counsel.

Thank you to all of our songSLAM partners: Women on the Verge (Toronto), Buffalo Chamber Players, Art Song Lab (Vancouver), Fourth Coast Ensemble (Chicago), Source Song Festival (Minneapolis), Per Artem (Ljubljana), Re-Sung (London), Kerrytown Concert House (Ann Arbor), Cincinnati Song Initiative, and the National Association of Teachers of Singing.

Thank you to all of the administrative staff at Sparks, past and present: Victoria Browers, Lucy Fitz Gibbon, Jardena Gertler-Jaffe, Jesse Goldberg, Jennifer Hinnell, Michael Hoffman, and Amy Petrongelli.

— Martha Guth & Erika Switzer

Introduction

Sparks & Wiry Cries promotes the advancement and preservation of art song by providing opportunities to its creators and performers. Its activities include:

- Presentation of the *song*SLAM Festival in NYC
- Commission and premiere of new works
- Publication of the *Art Song Magazine*

Creation and co-production of the *song*SLAM competition for emerging composers, poets and performers around the world

The *Sparks & Wiry Cries* NYC *song*SLAM is a unique competition for emerging composer/performer teams to premiere new art song. With an eye to the democratic process and equality of access, sign-up is first come, first served, and the registration fee is nominal. During the competition itself, carried out in the poetry-slam tradition, audience members vote on their favorite performances. Cash prizes are awarded.

First premiered in NYC in 2015, the *song*SLAM has now been or will be presented in four countries and 10 different cities around the globe: NYC, Toronto, Vancouver, London, Ljubljana, Ann Arbor, Cincinnati, Chicago, Minneapolis, and Buffalo, with even more growth on the horizon. The songbook is a selection of sexteen of the most promising songs premiered since its inception. Many of them were prize winners, though not all.

— Martha Guth & Erika Switzer

Performance Notes

Liam Moore: Crepuscule

I will wade out
                    till my thighs are steeped in burn-
-ing flowers
I will take the sun in my mouth
and leap into the ripe air
                                Alive
                                        with closed eyes
to dash against darkness
                                in the sleeping curves of my
body
Shall enter fingers of smooth mastery
with chasteness of sea-girls
                                  Will I complete the mystery
of my flesh
I will rise
            After a thousand years
lipping
flowers
          And set my teeth in the silver of the moon

— E.E. Cummings, 1917

Composer's Note:

The rhythm and order of sonorities in the RH piano part in mm. 1-4 and both hands in mm. 56-59 may be modified at the performer's pleasure so long as the written "feel" of the music and first sonority in each measure are retained.

Haley Olson: at this time i could not breathe like the others

At this time I could not.
Breathe like the others perhaps.
It was from walking so close.
To the ground breaths always.
Came in gasps hitching as though.
A rope was pulling at my lungs.
But today a crack of thunder.
Not of Prospero but nature-made shook the isle.
And I stood to watch the sea swallow the rocks.
Breathing in the seawater with huge gulps.
This island is mine and the proof.
Is in my lungs.

Composer's Note:

This song is part of an ongoing cycle of songs about Caliban, an antagonist and the "monster" character in William Shakespeare's "The Tempest." Often seen and marginalized through the eyes of others for the entirety of the story, the island's original inhabitant and true heir is left alone at the play's conclusion. What then? Whether he reclaims his world with zeal or flees in fear is up to the director--and the audience. The seven poems, originally written by the composer in 2013, explore how Caliban grapples with a new identity, the remnants of cosmopolitan life, and the deafening solitude that follows. In this poem, the second in the cycle, Caliban recalls how he was seen as subservient, and how he is now finding his selfhood in his ownership of the island.

for Chloë, for Judith, and for Adrian
composed for songSLAM NYC III 2019

nothing at all

adapted from the cycle *Death is nothing at all.*

from a sermon by Henry Scott-Holland

DANIEL CASTELLANOS
(2019)

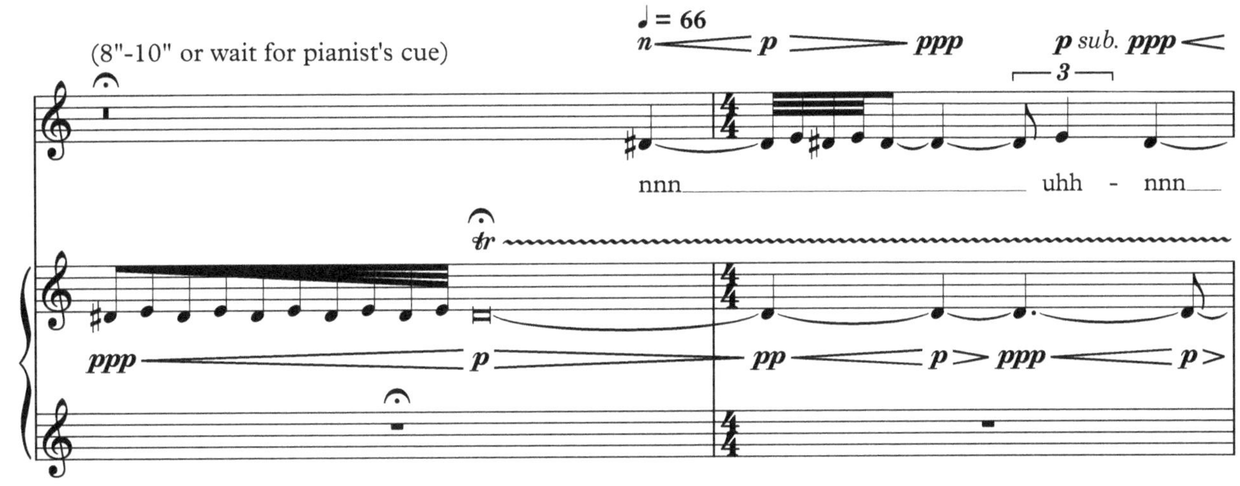

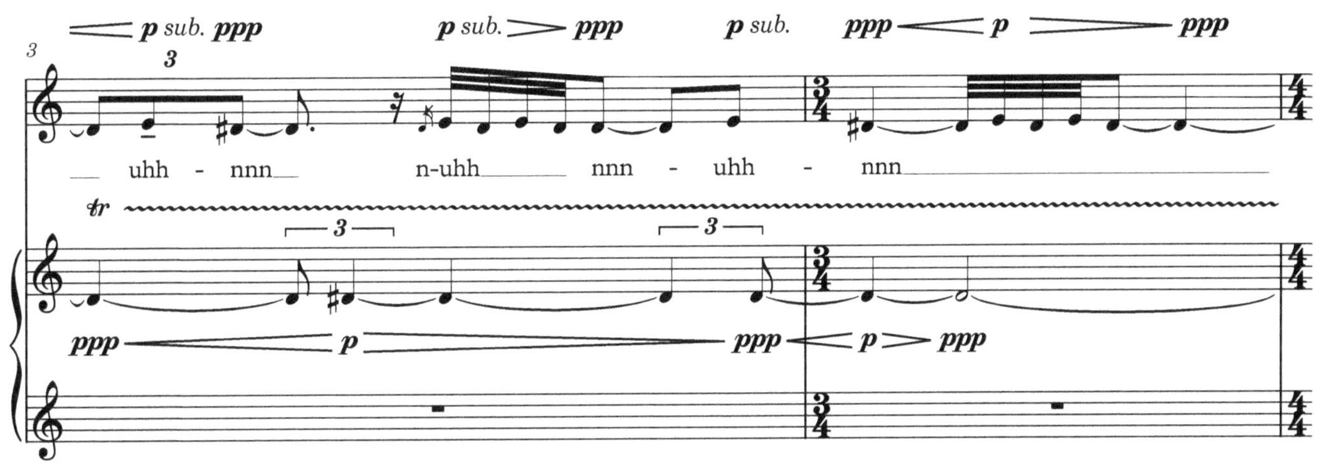

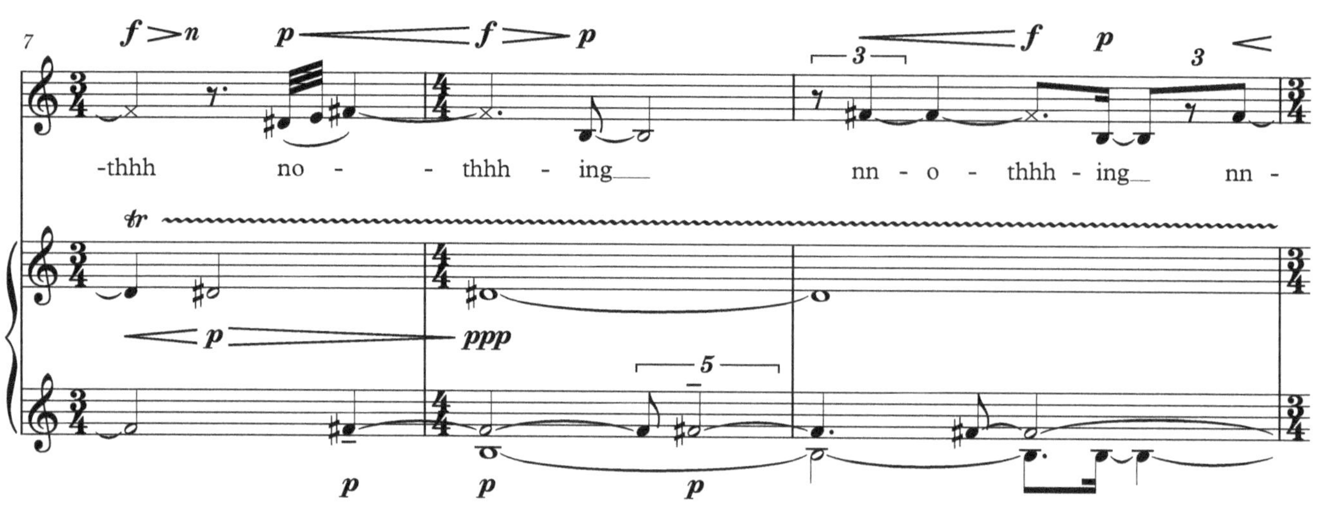
7
f
n
p
f
p
f
p
3
3
-thhh
no
thhh
ing
nn
o
thhh
ing
nn
tr
p
ppp
5
p
p
p

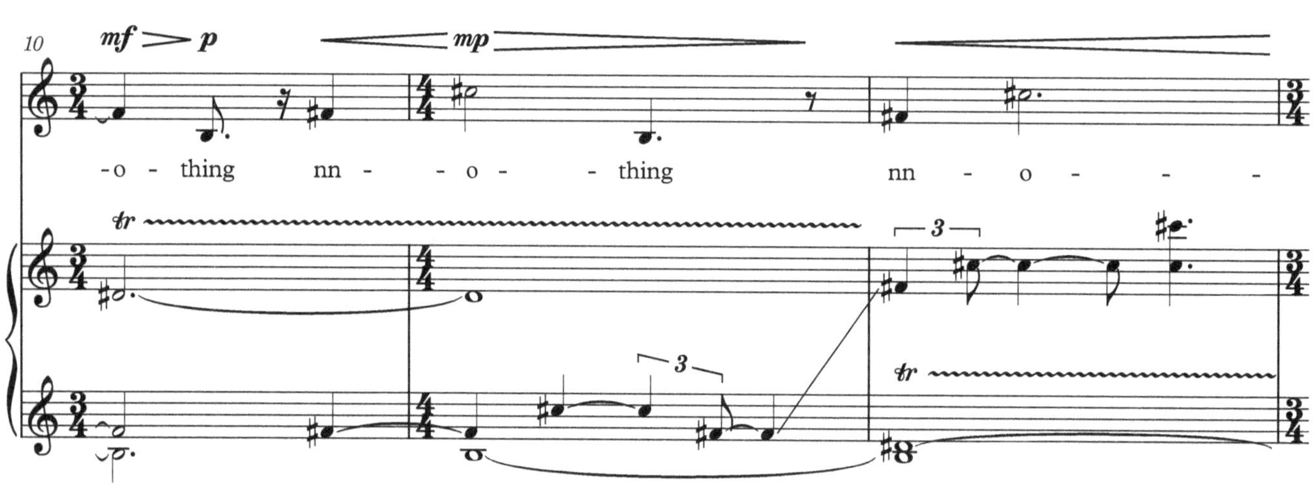
10
mf
p
mp
-o
thing
nn
o
thing
nn
o
tr
3
3
tr

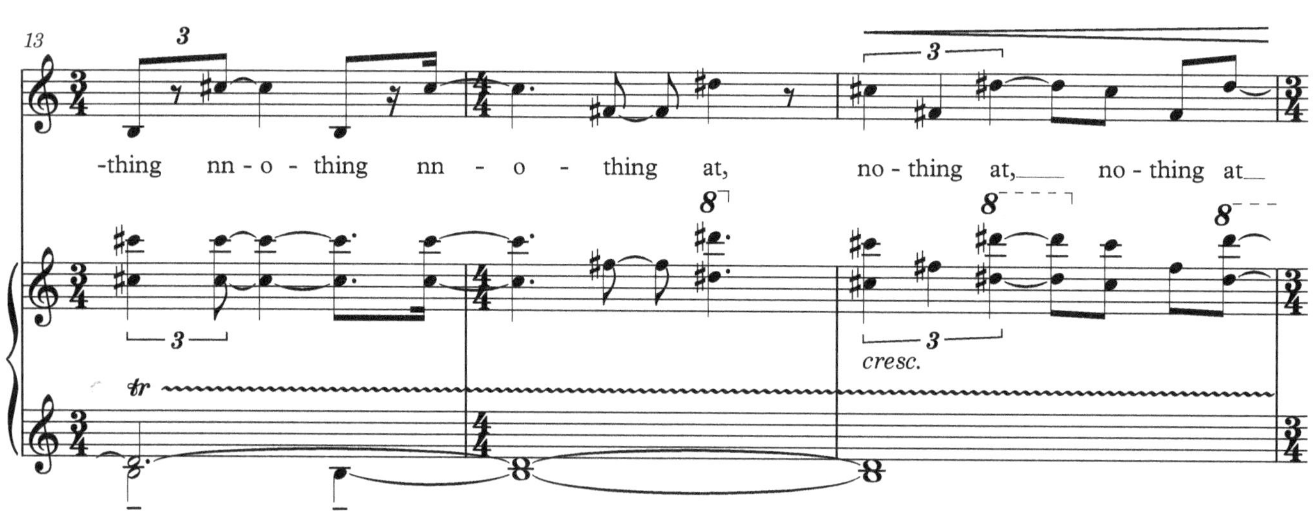
13
3
3
-thing
nn - o - thing
nn
o
thing
at,
no - thing
at,
no - thing
at
8
3
3
cresc.
tr

16
p
all,
no - thing at, no - thing at
(8)
8
3
tr

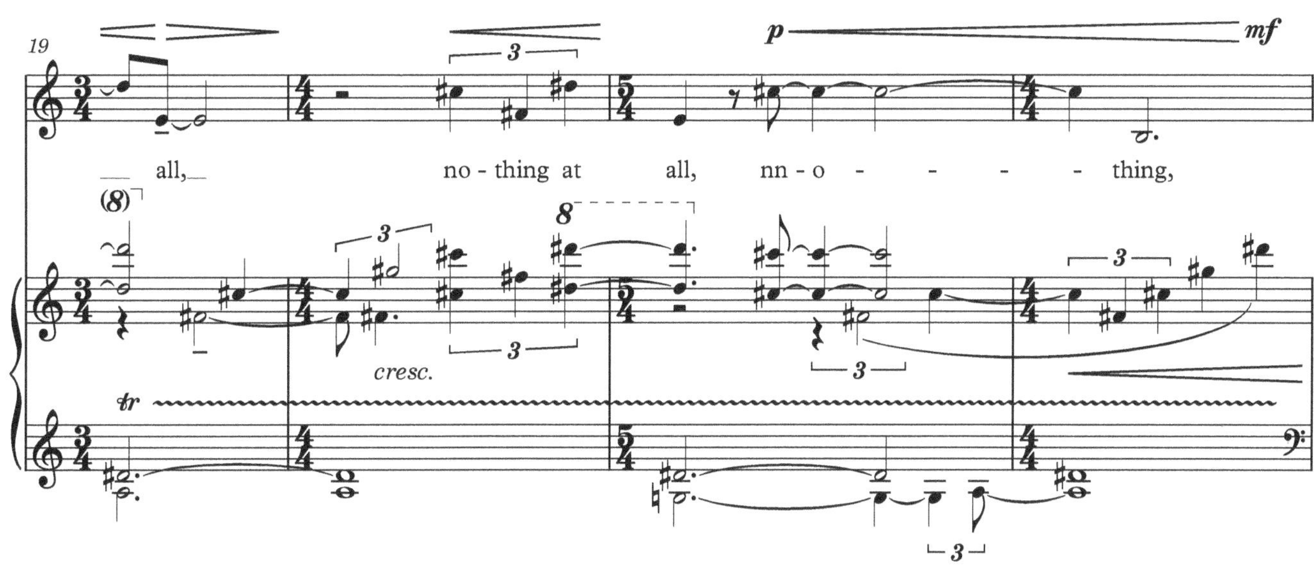

19
p
mf
all,
no - thing at all, nn - o - - - - thing,
(8)
8
3
cresc.
tr

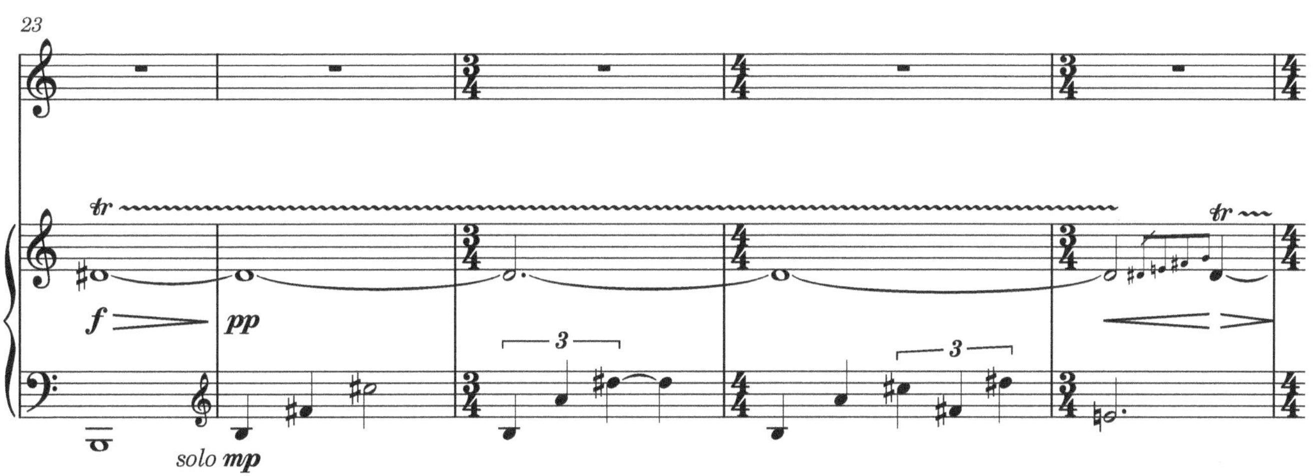

23
tr
f
pp
solo mp
3

28
tr

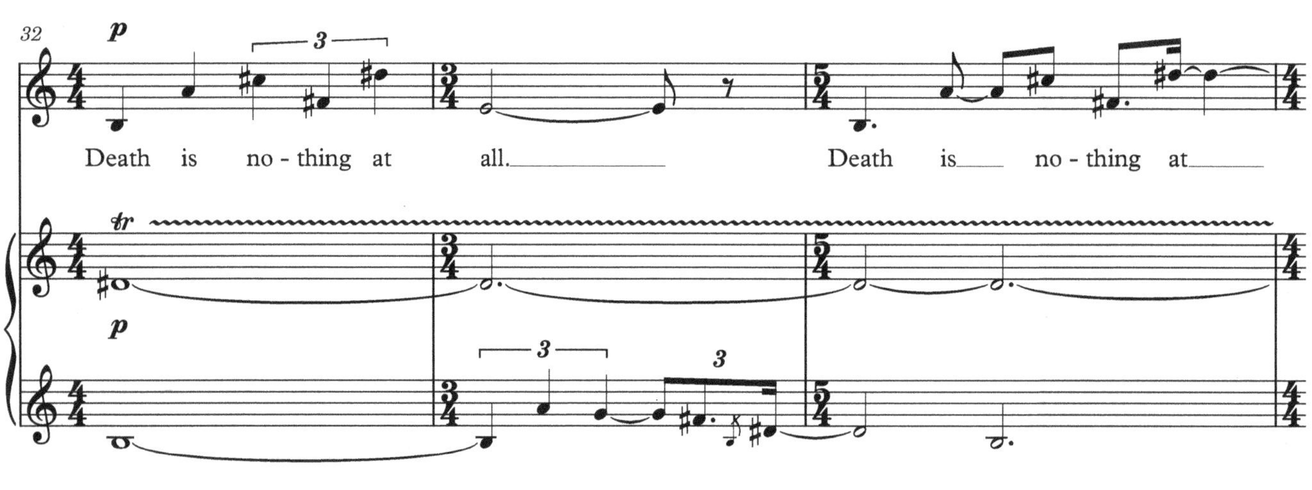
32
p
Death is no - thing at all.
Death is no - thing at
tr
p

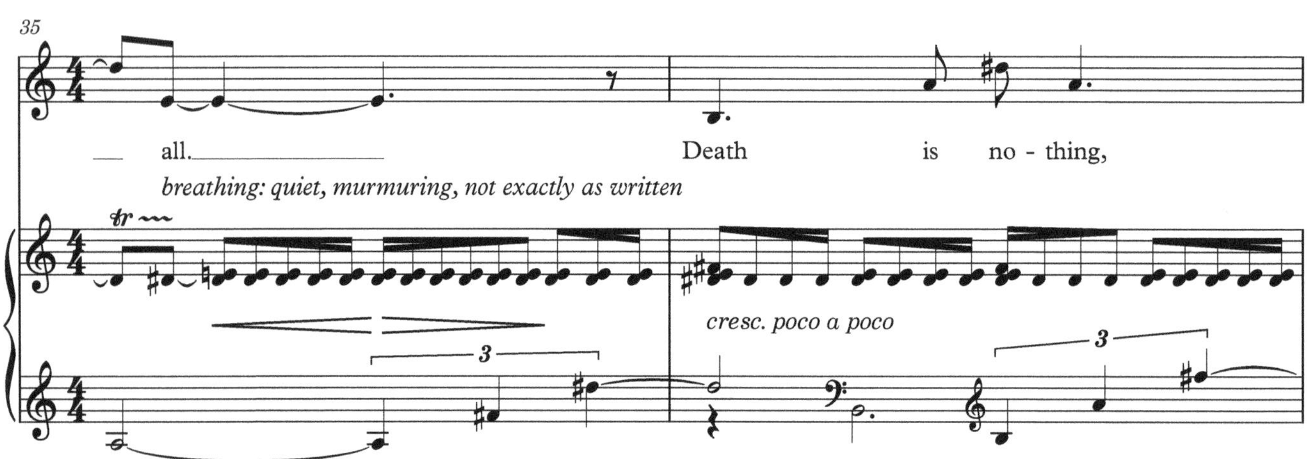
35
all.
Death is no - thing,
breathing: quiet, murmuring, not exactly as written
tr
cresc. poco a poco

37
3
mf
3
no - thing at all, Death is no - thing at
LH
LH
3

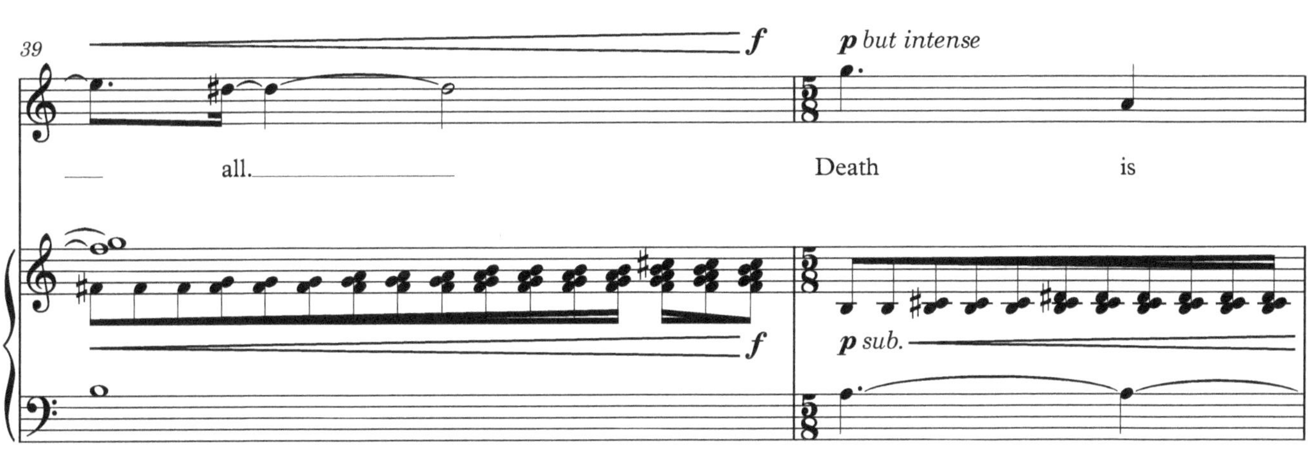
39
f
p but intense
all.
Death is
f
p sub.

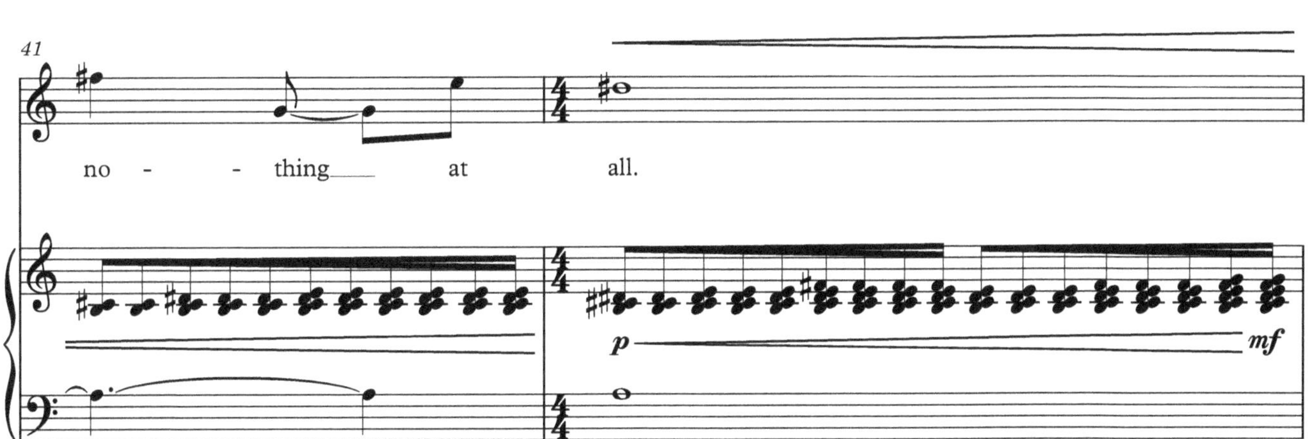
41
no - - thing at all.
p
mf

43
further intensifying
Death is no - thing at
p

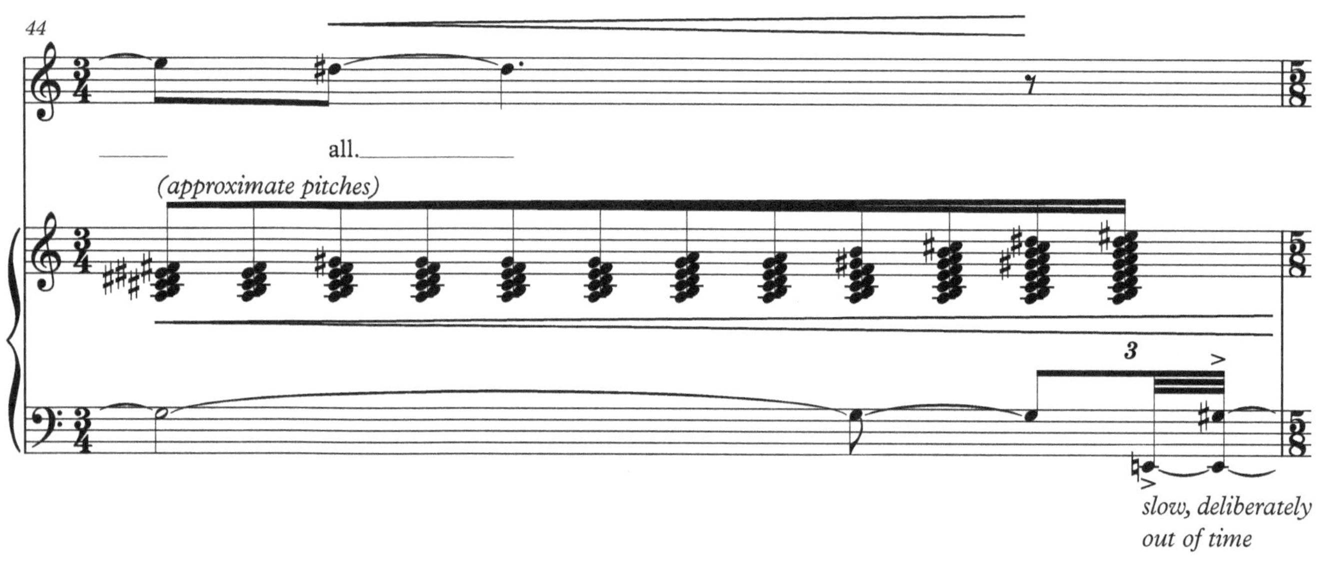
44
all.
(approximate pitches)
3
slow, deliberately
out of time

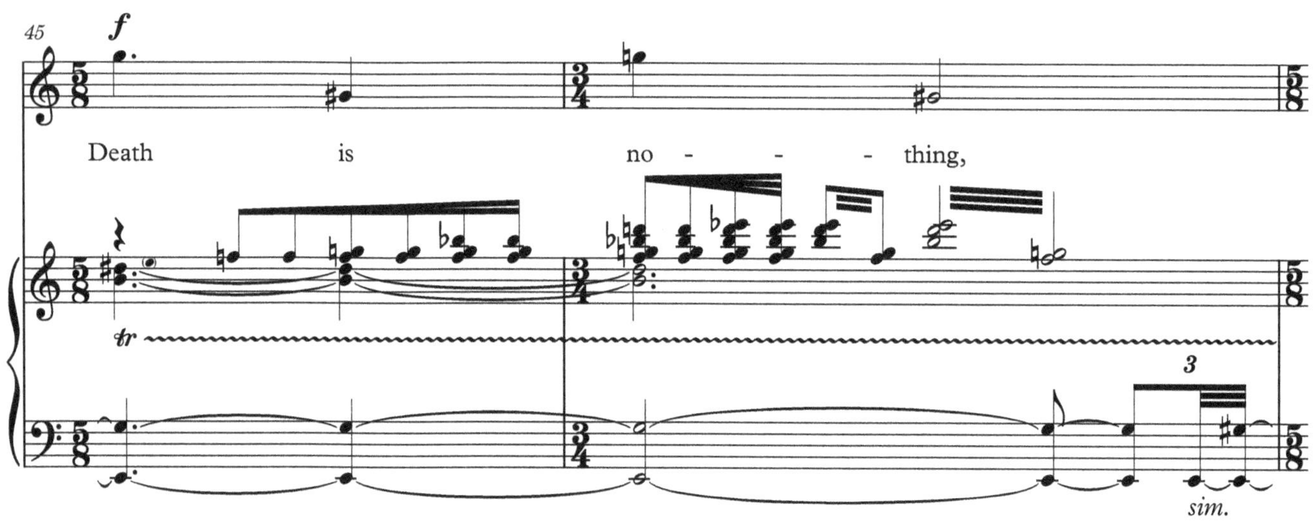
45
f
Death is no - - - thing,
tr
3
sim.

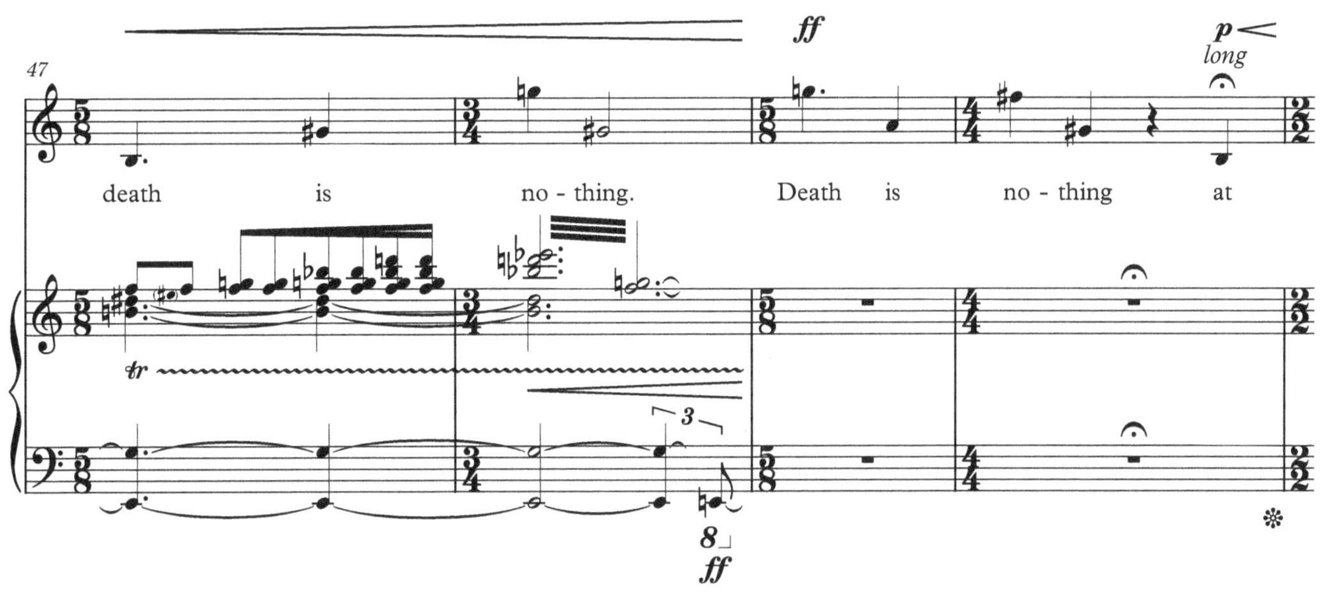

Faster, lighter (𝅗𝅥 = 80)

rit.................................

a tempo
ff
58
no - - - - - - - - - - - - - thing, no - - -
f
ff
61
3
3
- - - - - - - - - - - - thing, no - -
64
- - - - - - - - - thing, no - - thing,

p sub.
cresc. poco a poco
growing with excitement
67
no - - - - - - - - - - - - - - thing,
p sub.
cresc. poco a poco

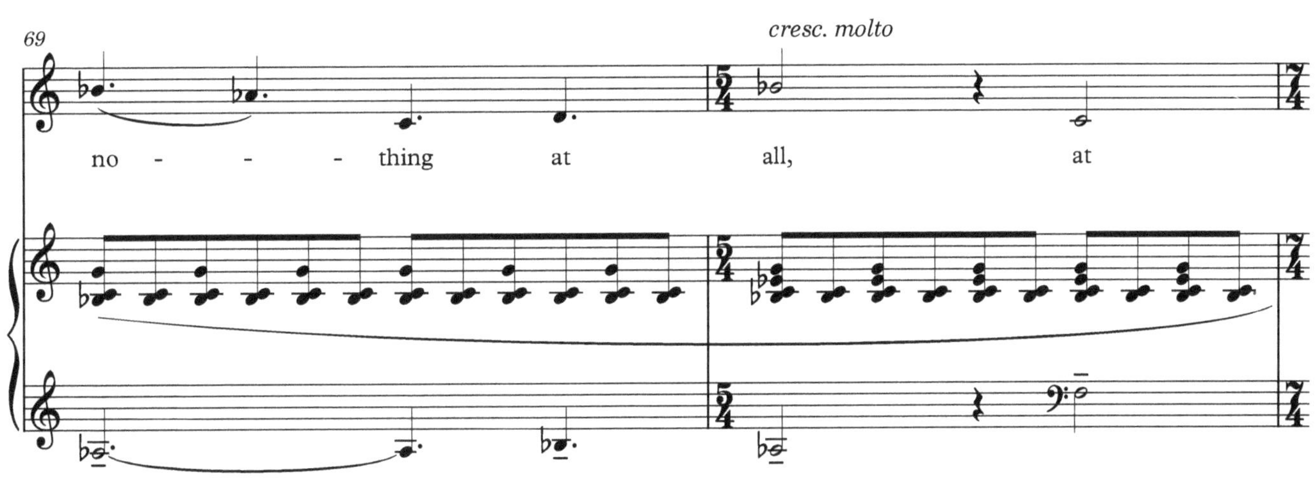
69
cresc. molto
no - - - thing at all, at

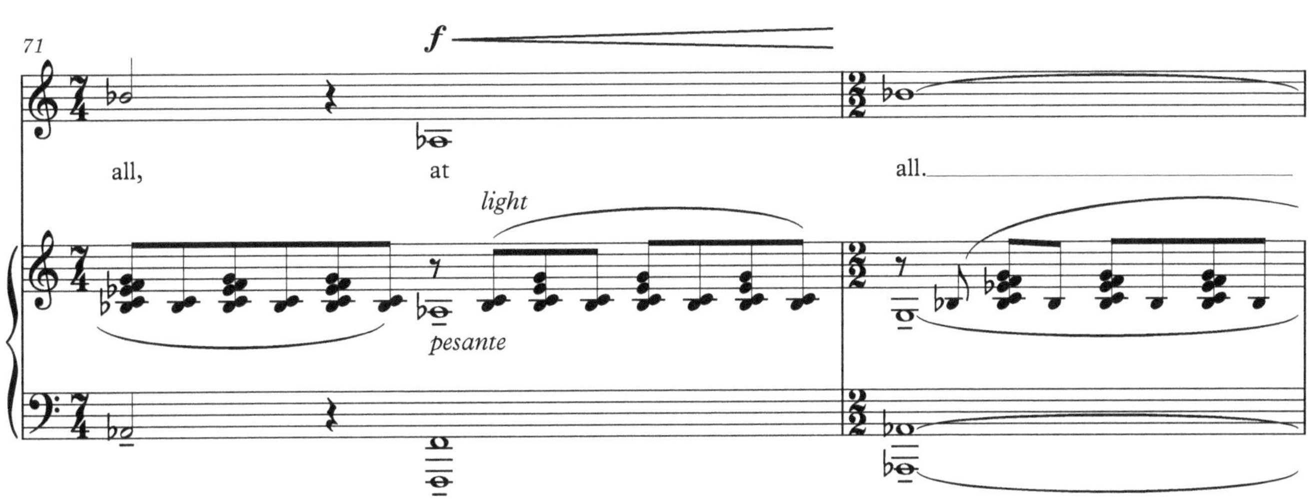
71
f
all, at all.
light
pesante

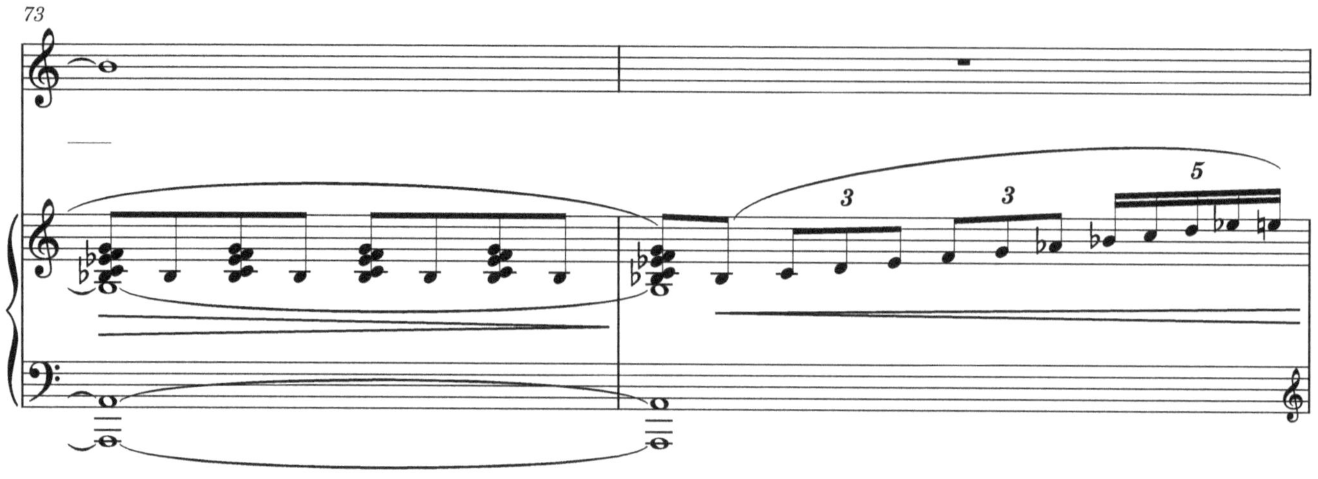
73
3
3
5

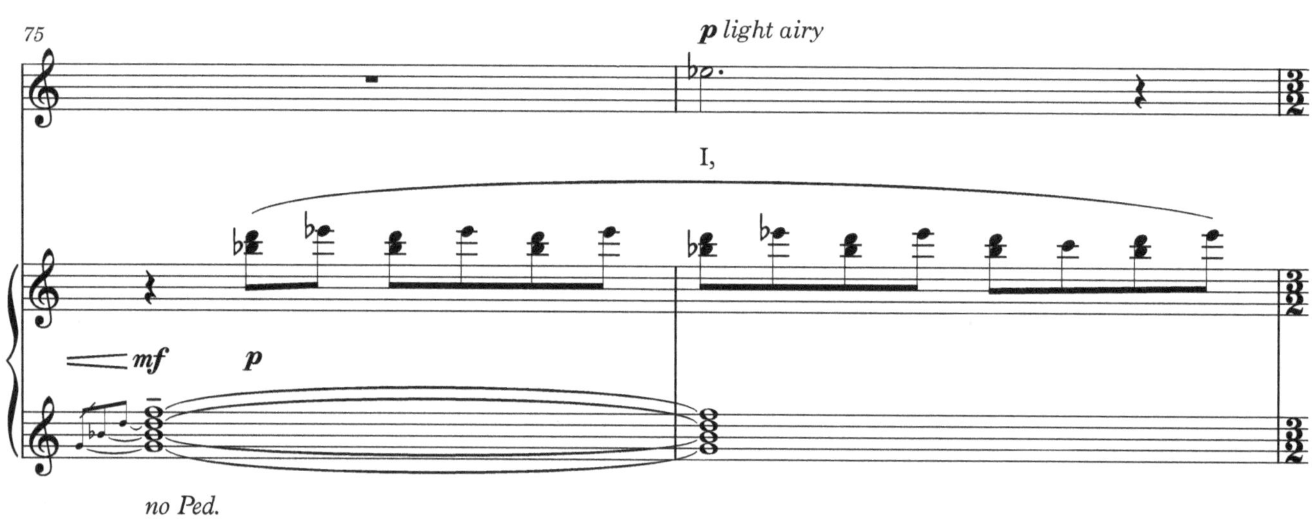
75
p light airy
I,
mf
p
no Ped.

77
gliss.
3
gliss.
I,
I
have,
mf
p
mf
p
a little more Ped.
even more Ped.

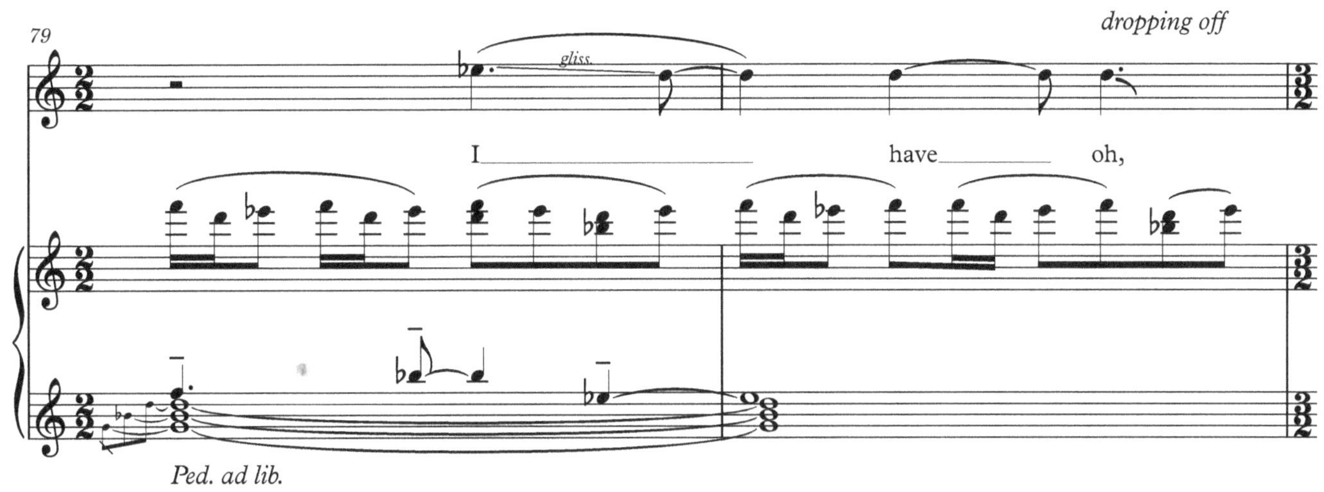
79
dropping off
gliss.
I have oh,
Ped. ad lib.

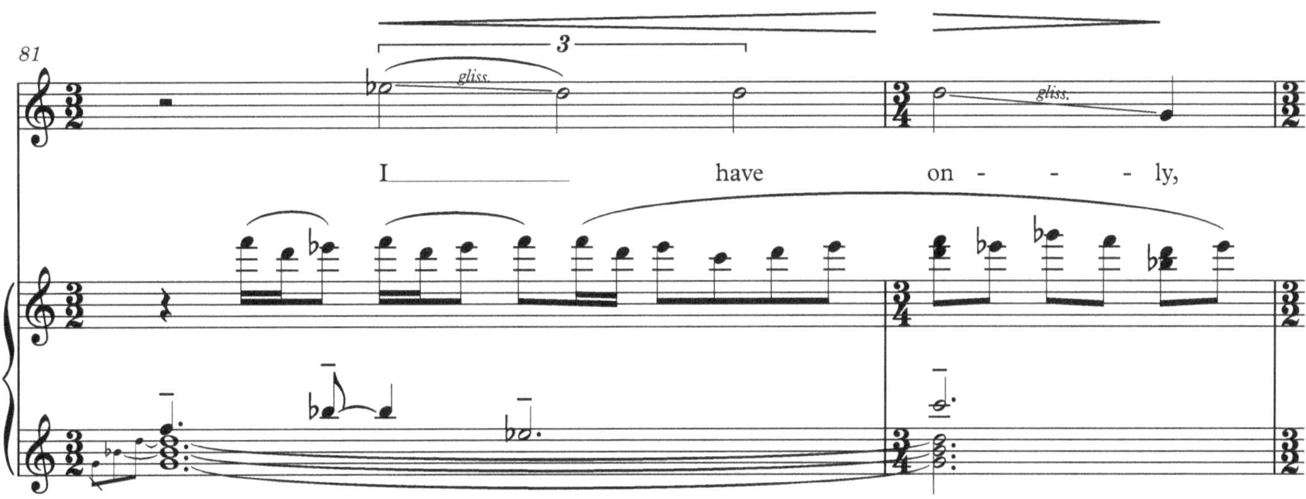
81
3
gliss.
gliss.
I have on - - - ly,

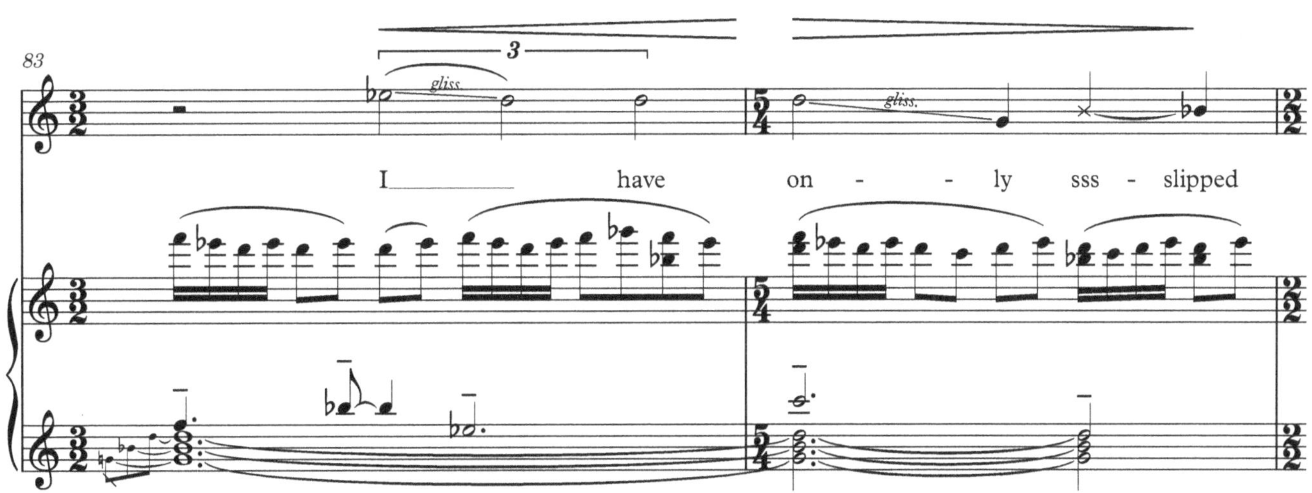
83
3
gliss.
gliss.
I have on - - ly sss - slipped

85
gliss.
I have on - - - ly sss -

88
gliss.
-slipped a - - way, a -

91
gliss.
-way a - - way
pp precise

94
in - - to the next room.
poco fp

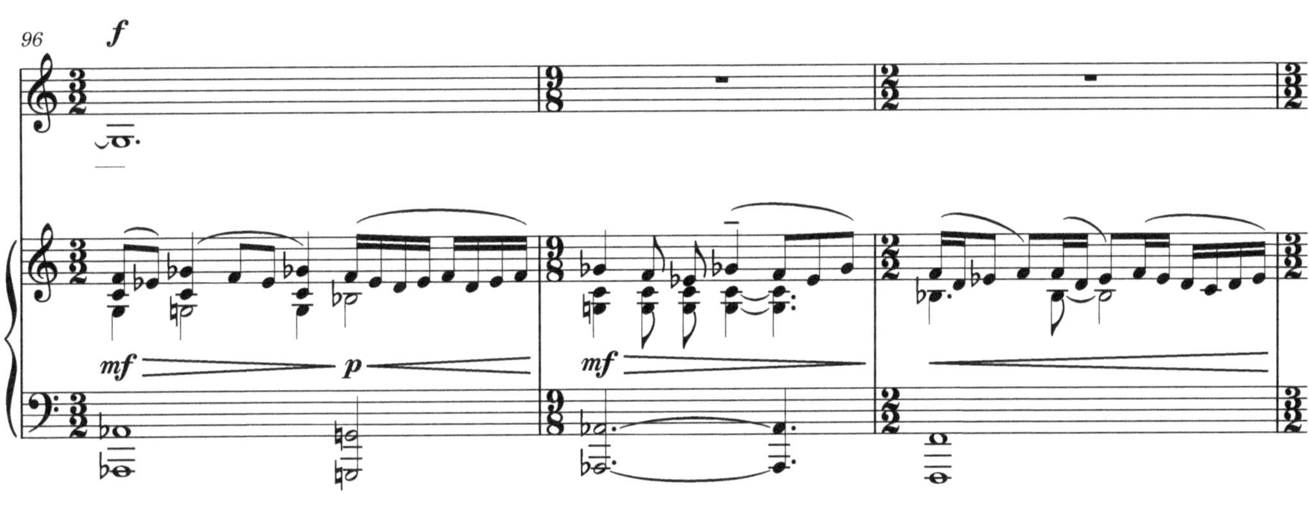
96
f
mf
p
mf

99
f

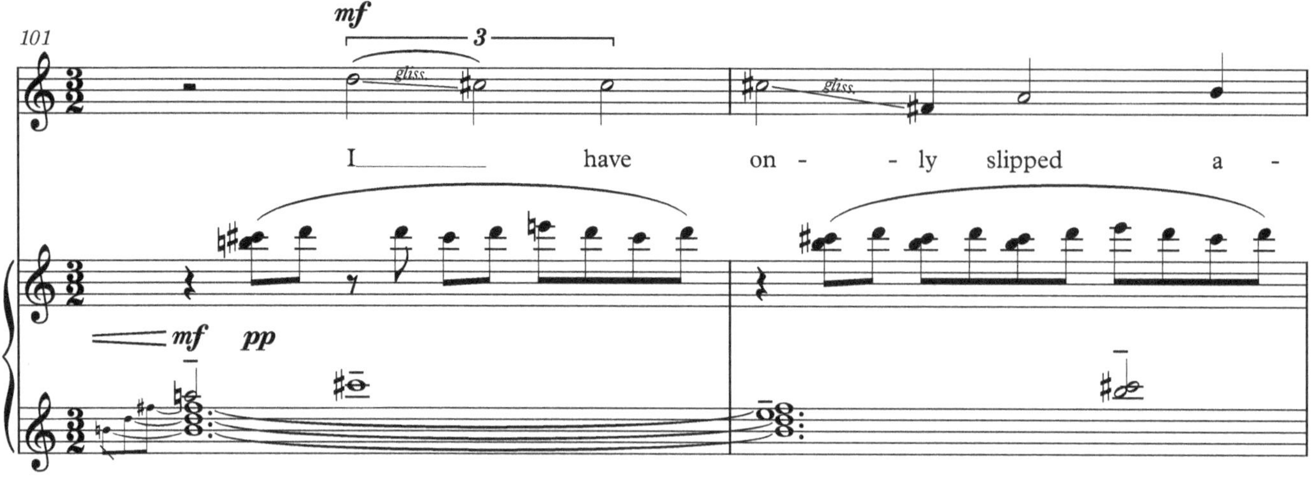
101
mf
3
gliss.
gliss.
I have on - - ly slipped a -
mf pp

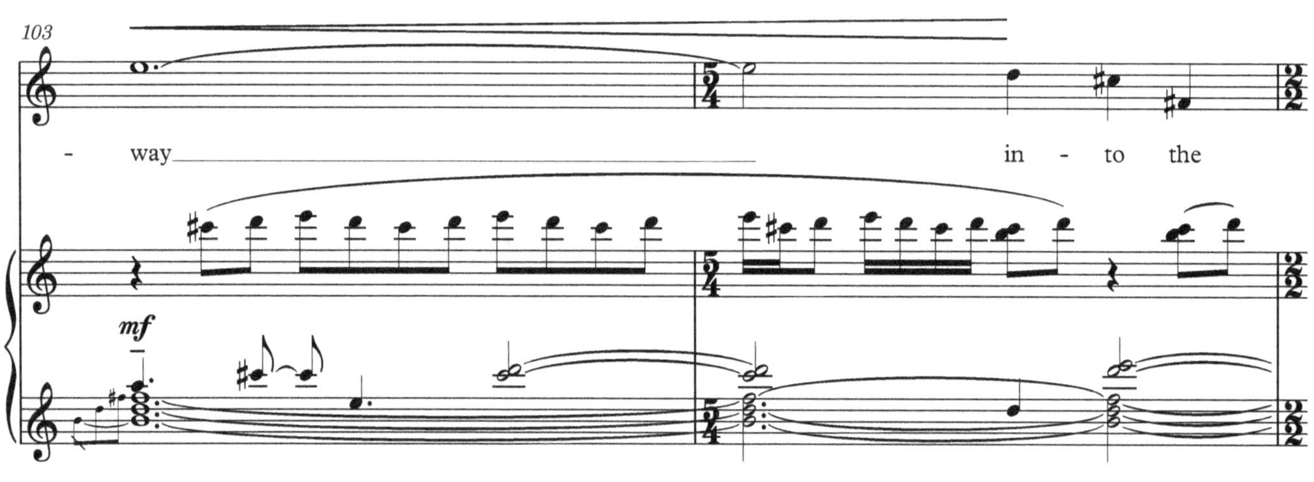
103
- way into the
mf

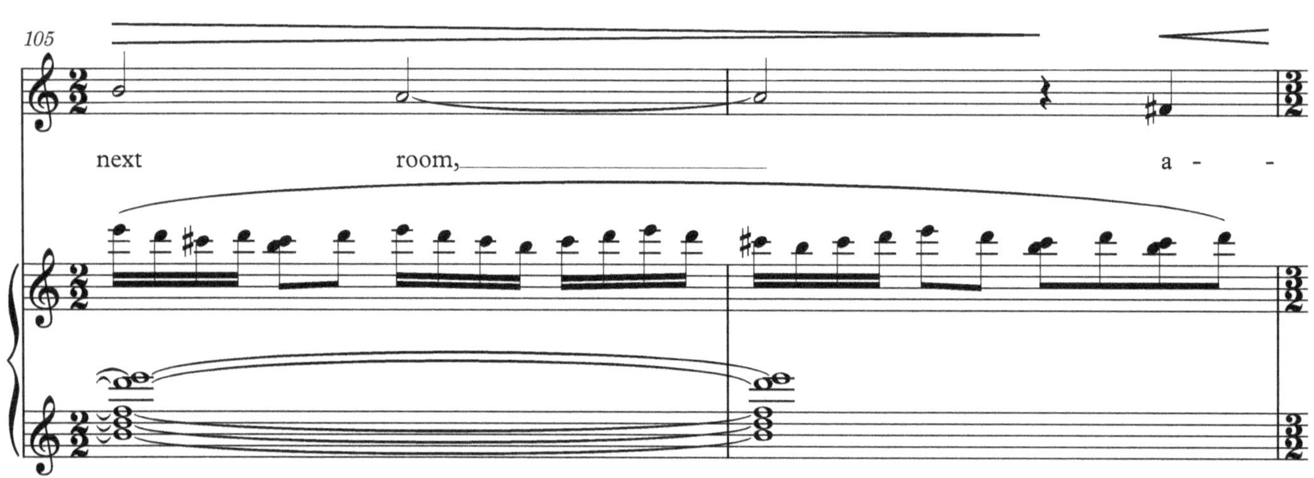
105
next room, a -

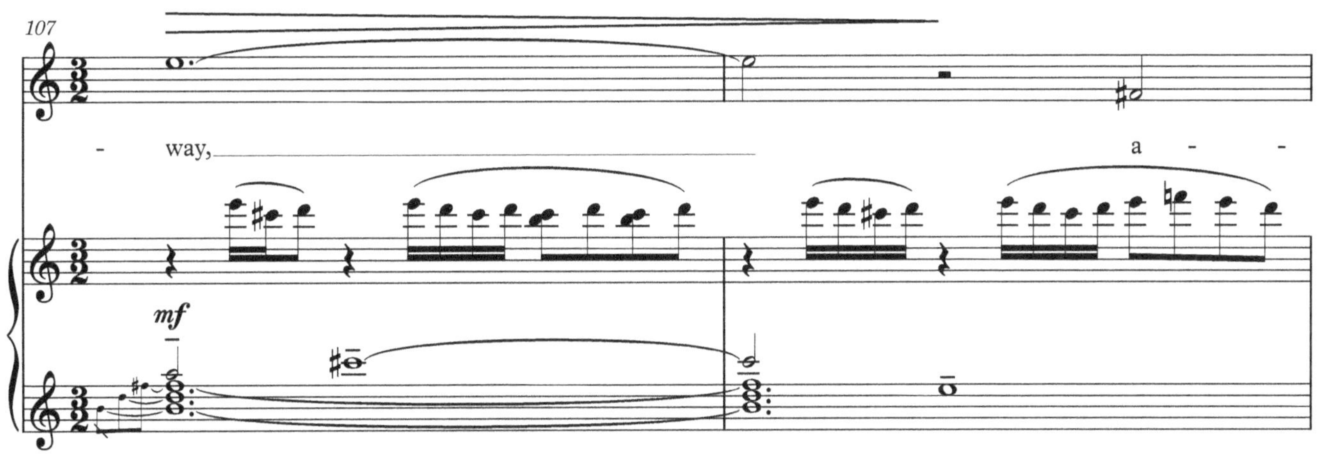
107
way,
a
mf

109
way,
a
mf

p sweetly
111
way.
8
pp
p

114
p
Death
is
no - thing at
(8)
loco
8

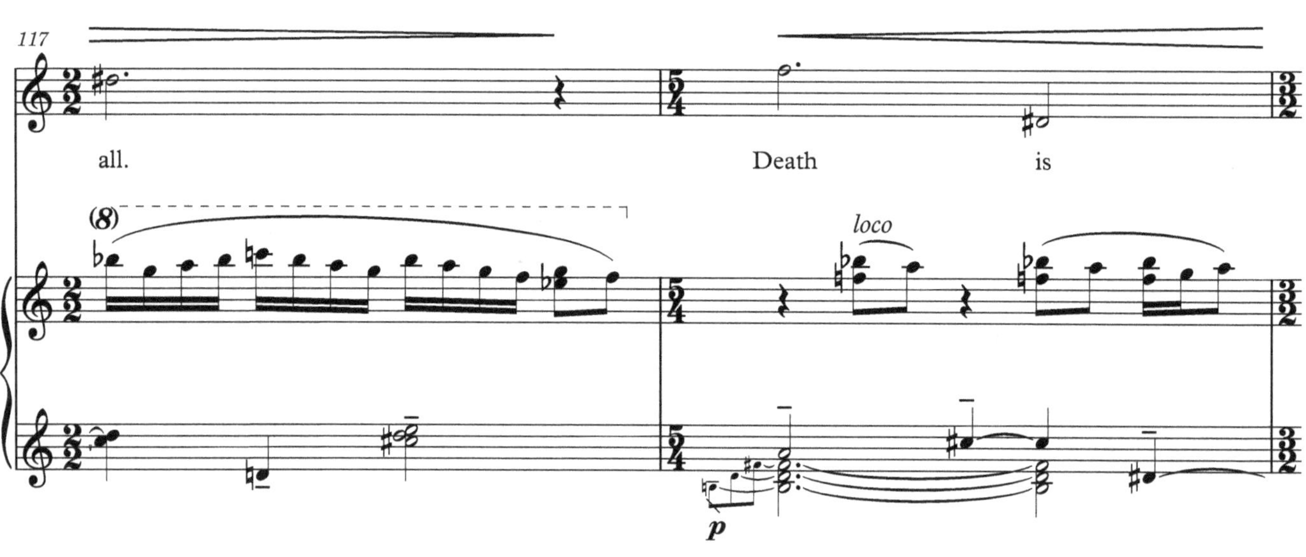
117
all.
Death
is
(8)
loco
p

119
no - - - thing
at
all,

121
3
no - thing at all, at all,
8
mf

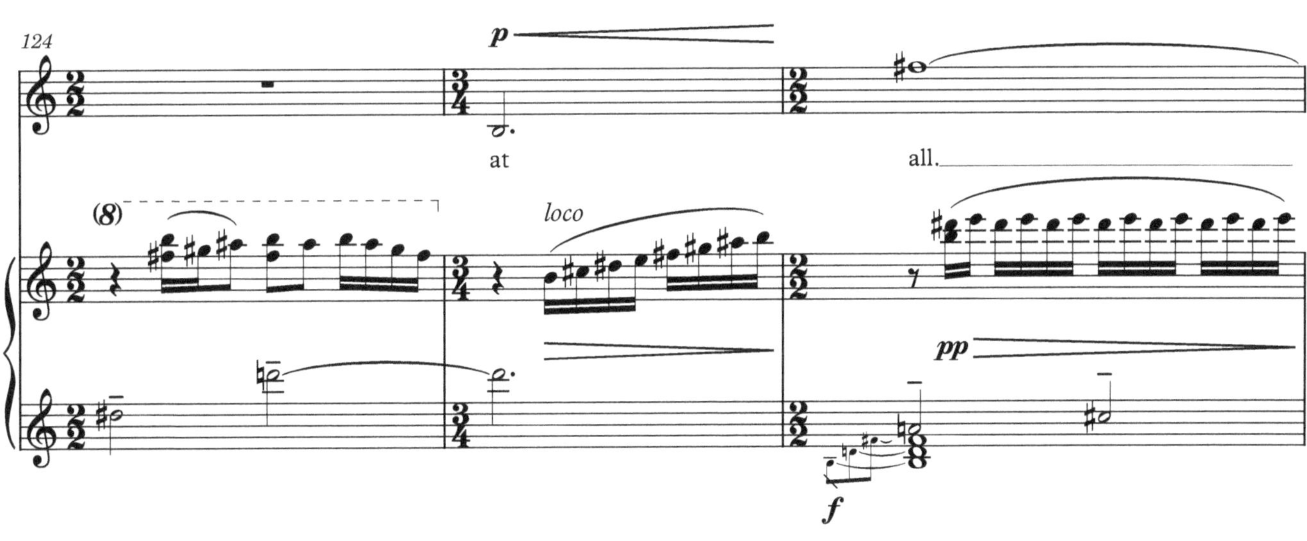
124
p
at all.
(8)
loco
pp
f

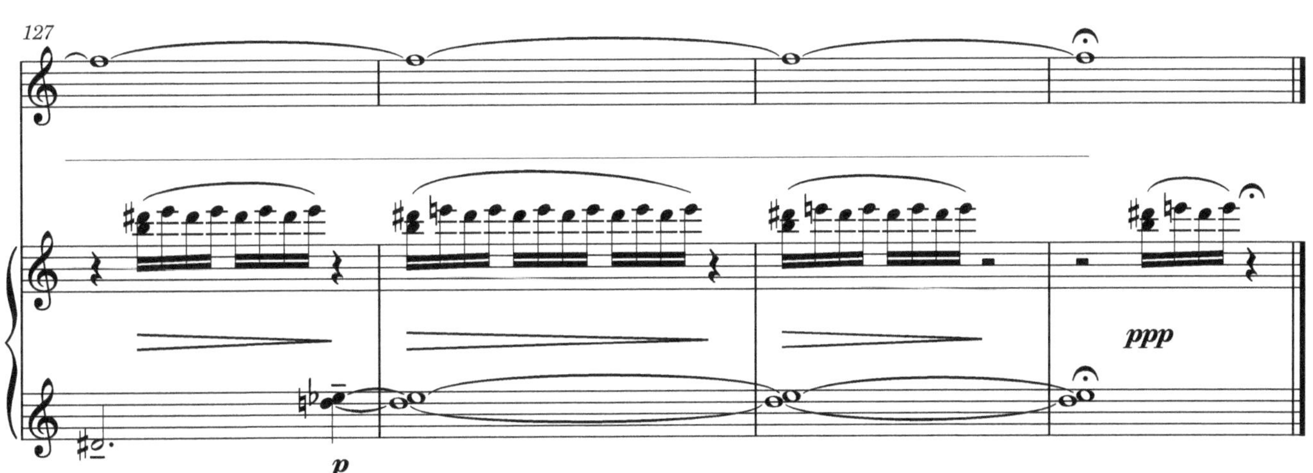
127
p
ppp

composed for songSLAM Toronto 2019

Stars

Marjorie Pickthall
(1883-1922)

ABIGAIL DE NIVERVILLE
(2018)

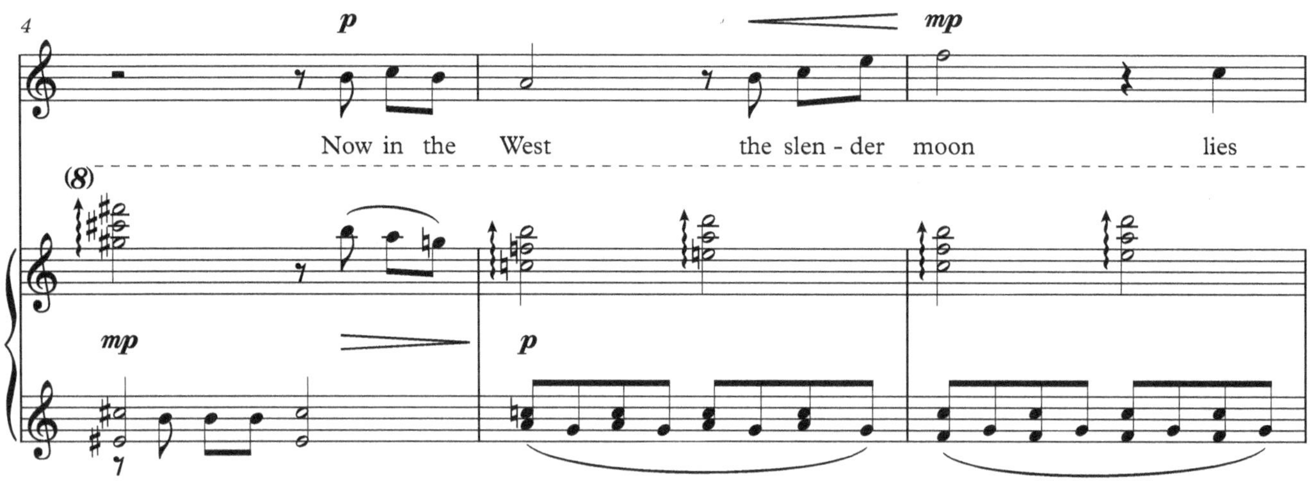

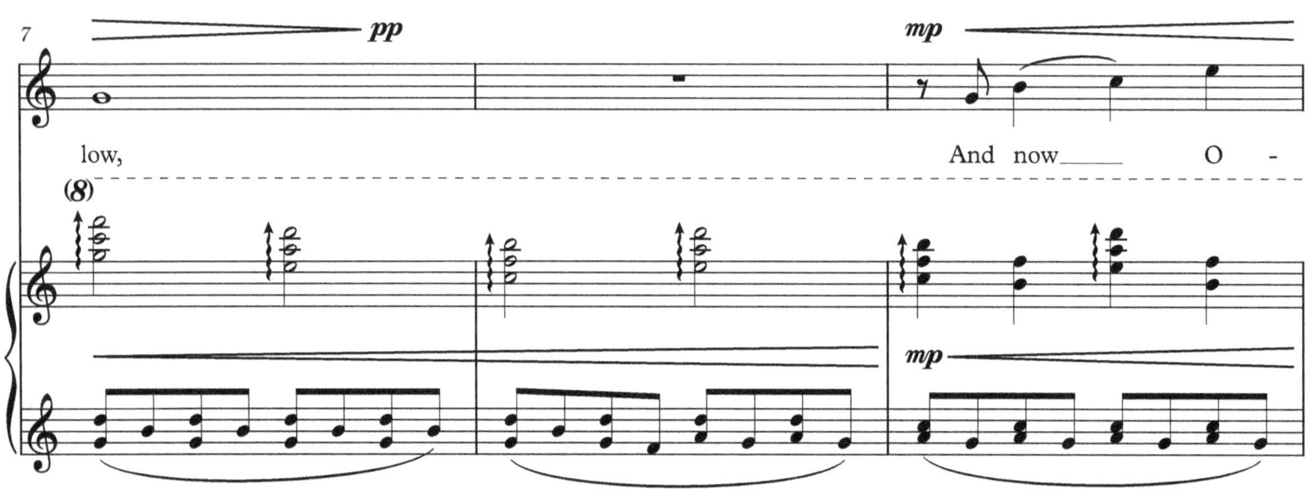

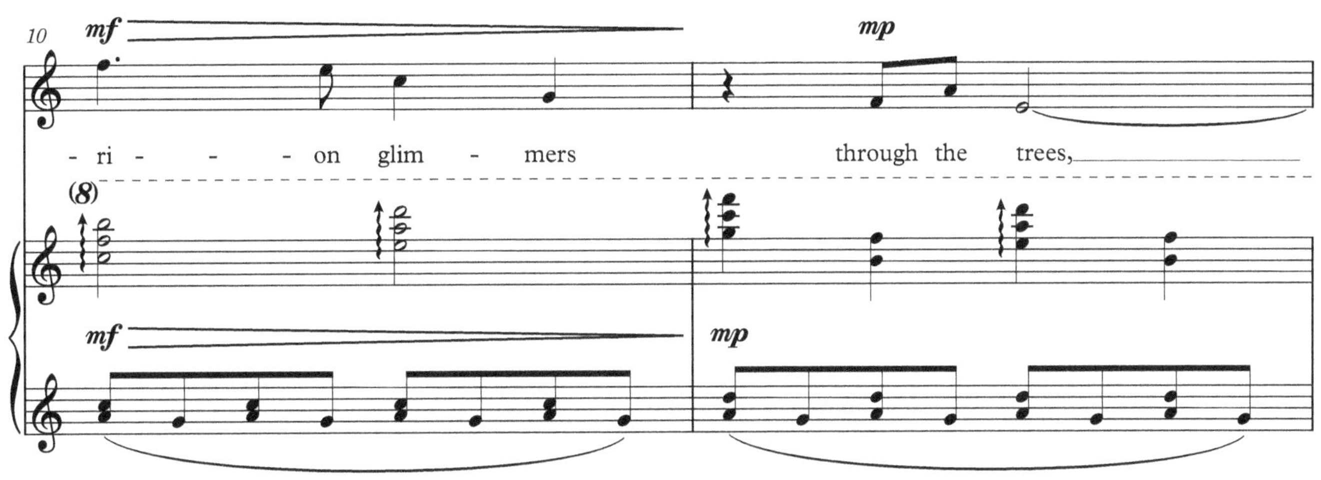
10
mf
mp
-ri - - - on glim - mers through the trees,
(8)
mf
mp

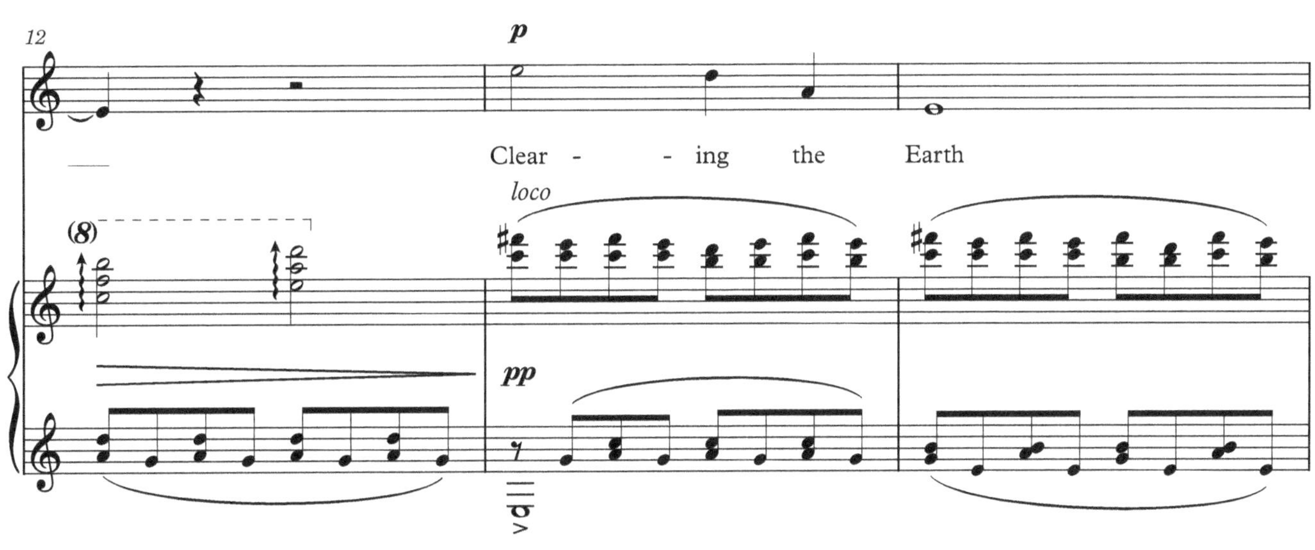
12
p
Clear - - ing the Earth
loco
(8)
pp

15
mf
with e - - ven pace and
mf

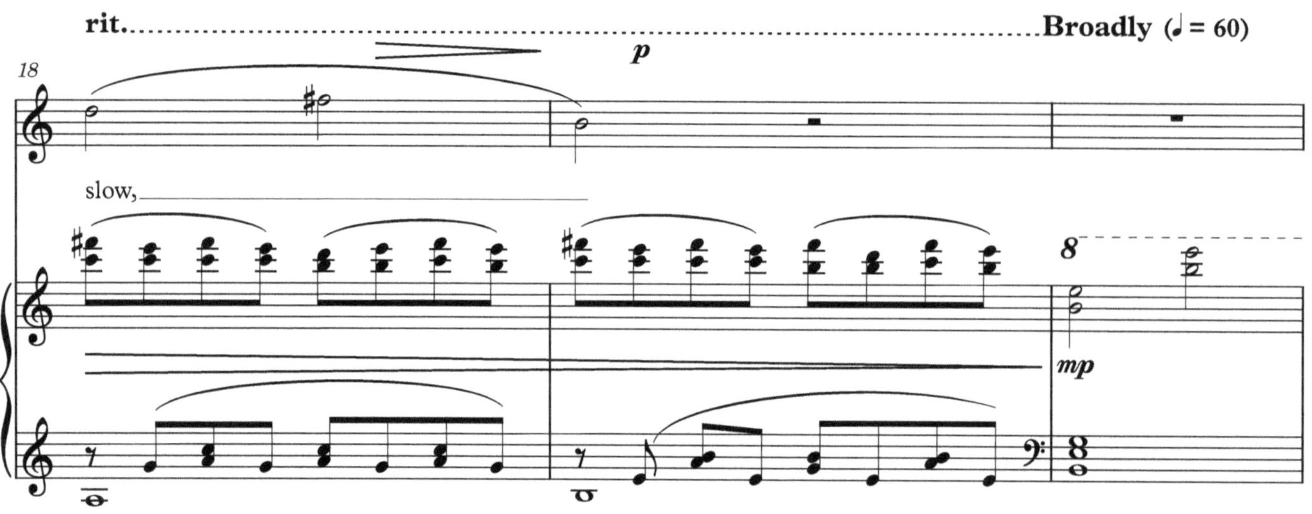

rit.
Broadly (♩ = 60)
18
p
slow,
8
mp

21
p
cresc.
And now the state - ly mo - ving Plei - a - des, In that
(8)

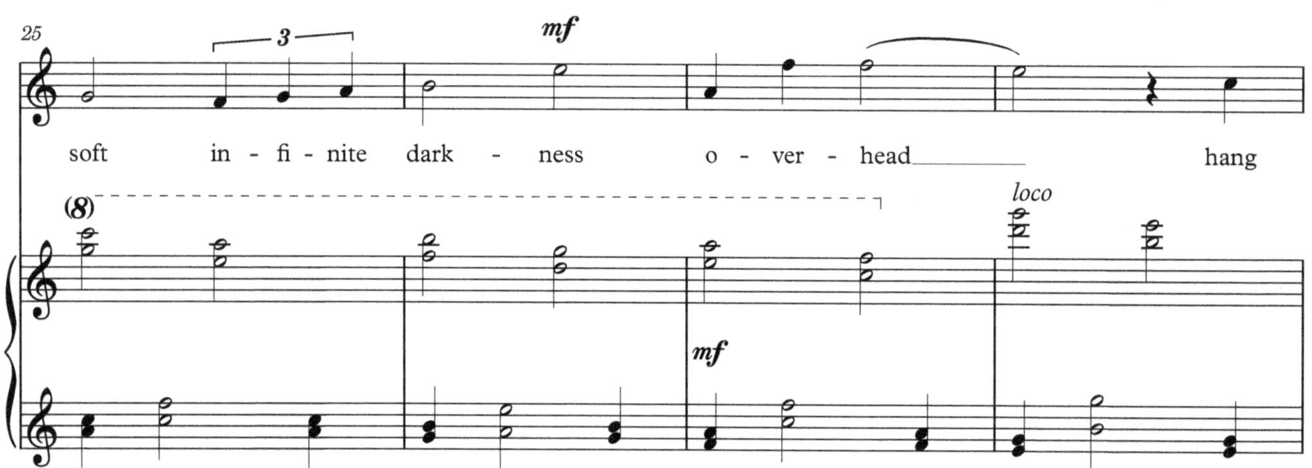

25
3
mf
soft in - fi - nite dark - ness o - ver - head hang
(8)
loco
mf

29
p
jewel - wise u - pon a sil - ver thread.
p

accel. With feeling (♩ = 84)
33
cresc.

36
f
And all the
f

39
3
lone - li - er stars that have their place, Calm

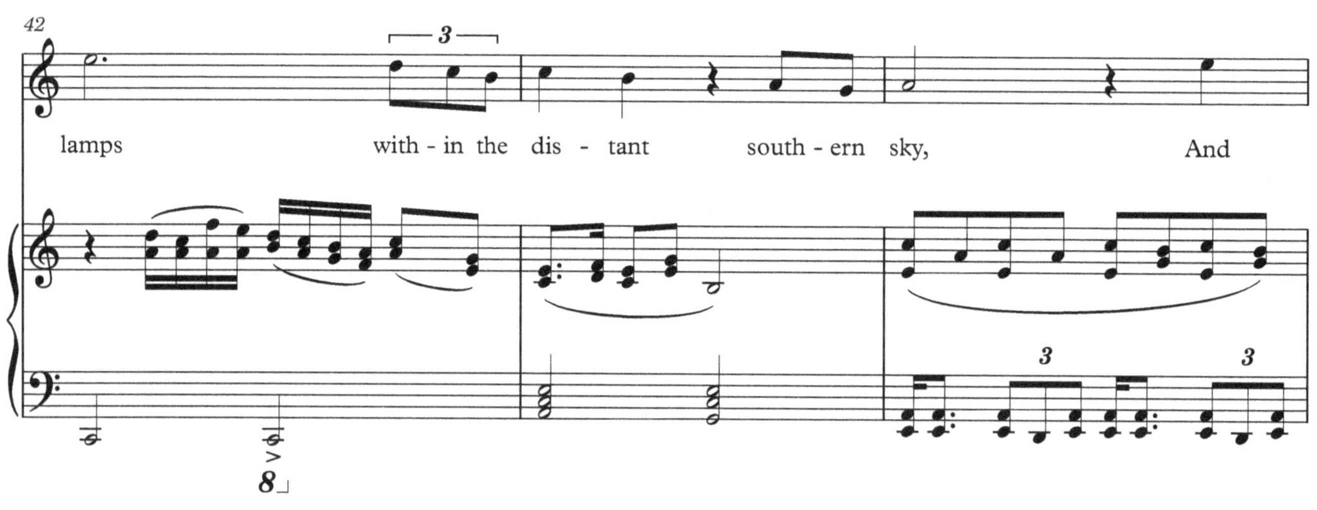
42
3
lamps with - in the dis - tant south - ern sky, And
8

45
plan - et dust u - pon the edge of
3
3

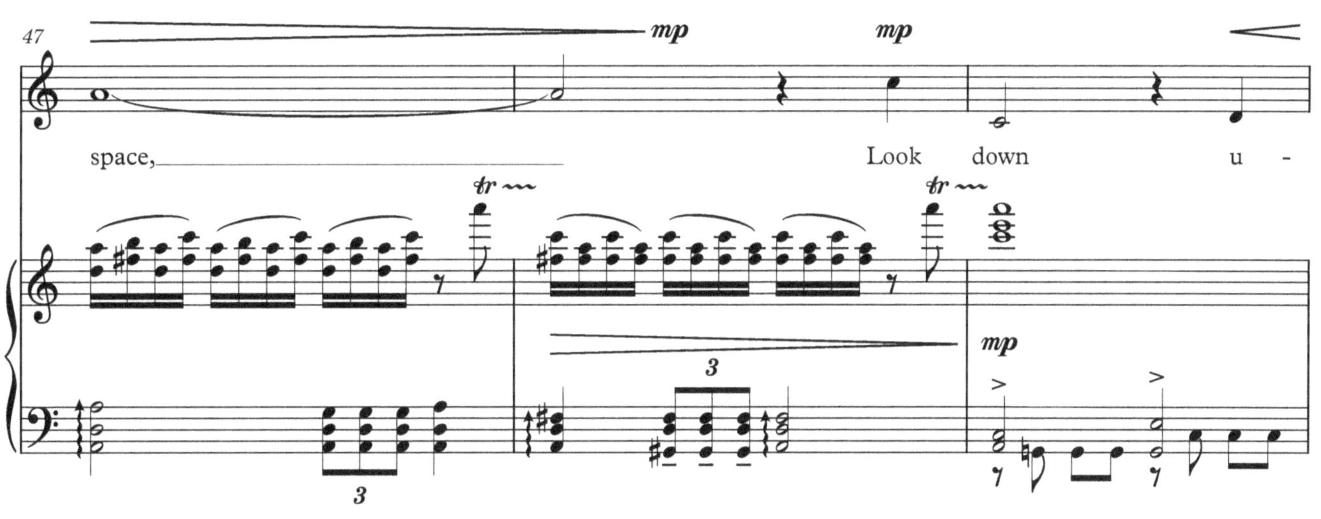
47
mp
mp
space,
Look down u -
tr
tr
3
mp
3

50
- pon the fret - ful world, and I Look

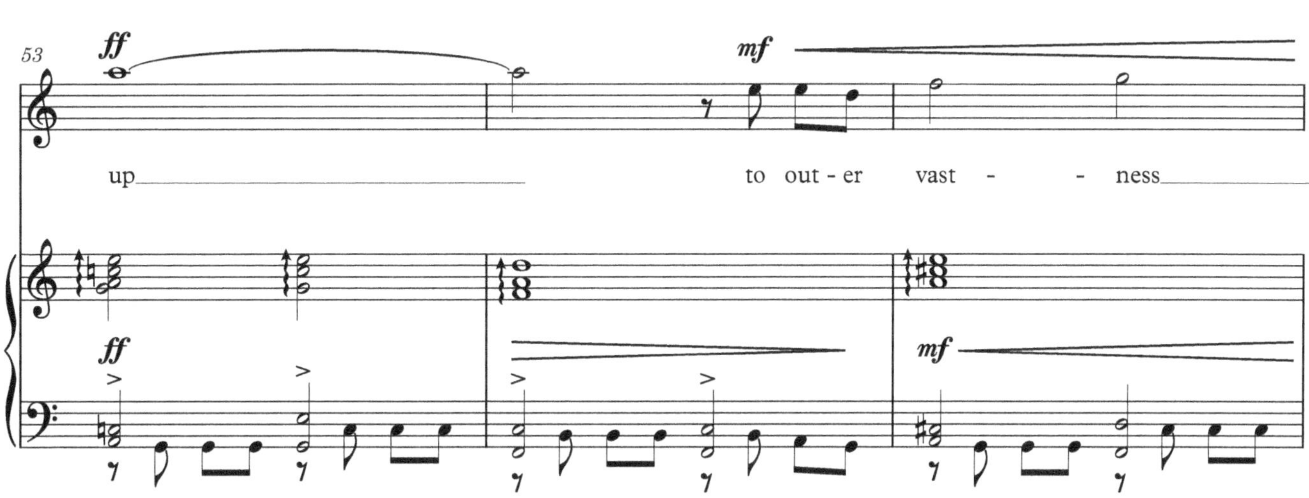
53
ff
mf
up
to out - er vast - - ness
ff
mf

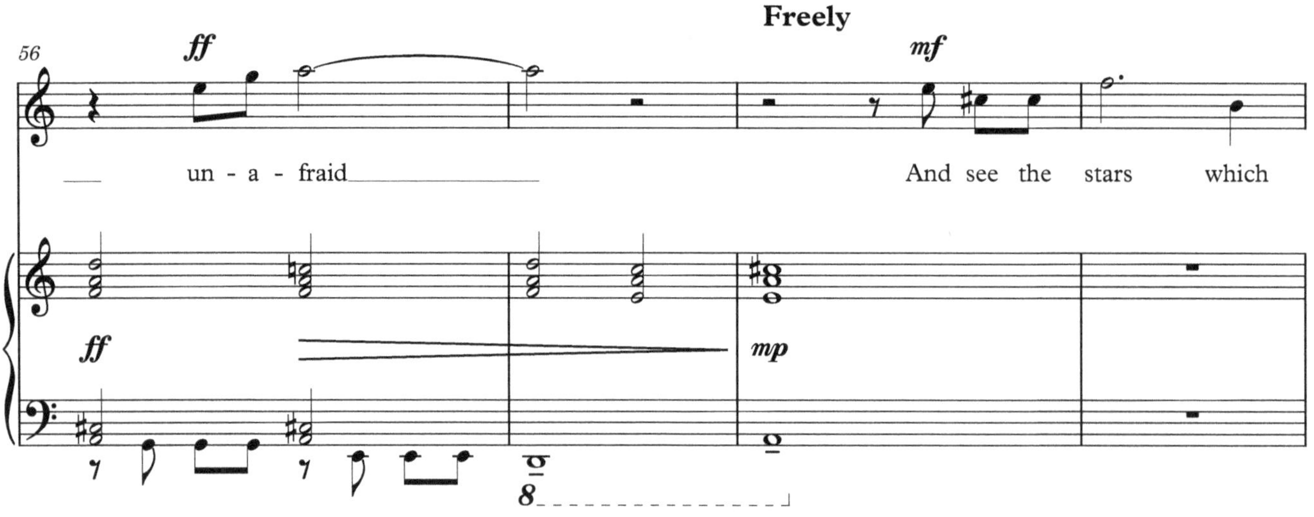
Freely
ff
mf
un - a - fraid
And see the stars which
ff
mp
8

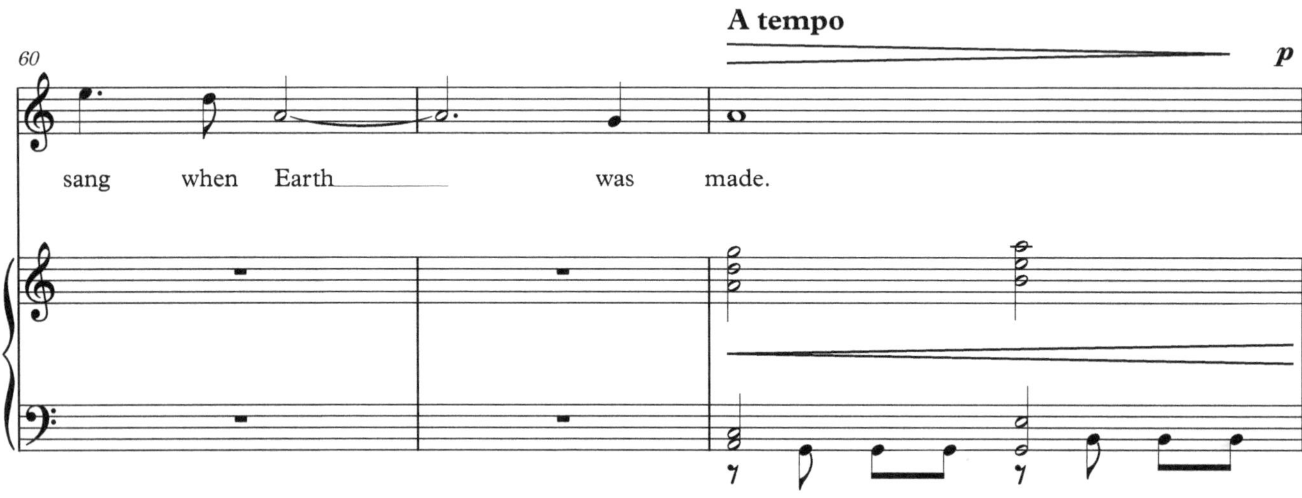
A tempo
p
sang when Earth was made.

rit.
8
f
mp
f
p

composed for songSLAM NYC I 2017

V. Postlude

from *O sea-starved, hungry sea*

William Shakespeare

NATALIE DRAPER
(2017)

12
mp
No - thing of him that doth fade
p

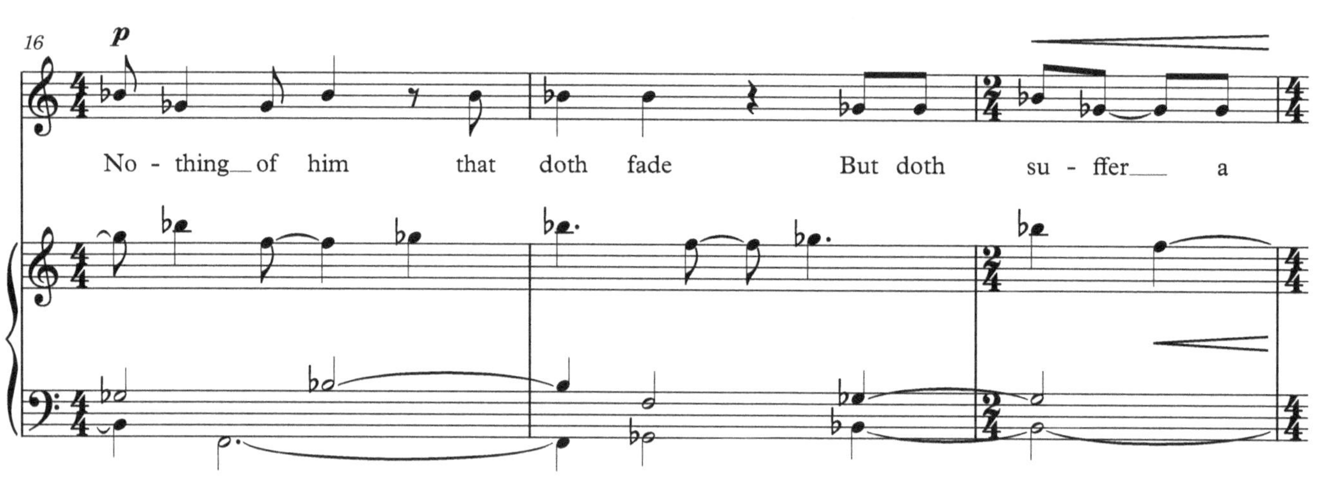
16
p
No - thing of him that doth fade But doth su - ffer a

19
f
sea change
mf

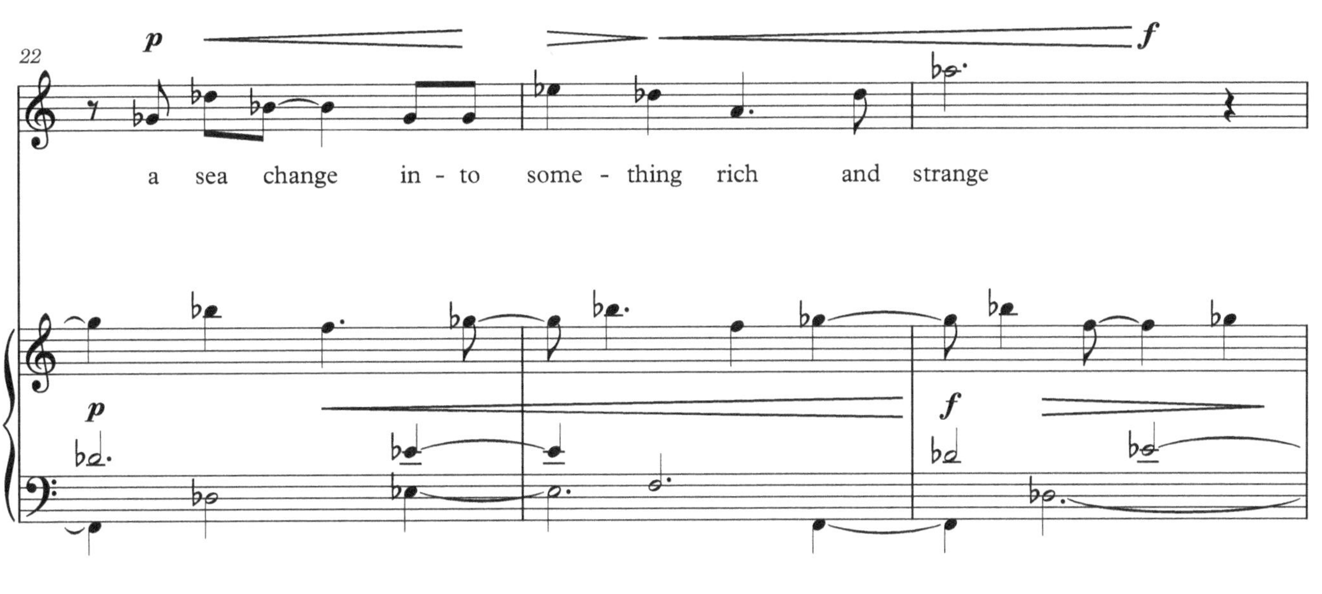
22
p
f
a sea change in - to some - thing rich and strange
p
f

25
mf
p

29
f
Sea nymphs hour - ly ring his knell

33
mf
Hark! now I hear them ding dong bell

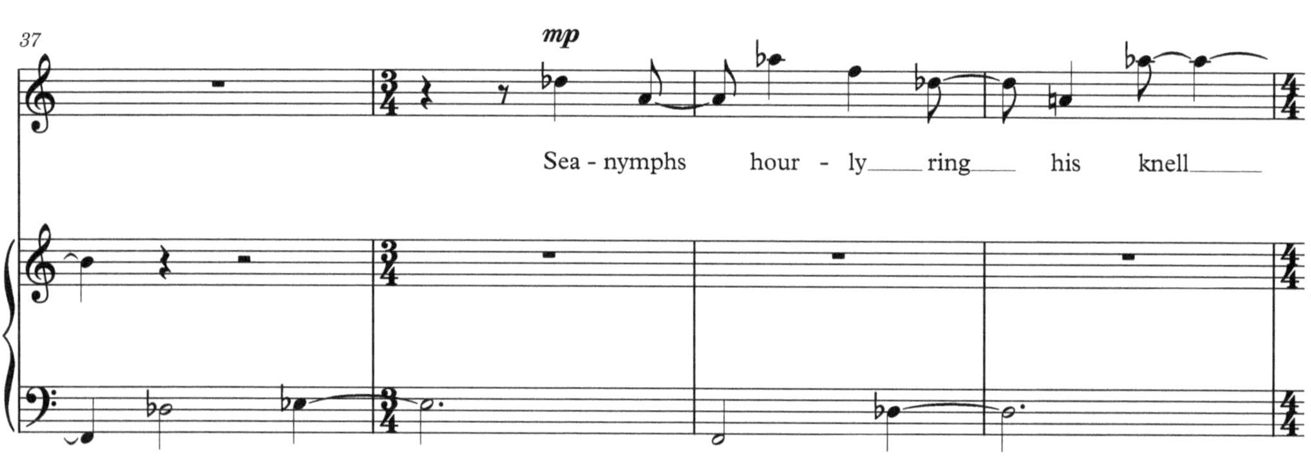
37
mp
Sea - nymphs hour - ly ring his knell

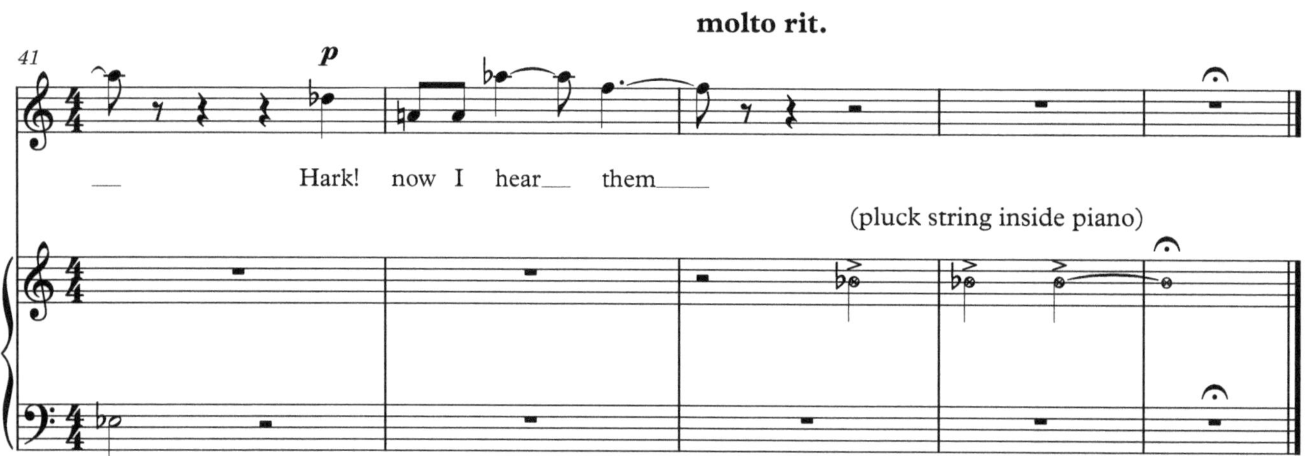
molto rit.
41
p
Hark! now I hear them
(pluck string inside piano)

composed for songSLAM NYC I 2017

in New York

Johnny Call

WHITNEY E. GEORGE
(2017)

Unnecessarily Grand (♩ = c. 102)

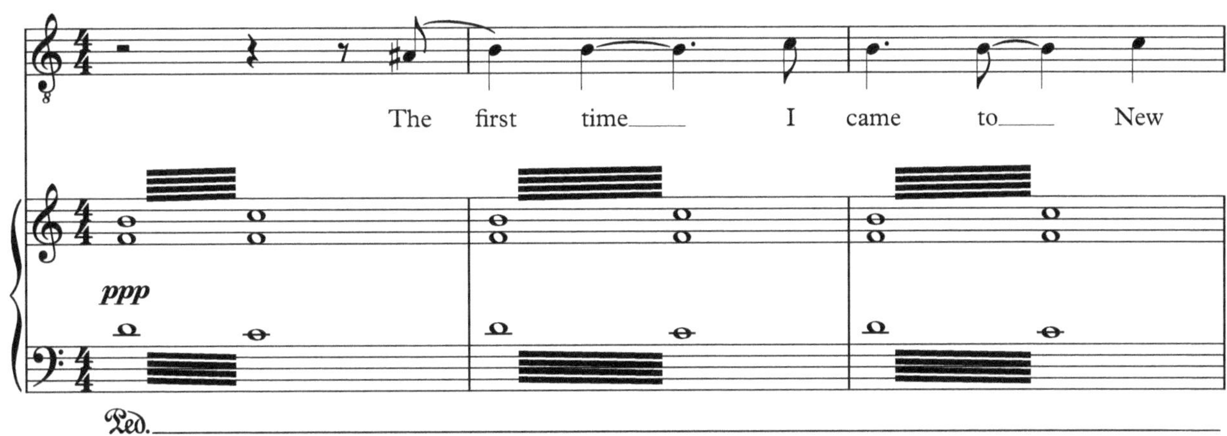

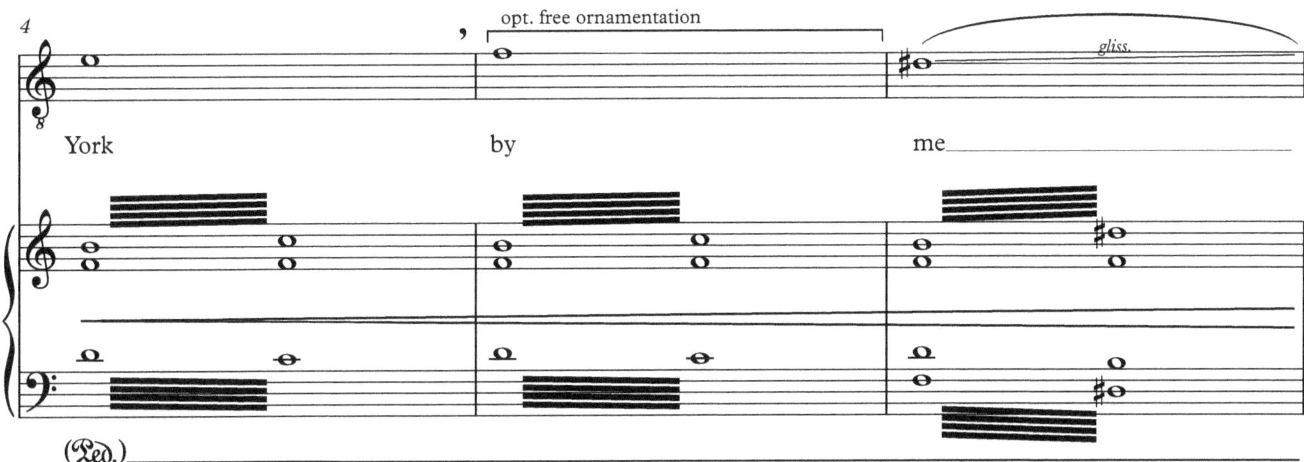

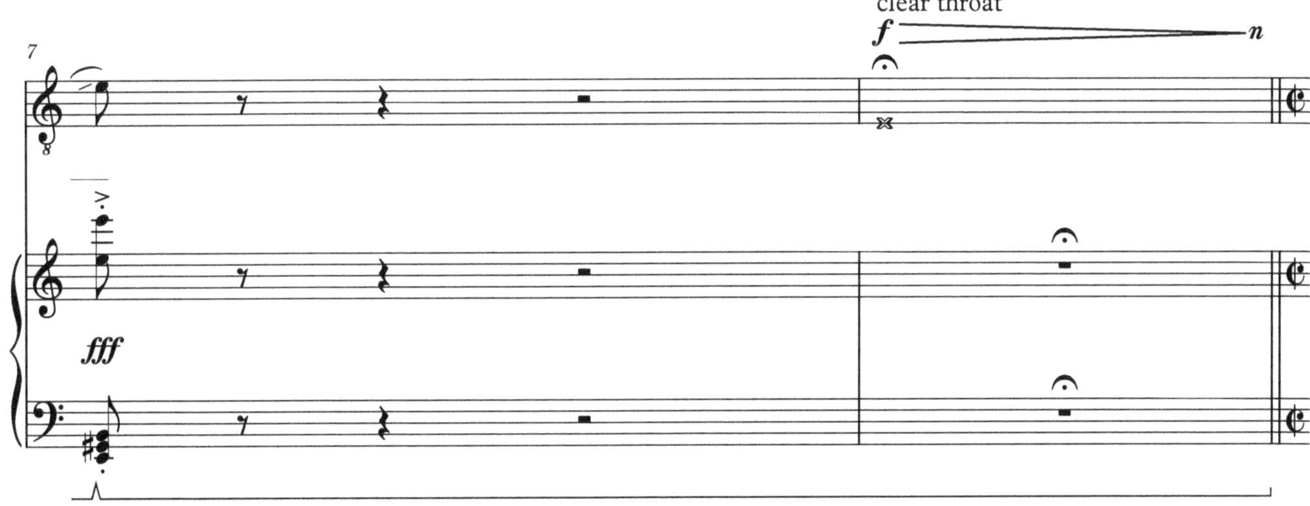

A
mp sub.
p
mf
mp sub.
fff
13
The first time I came to New York
p sub.
fff
p sub.
17
it was snow - ing at J - F - K.
mf sub.
fff

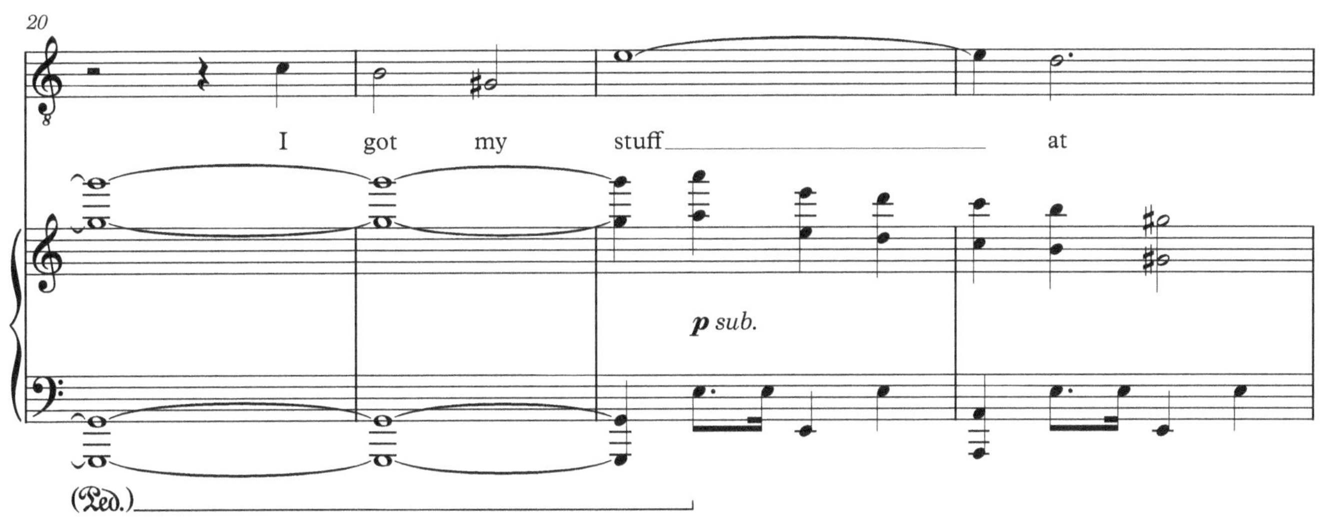
20
I got my stuff at
p sub.
(Ped.)

24
bag - gage claim five af - ter post - ing some sel - fies in the
3
fff
Ped.

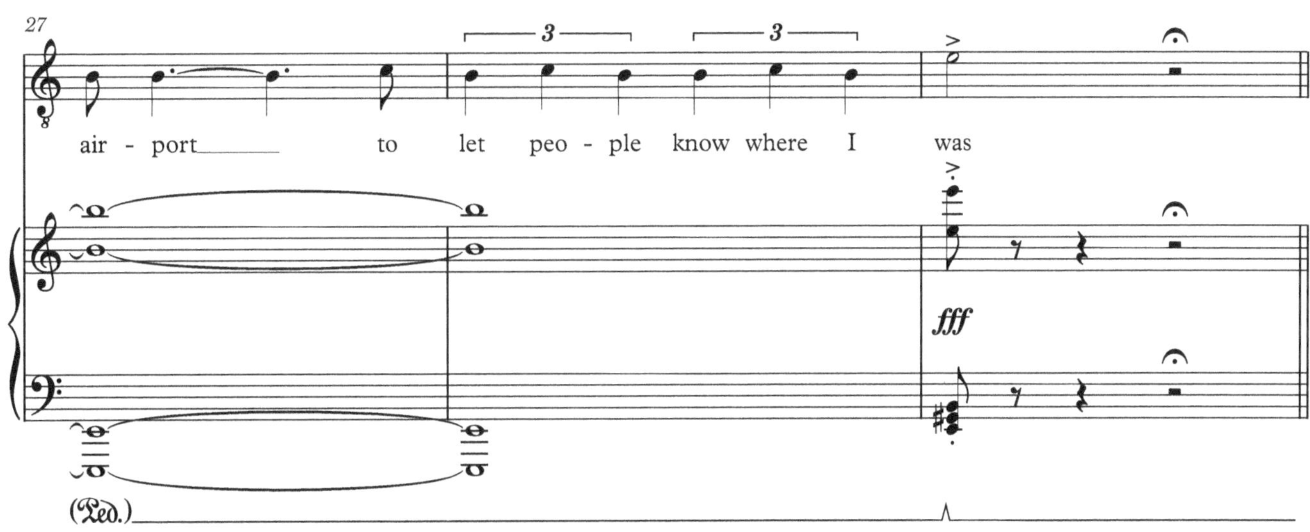
27
air - port to let peo - ple know where I was
3
fff
(Ped.)

B
ad lib.
New York! New York! New
gliss.
(Ped.)

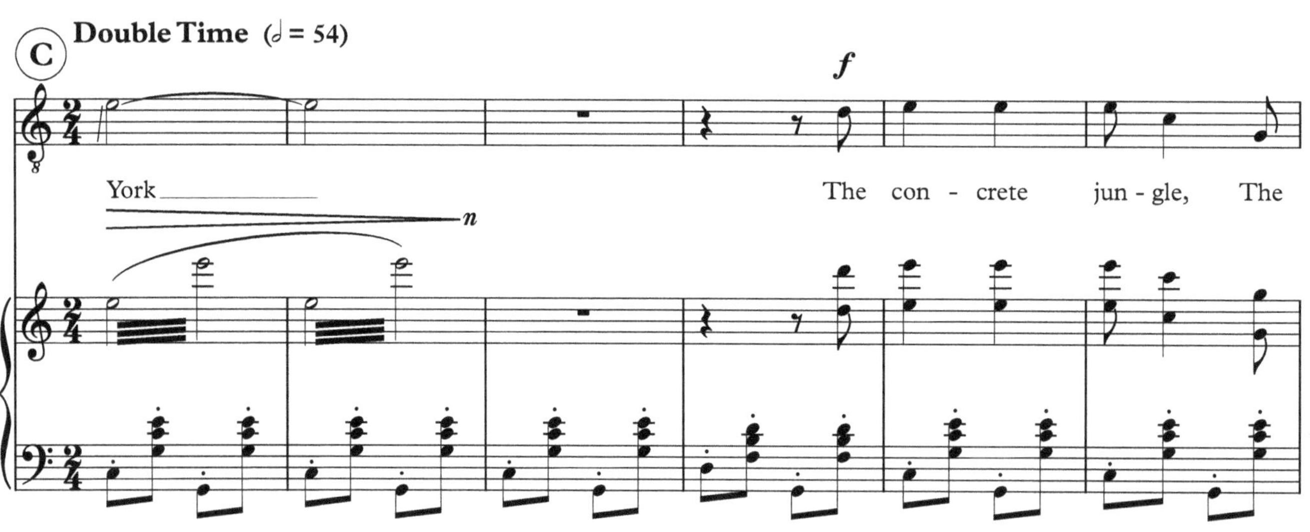
C
Double Time (𝅗𝅥 = 54)
f
York
The con - crete jun - gle, The
n

39
Em - pi - re State, the Big Ap - ple it - self.

46
I dropped my things at my Air B-'n-

52
-B and set out a-mong the old
p sub.
Ped.
sim.

57
stones and the his-to-ry
f

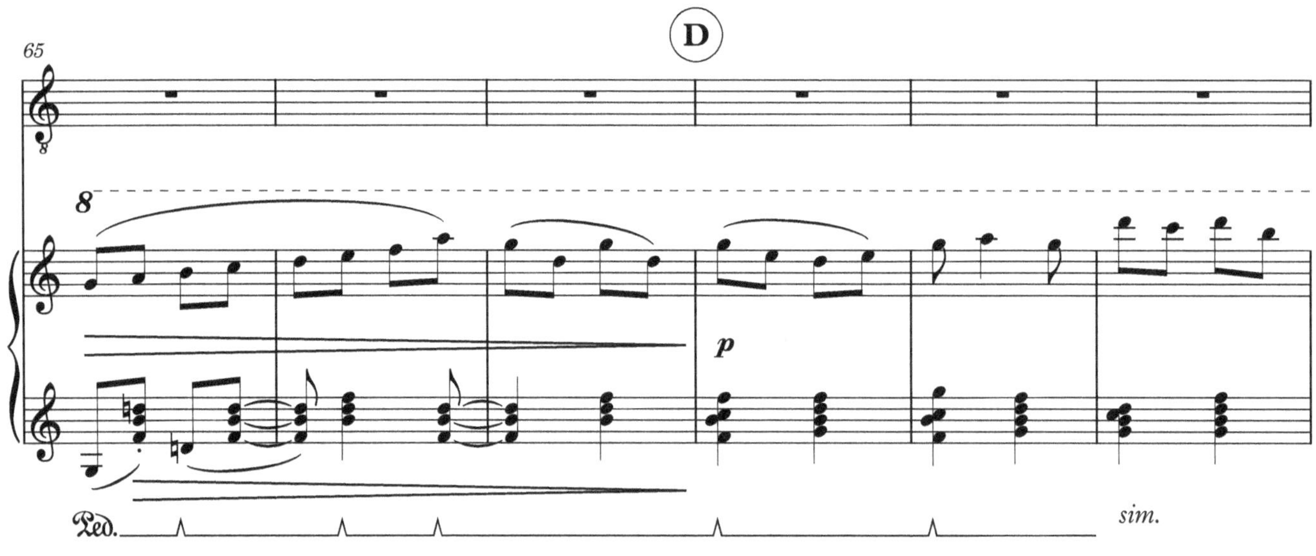
65
D
8
p
Ped.
sim.

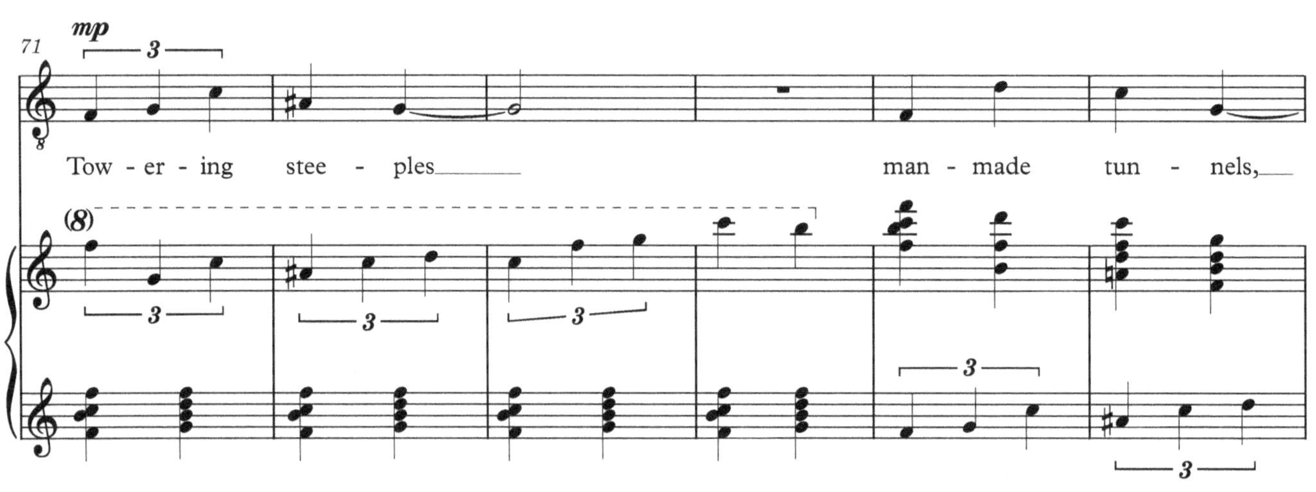
71
mp
Tow - er - ing stee - ples
man - made tun - nels,
(8)

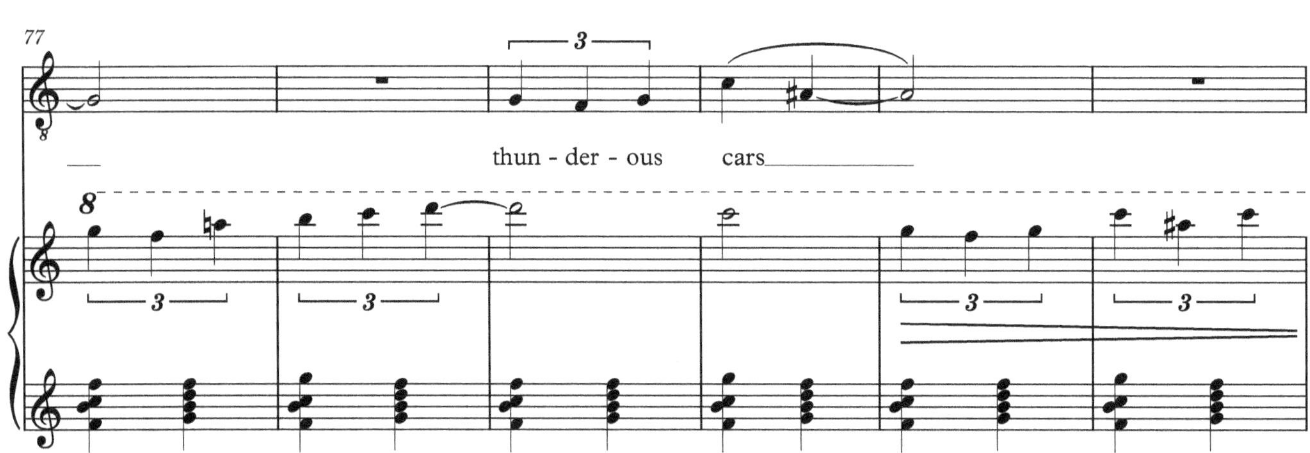
77
thun - der - ous cars
8

83
3
I took a wa - ter ta - - xi so I could see
(8)
3
ppp
3

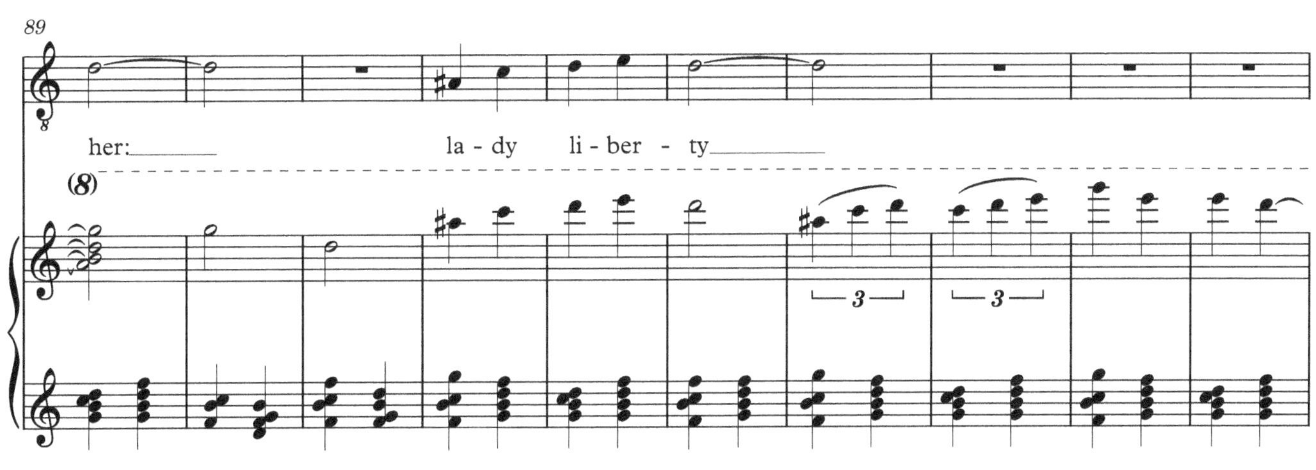
89
her:
la - dy li - ber - ty
(8)
3
3

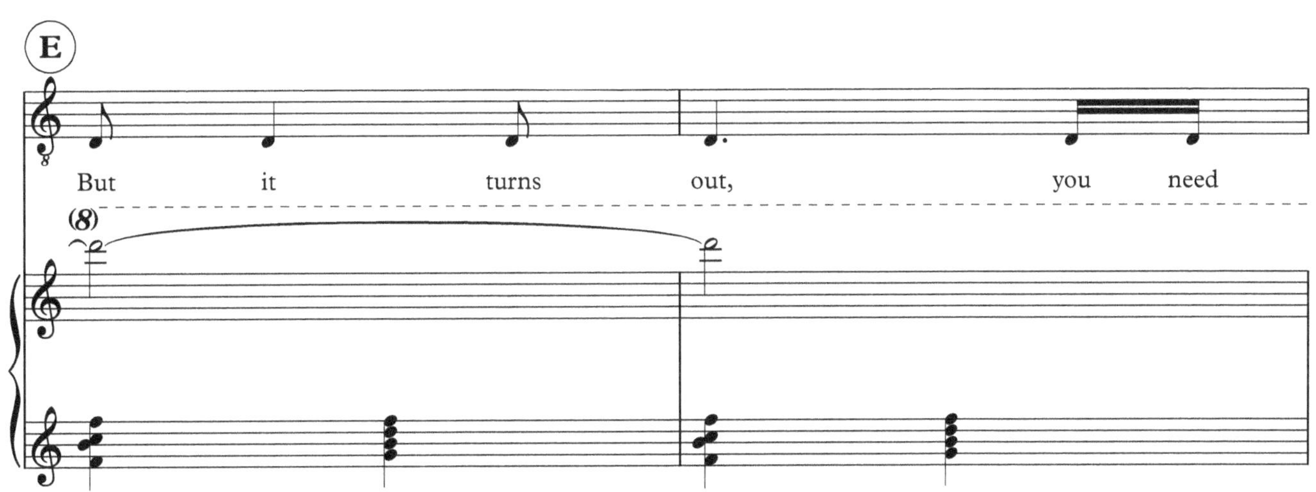
E
But it turns out, you need
(8)

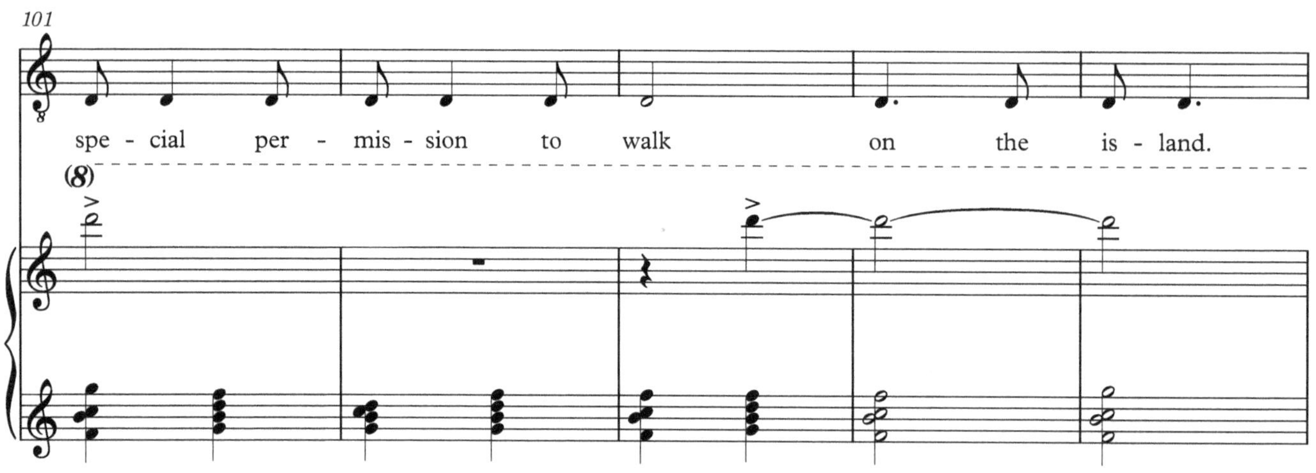
101
spe - cial per - mis - sion to walk on the is - land.
(8)

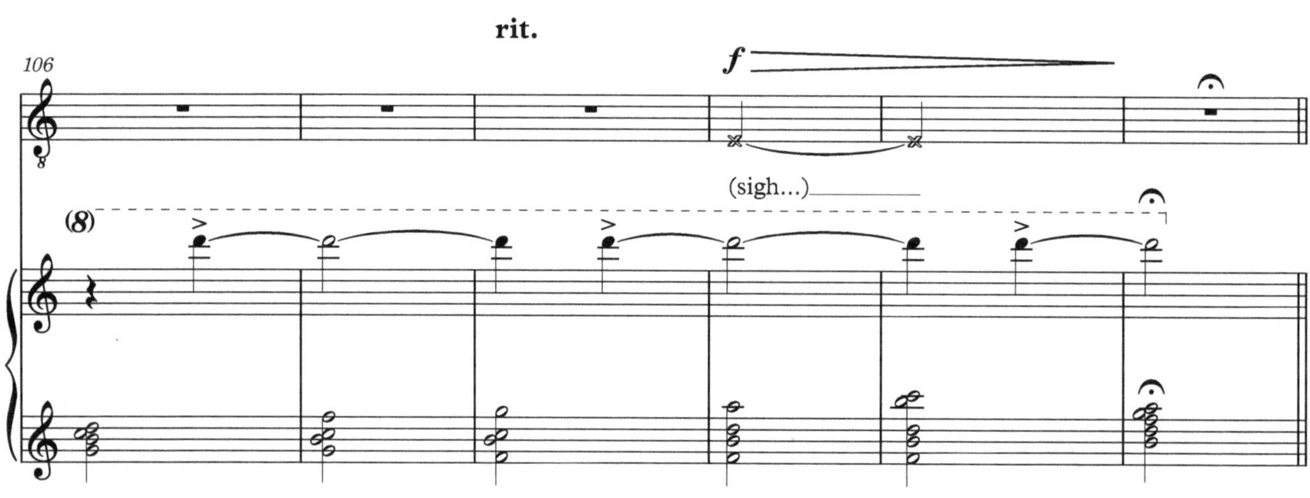
rit.
106
f
(sigh...)
(8)

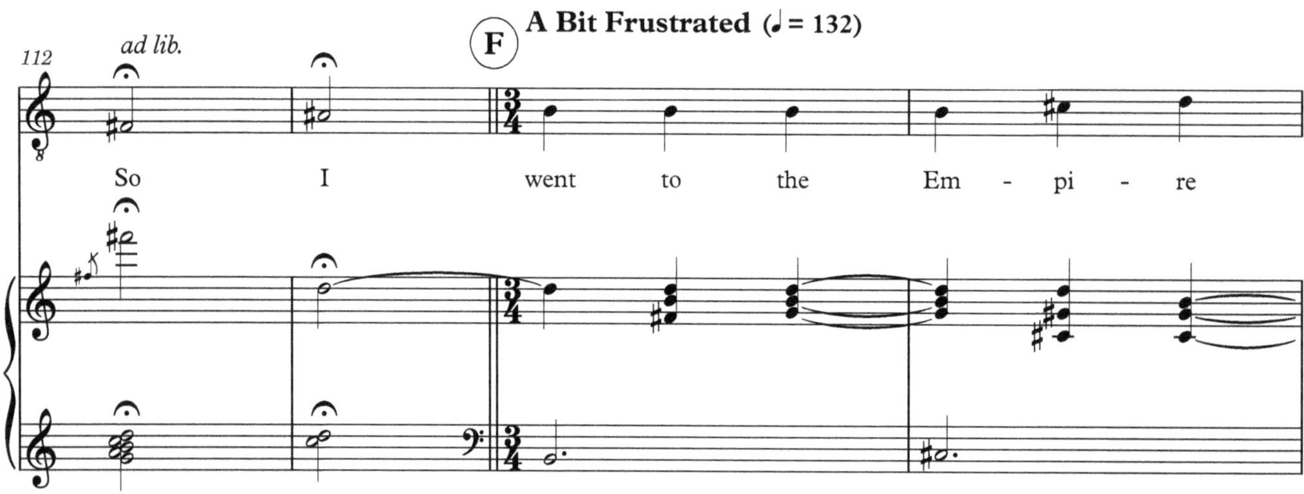
F
A Bit Frustrated (♩= 132)
112
ad lib.
So I went to the Em - pi - re

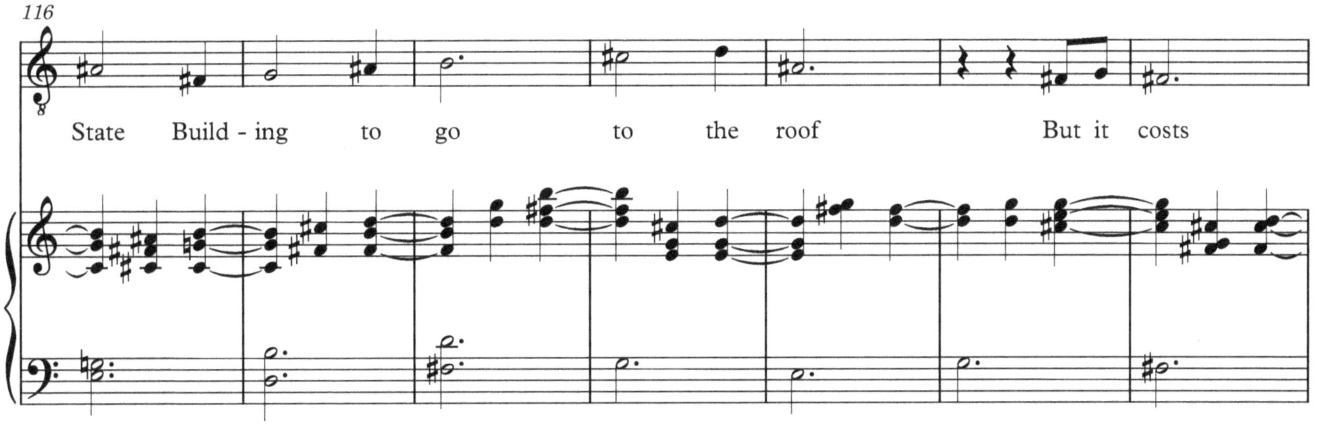
116
State Build - ing to go to the roof But it costs

rit.
accel.
123
thir - ty - five dol - lars and you have to buy your tick - et in ad - vance!

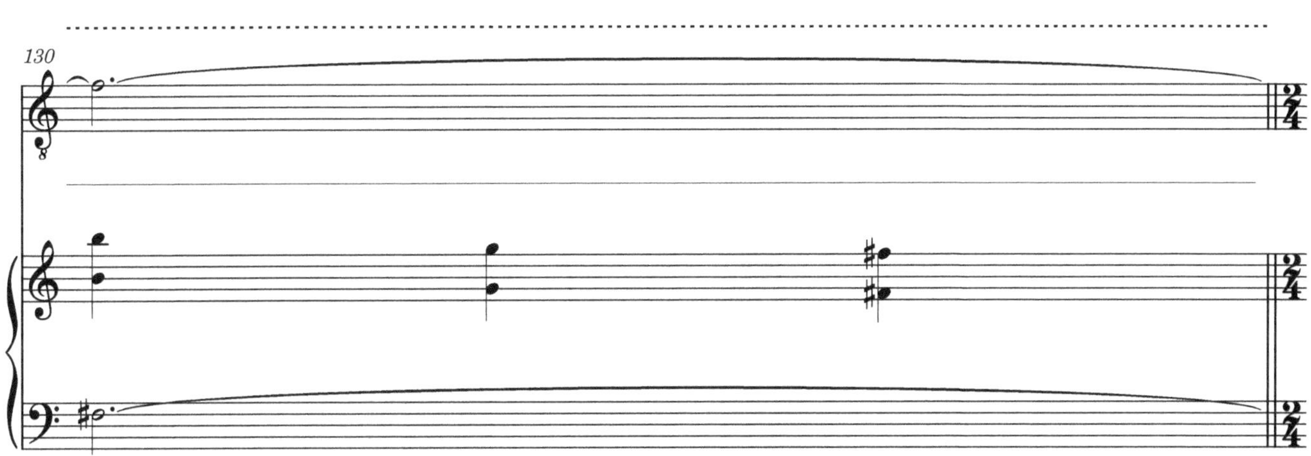
130

G
A Tempo (♩= 120)
So I walked a - round The

136
Ci - ty in - stead The food in Hell's

141
Kit - chen The shop - ping in So - ho.

146
The lights of Broad - way. And

152
sud - den - ly I was there: the cross - roads of the world

rit.
157
it - - - self Times

H
Double Time Feel (𝅗𝅥 = 54)
f
Square
The hust - le, the

168
bust - le
So man - y dif - ferent fa - ces.
Some bus - y, some

173
lin - ger - ing

178
I took a pho - to of a nice ol - der coup - le

183
From some place called Wee - hauk - en
p sub.
f
Ped.
sim.

188
semi-spoken
Ne - ver heard of it.
The

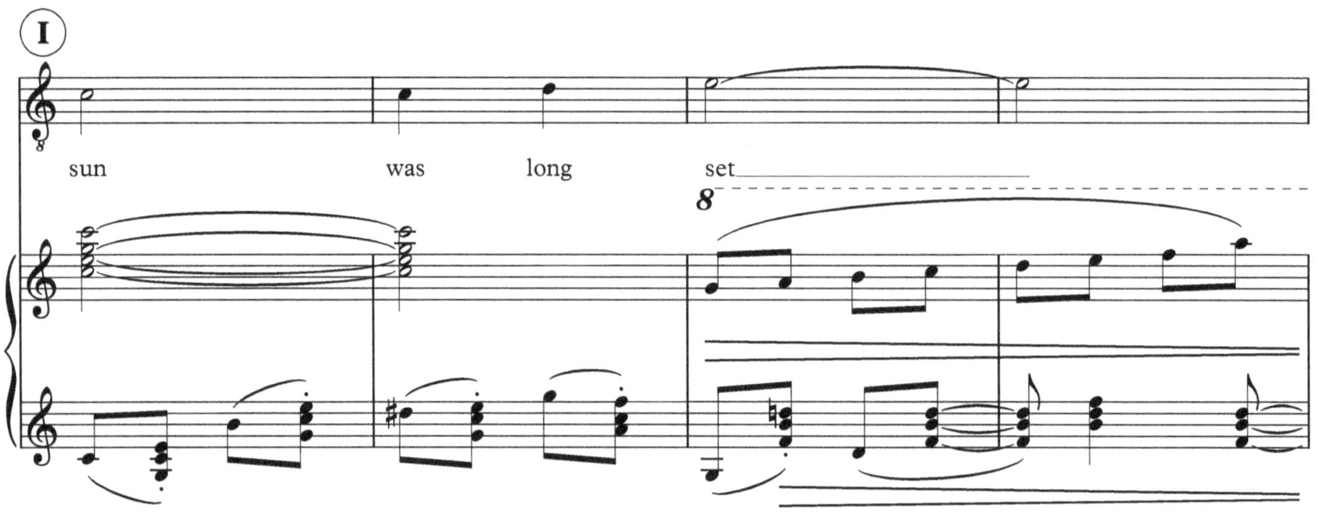
I
sun was long set
8

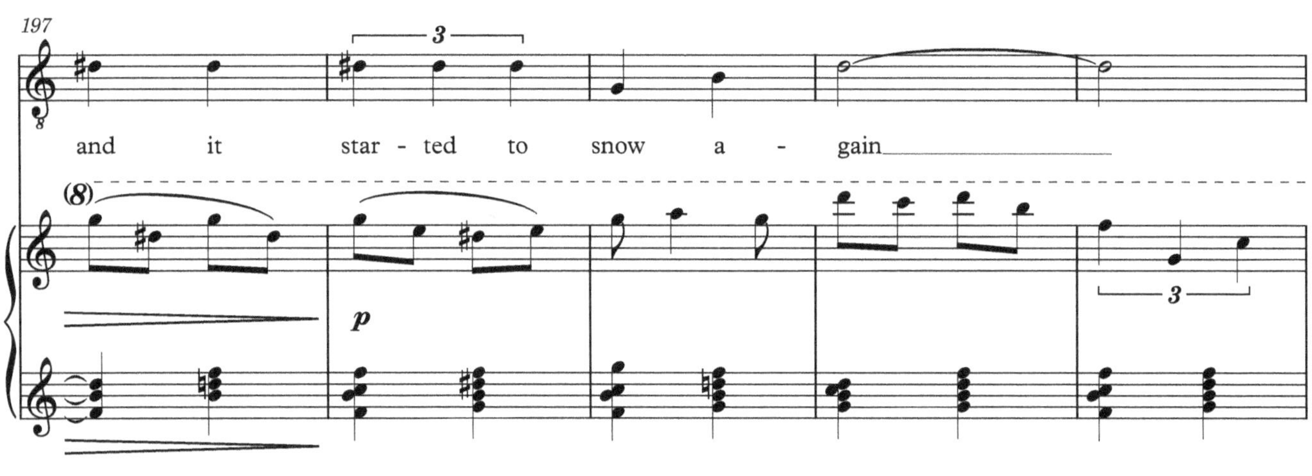
197
3
and it star - ted to snow a - gain
(8)
p
3

202
3
I felt such joy
(8)
3
3
3
3

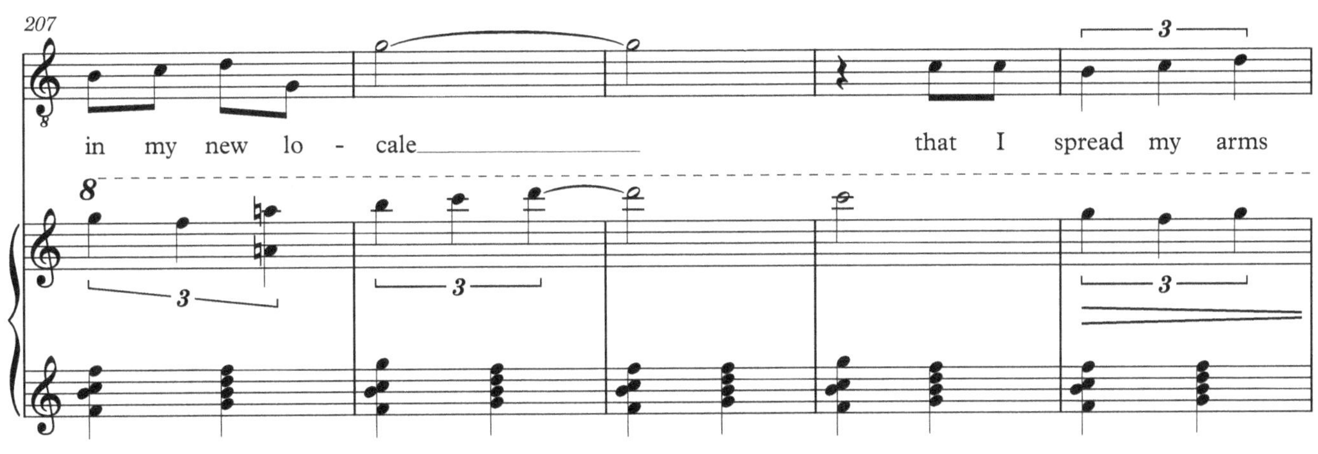
207
in my new lo - cale
that I spread my arms
8
3
3
3
3

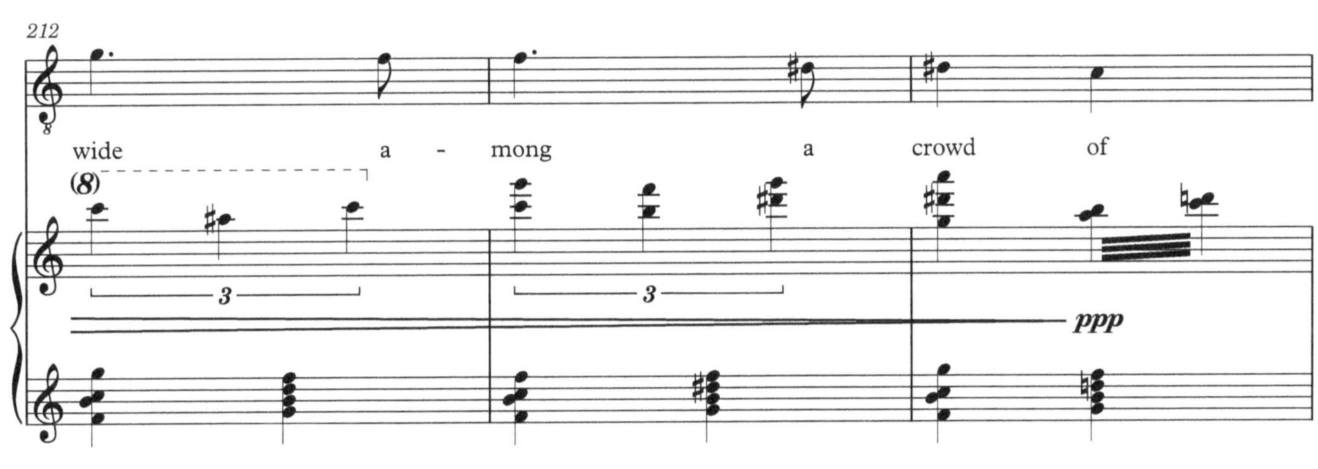
212
wide a - mong a crowd of
(8)
3
3
ppp

215
peo - ple
and ex - claimed:
8
3
f

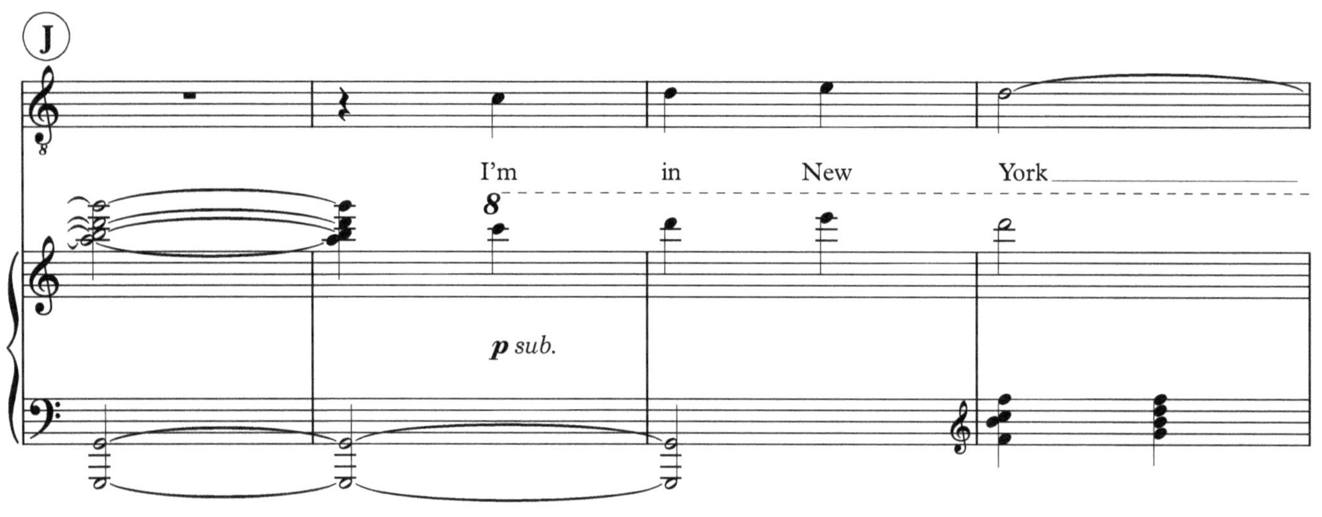
J
I'm in New York
8
p sub.

223
I'm in New York
(8)
3

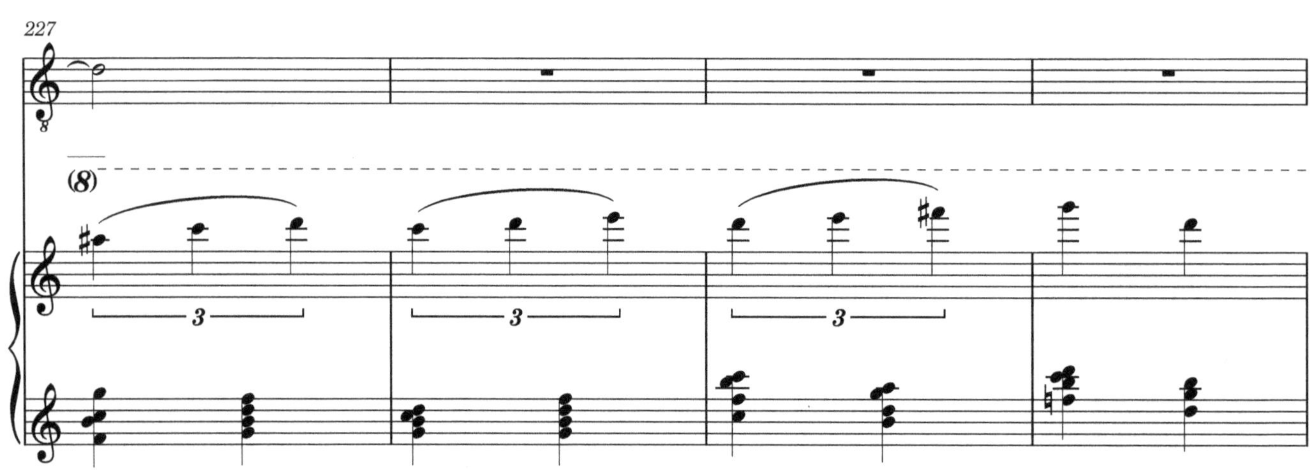
227
(8)
3
3
3

231
3
What hap - pened next, I will ne - ver for - get.
(8)
8

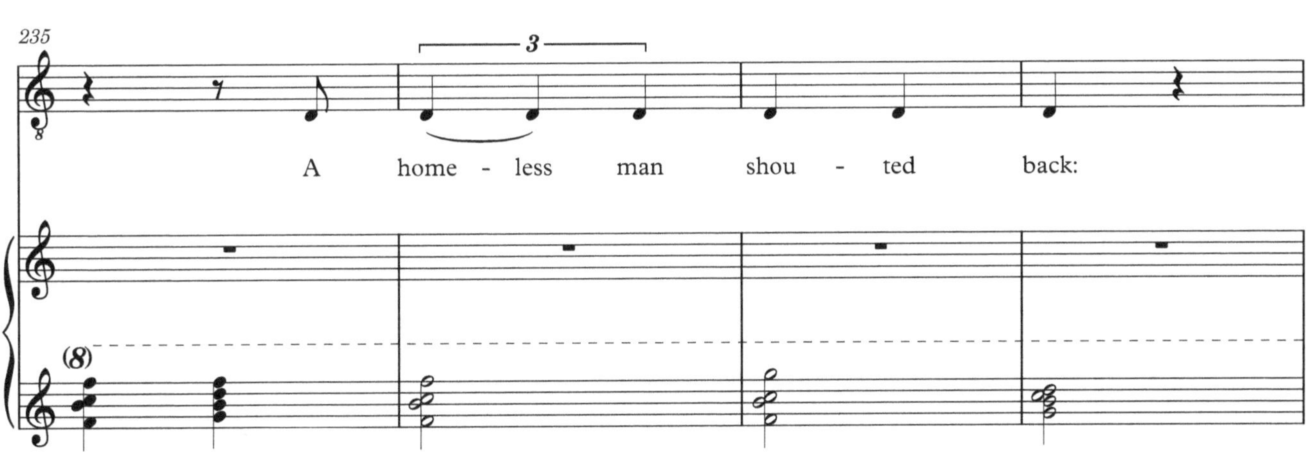
235
3
A home - less man shou - ted back:
(8)

semi-spoken
f
239
3
"Shut the fuck up!"
8
ff
(8)

composed for songSLAM NYC I 2017

One Good Life

Maria Zajkowski

WALLY GUNN
(2017)

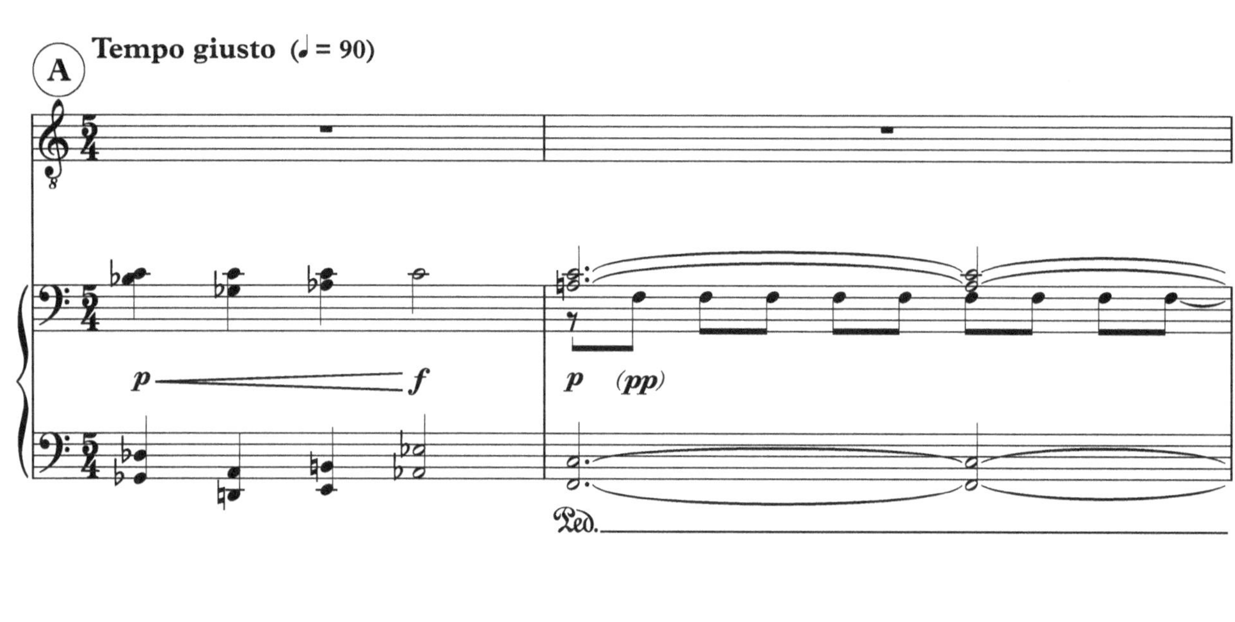

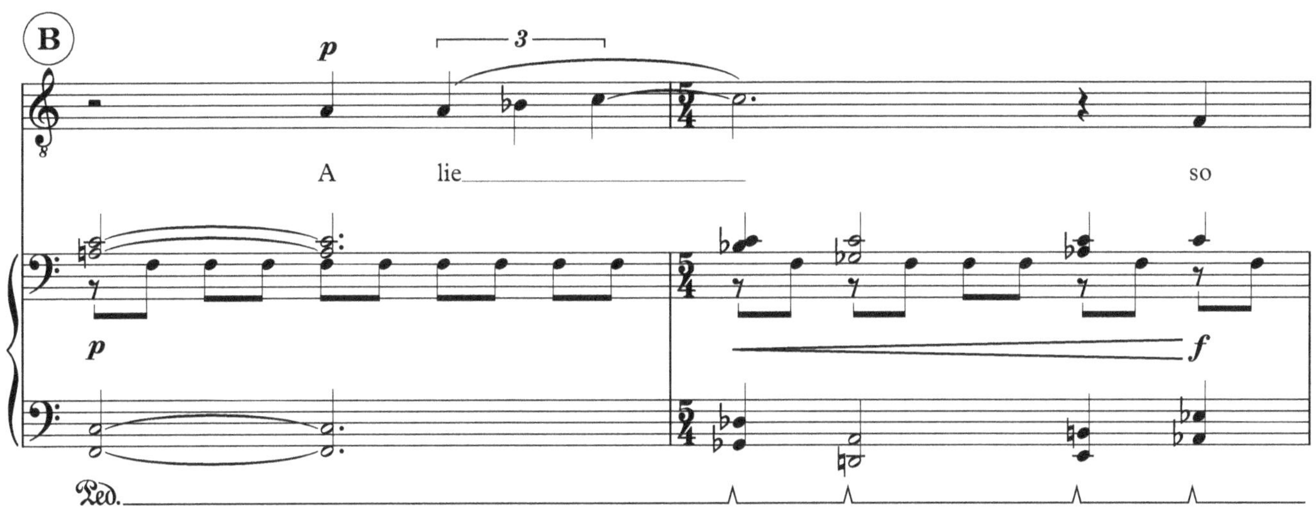
B
p
3
A
lie
so
p
f
Ped.

10
gliss.
hand - some
a boy might
3
p
f

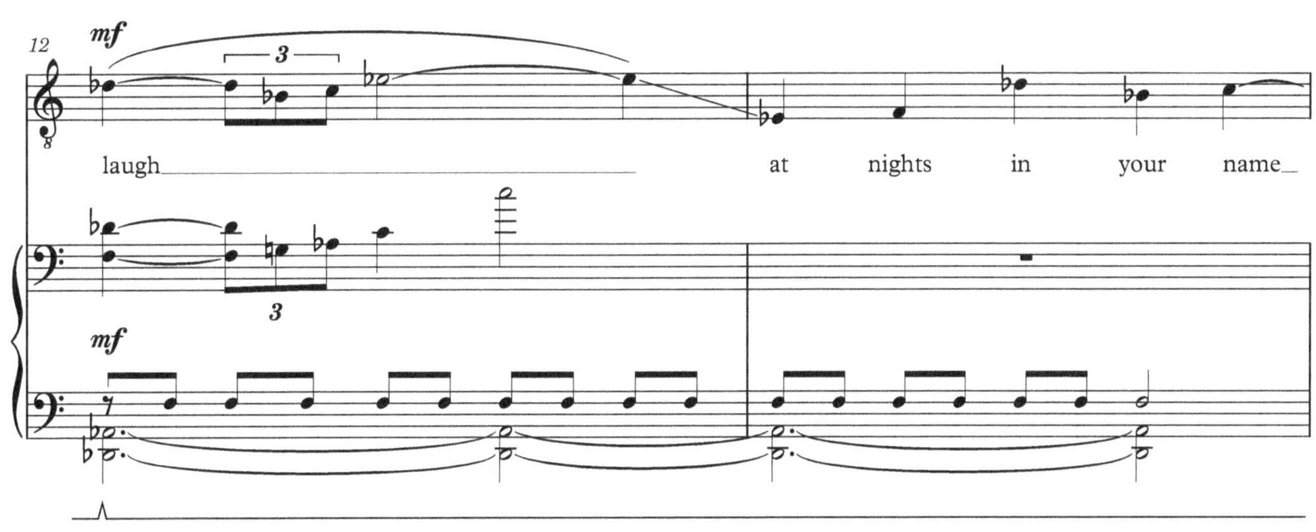
12
mf
3
laugh
at nights in your name
3
mf

14
p
p
the
p
f
sim.

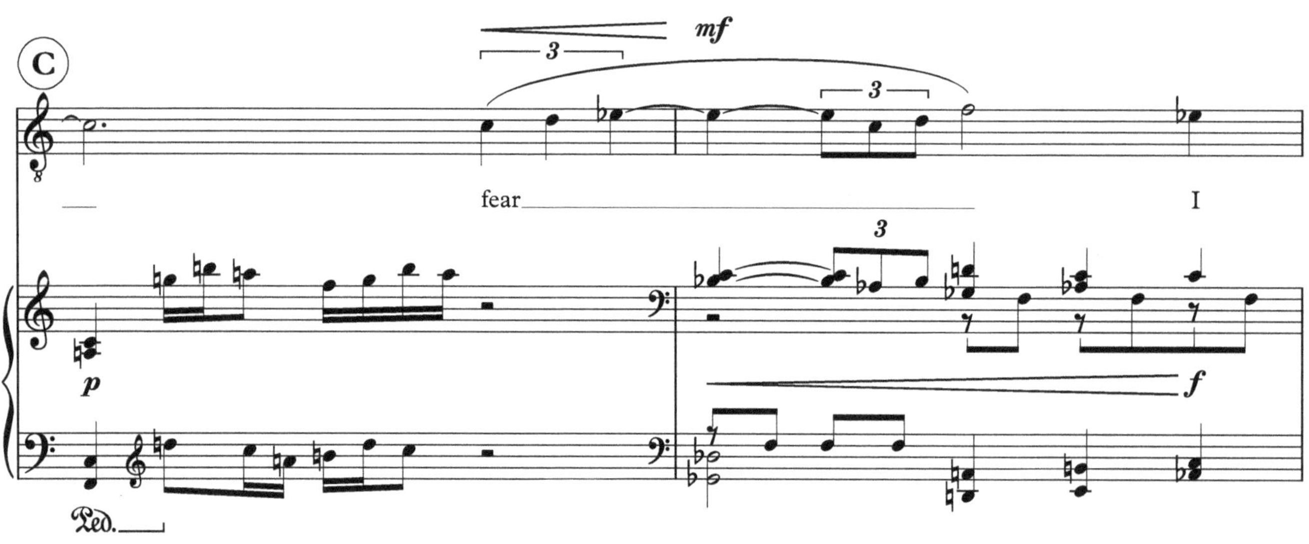
C
3
mf
3
fear
I
3
p
f
Ped.

18
p
gliss.
3
don't be - lieve
comes from the
p
f
Ped.

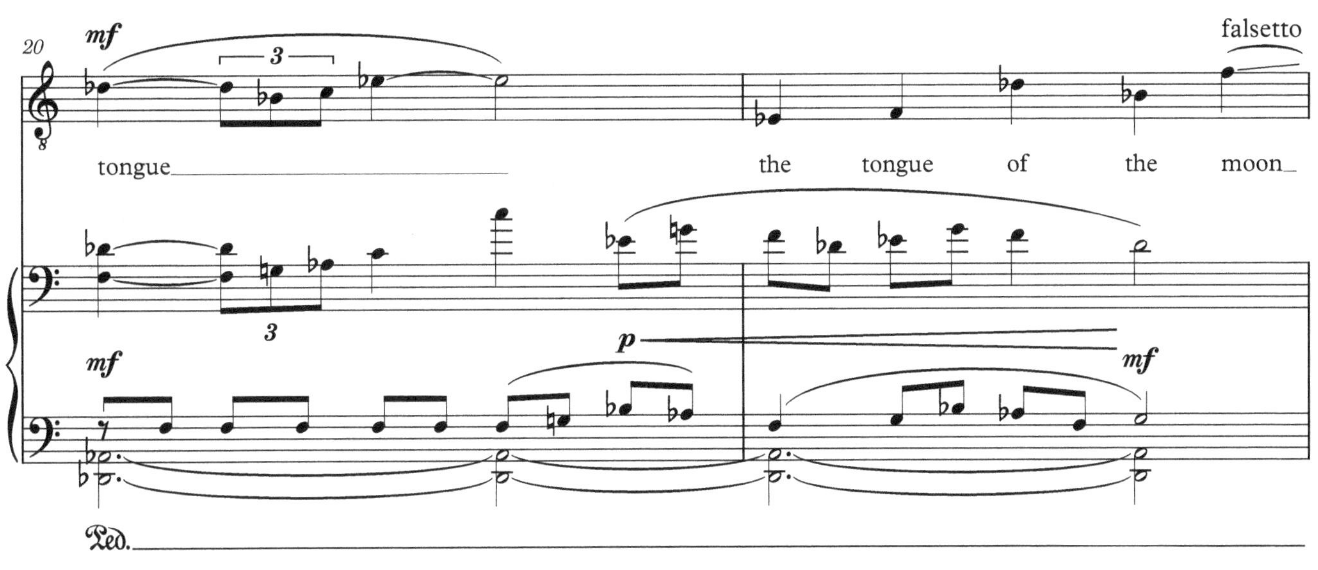
20
mf
3
falsetto
tongue
the tongue of the moon
3
p
mf
mf
Ped.

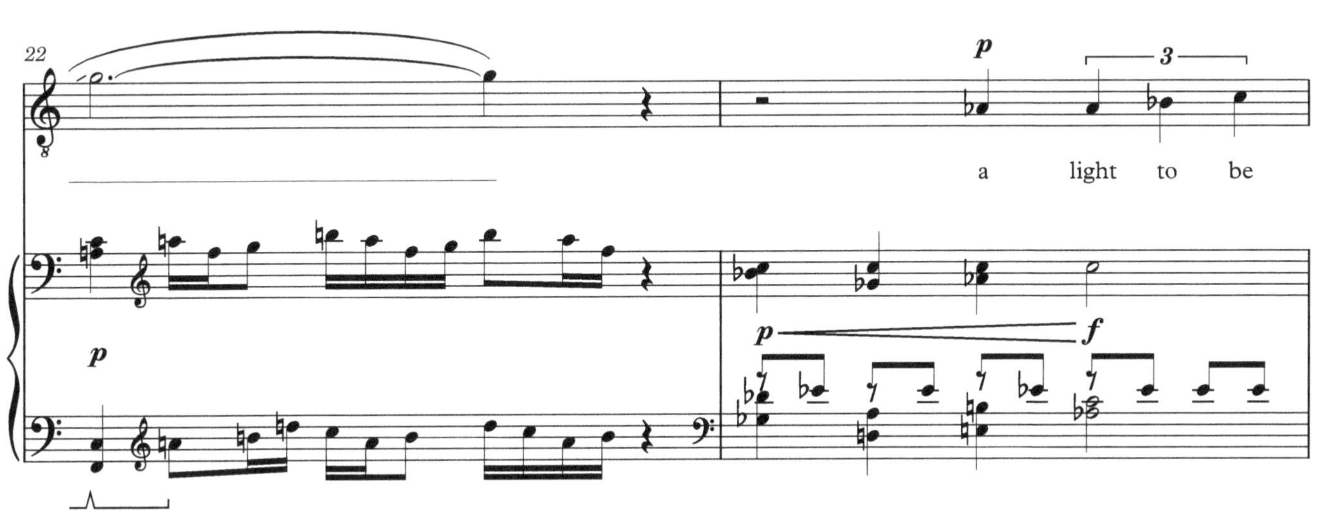
22
p
3
a light to be
p
f
p

24
gliss.
spo - ken
p
p
f
Ped.

D
mf
3
The sin of the sun and the way we look
3
f
p
Ped.
29
f mf p
gliss.
to it
mf
free
8
p
f
Ped.
31
3
will
gliss.
so far in your eyes
3
mf
p mf
Ped.

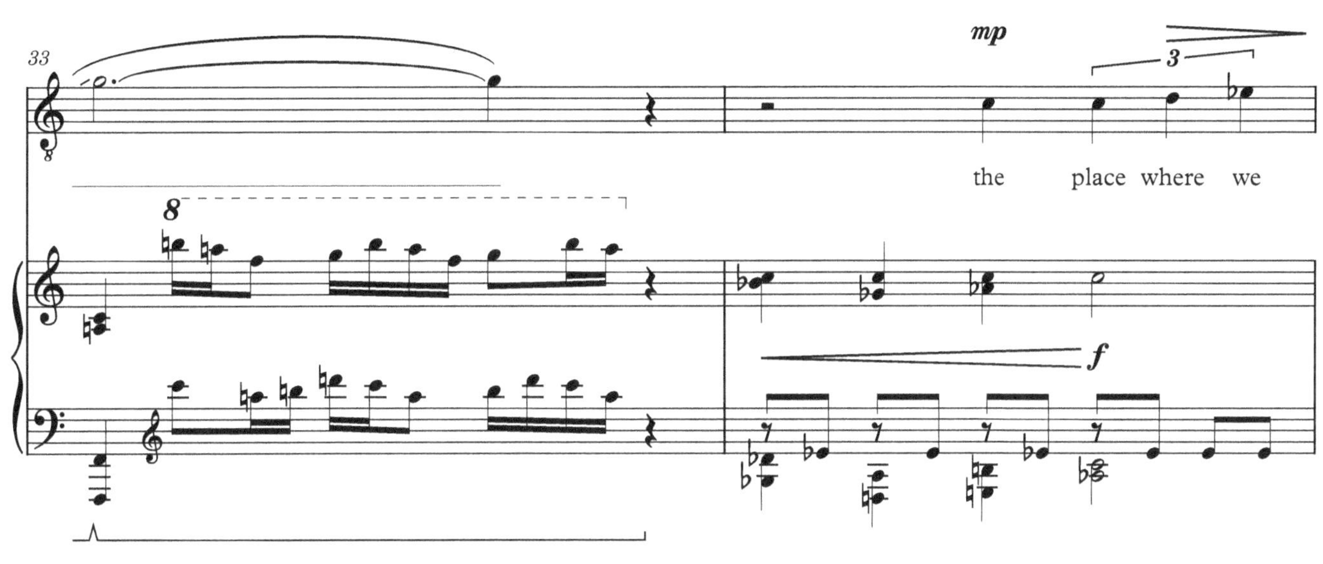
mp
3
the place where we
8
f

p
meet
p
Ped.

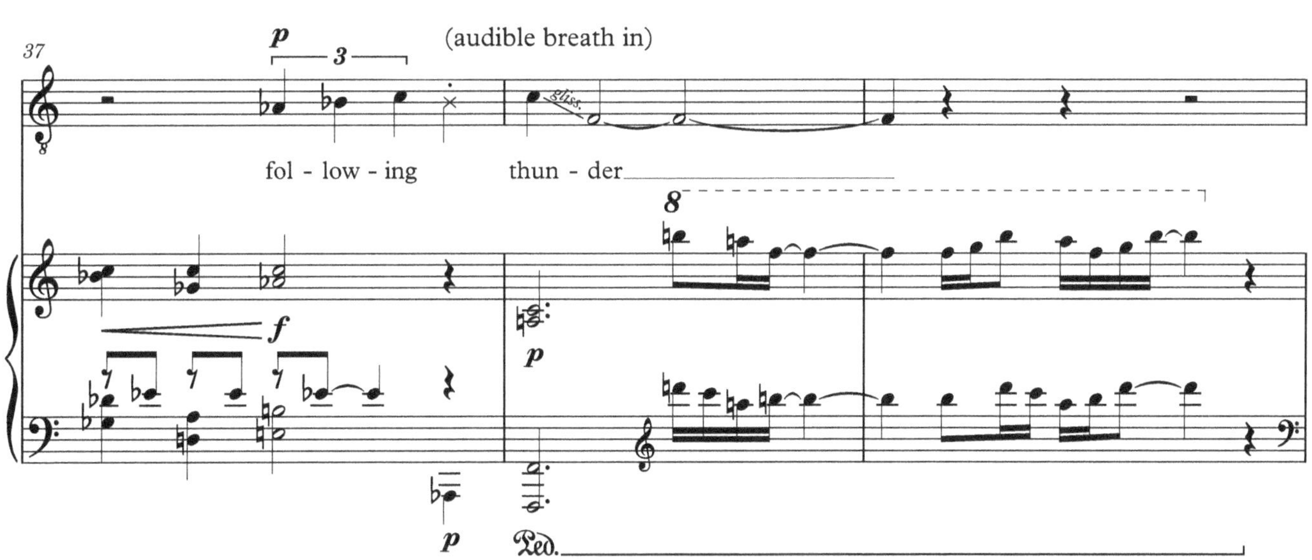
p
3
(audible breath in)
gliss.
fol - low - ing
thun - der
8
f
p
p
Ped.

E
40
Do you know this one good life
Sost.
42
and its tak - ing
(Sost.)
Sost.
44
the beats of our
(Sost.)

45
3
3
flight
un - der
fall -
- ing of fear
Sost.
47
3
be - tween
Sost.
49
3
3
dark - - - ness that calls
from my
Sost.

51
3
pris - - - on to yours
3
mine to
Sost.
53
yours
Ped.
55
p
(Ped.)

This page intentionally left blank to facilitate page turns

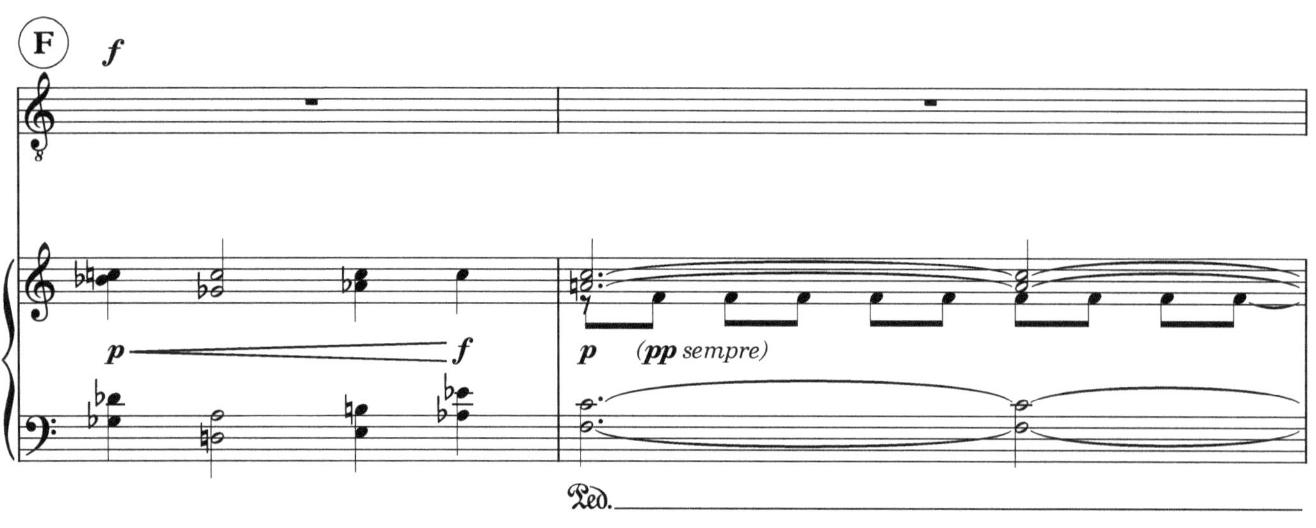
F
f
p
f
p
(pp sempre)
Ped.

59
f
3
If we run and
(Ped.)
f

61
3
run out of
3
time take this
3
3
Ped.

63
p
mf
3
pro - mise
and ride a - way
8
p
f
Ped.
65
3
gliss
stars
I'll al - ways lie true
3
mf
p
mf
Ped.
67
p
p
3
Do you know
8
p
f
(Ped.)

G
this
one
good
life
p
Ped.

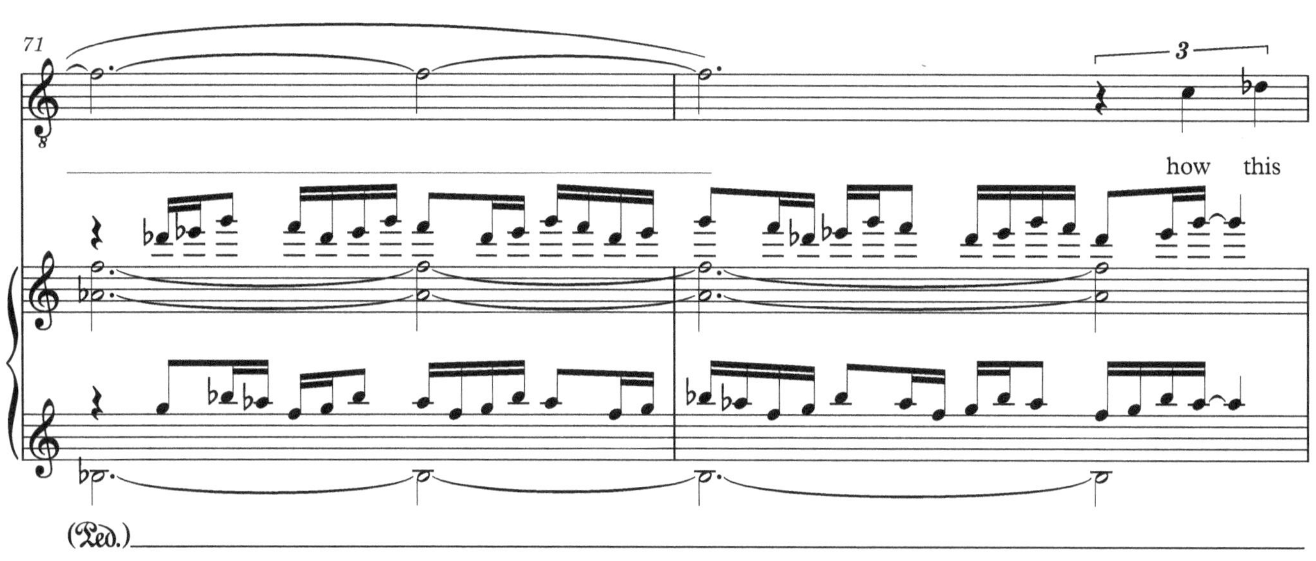
71
how
this
(Ped.)

73
moon
light
is
made
keep
me

This area intentionally left blank to facilitate page turns

H

3
ooh
pp
(Ped.)

79
3
ah
(Ped.)

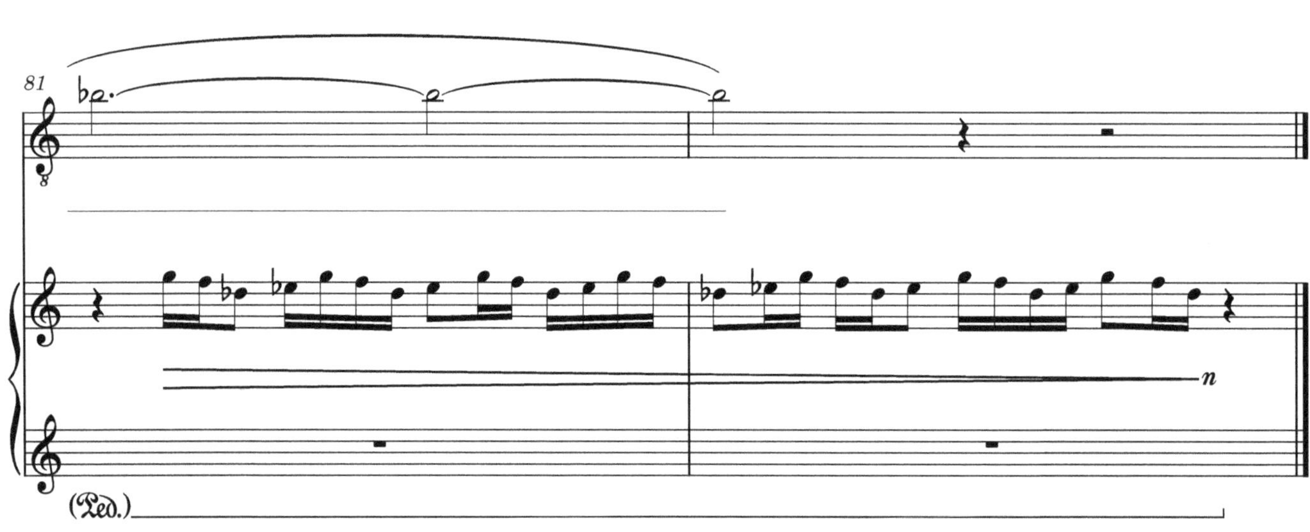
81
n
(Ped.)

This page intentionally left blank to facilitate page turns

composed for songSLAM Chicago 2019

Tikka Masala

Unfortunately Based on a True Story

Words and music:
MEG HUSKIN
(2019)

Freely (♩. = 60)

12
mf
ff
3
I've had al - ler - gic re - ac - tions more pleas - ant than love. Se - ri - ous - ly.

15
f
give me a pe - can and I'll break out in hives; a wal - nut will
mf

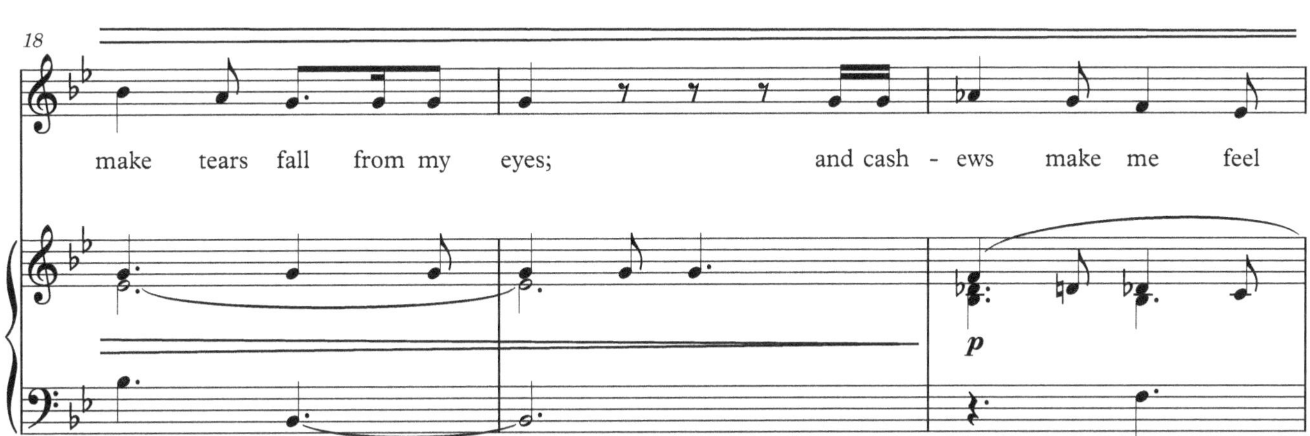
18
make tears fall from my eyes; and cash - ews make me feel
p

rit.
21
mp
sick in - side,
but noth - ing com - pares to love.
On the
f

A Brisk Walk (♩. = 70)
25
mf
day we ar - rived in Sing - a - pore we walked to the

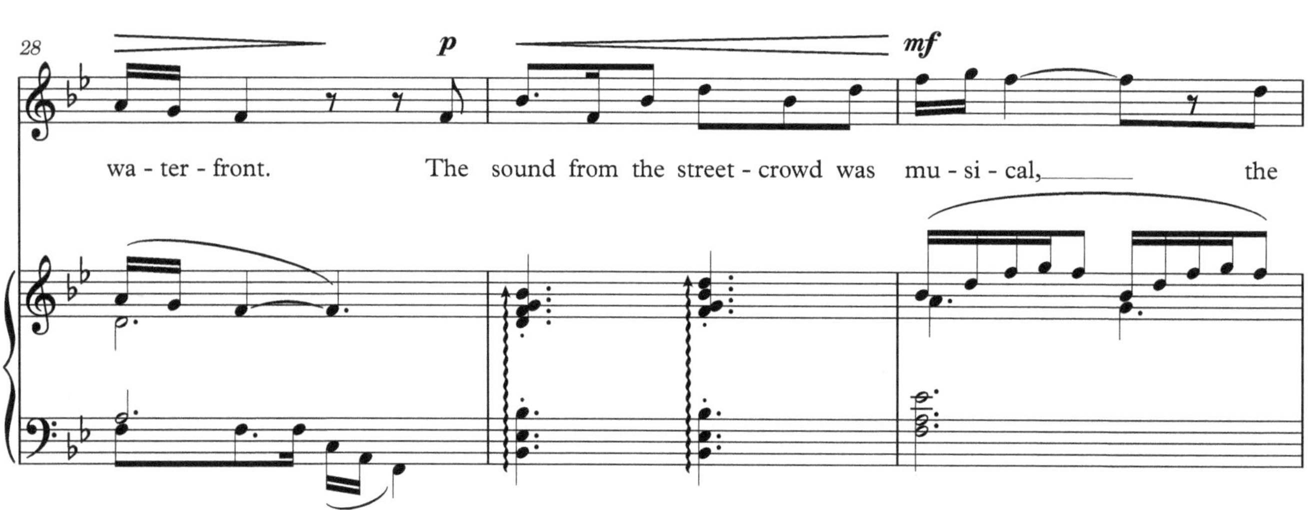
28
p
mf
wa - ter - front. The sound from the street - crowd was mu - si - cal, the

31
scents from the street - carts, sub - lime.
We walked
mp

34
hand in hand,
I wore my brand - new white dress,
the

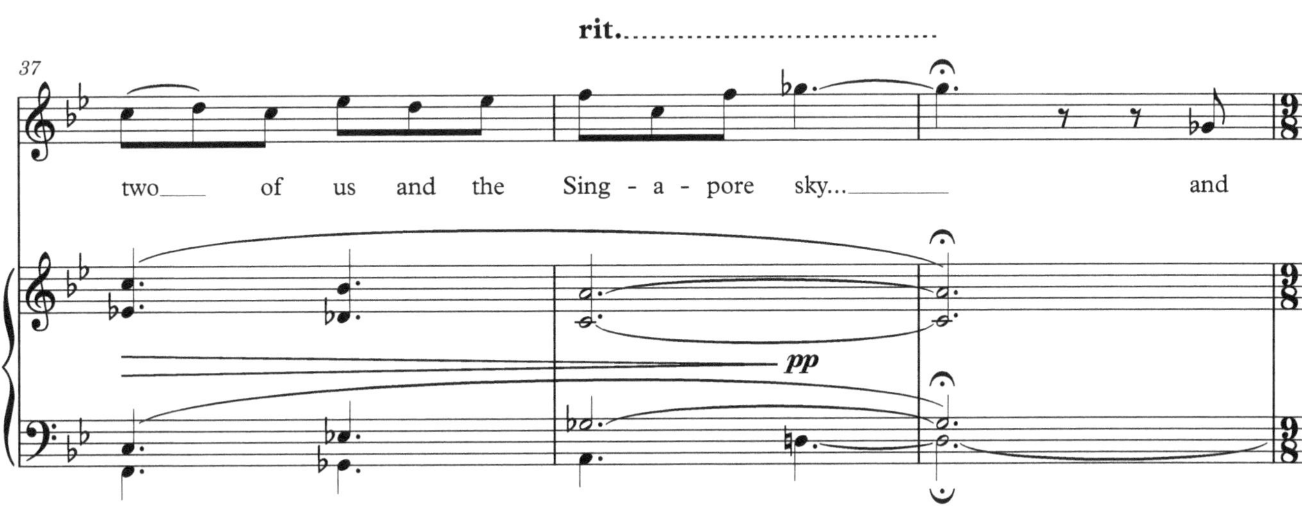
rit.
37
two of us and the Sing - a - pore sky...
and
pp

♩. = 60
40
mp
I thought I'm so in love. We
gentle, loving

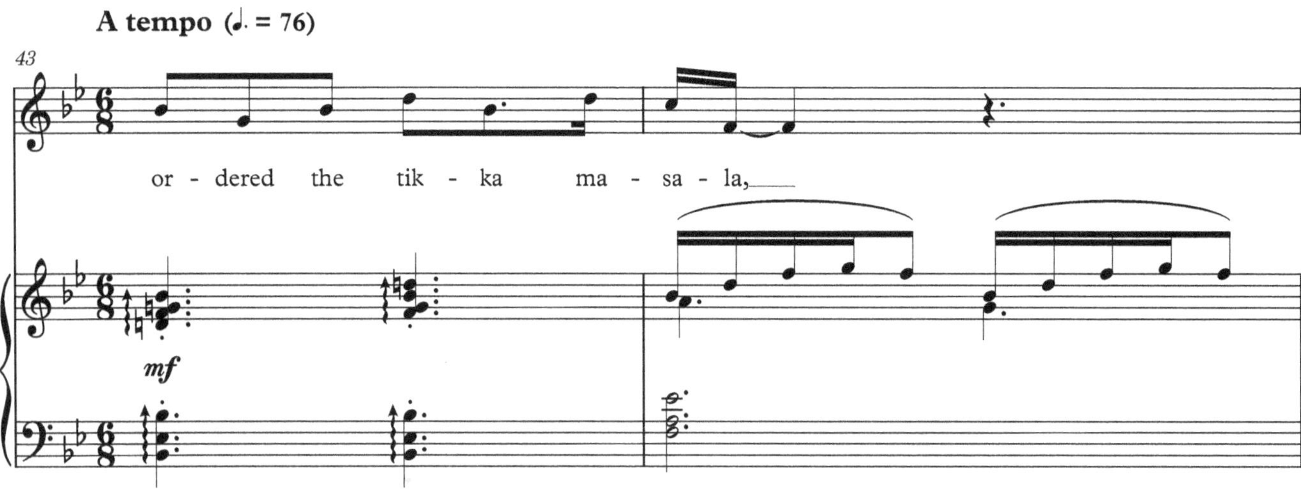
A tempo (♩. = 76)
43
or - dered the tik - ka ma - sa - la,
mf

Suddenly slower
a hint of sexy
45
siz - zl - ing, spic - y, red as the dev - il. The

a tempo
47
steam made my eyes and mouth wa - ter. Has a

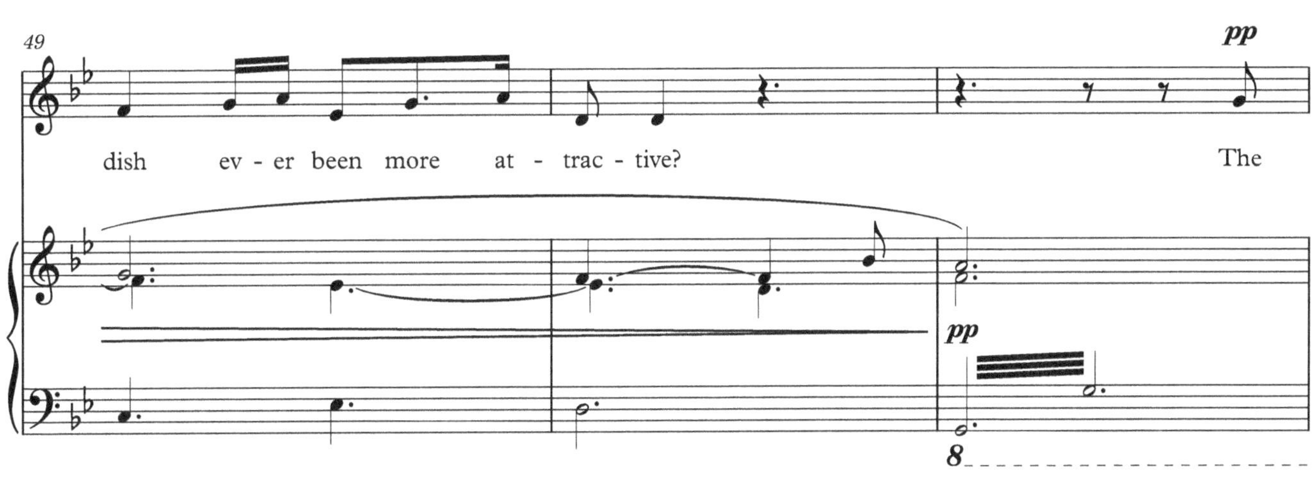
49
pp
dish ev - er been more at - trac - tive? The
pp
8

♩. = 69
52
p
with passion
first bite... like the first kiss... my lips be - gan to
(8)

accel.
55
tin - gle.
The next bite...
and the next one and soon it's al -
f
(8)

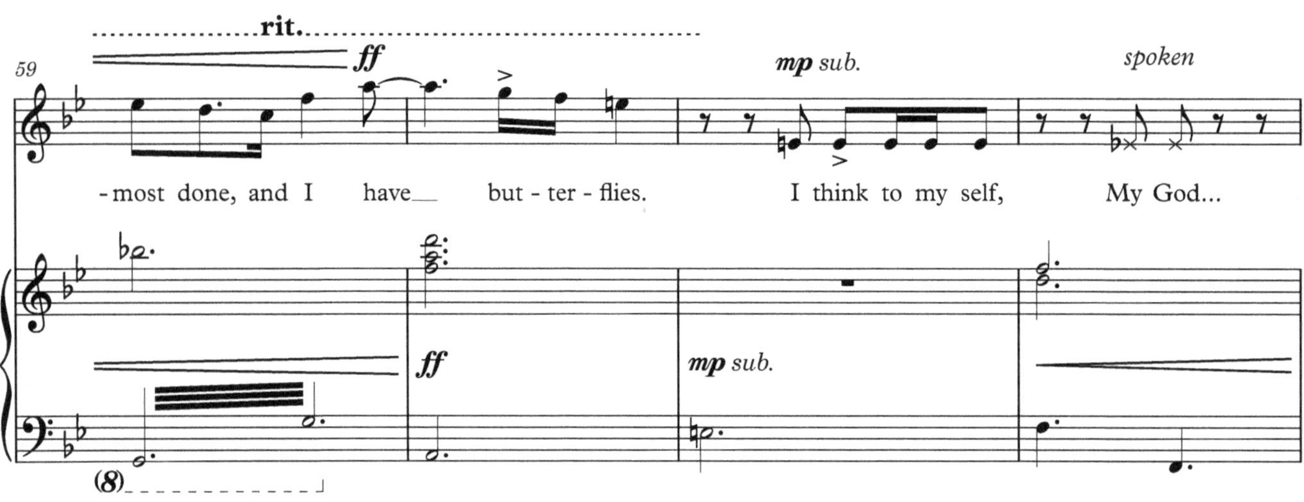
rit.
59
ff
mp sub.
spoken
- most done, and I have but - ter - flies.
I think to my self,
My God...
ff
mp sub.
(8)

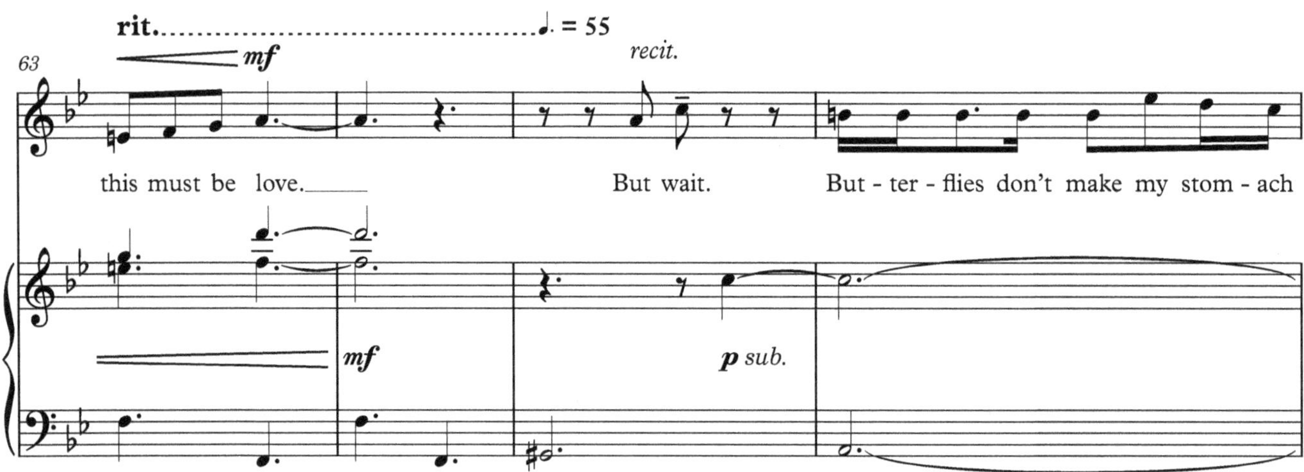
rit.
♩. = 55
63
mf
recit.
this must be love.
But wait.
But - ter - flies don't make my stom - ach
mf
p sub.

67
with growing concern
2
churn, or my lips be - gin to swell. That on - ly hap - pens when... could it be

rit.................................. = 50
71
true? Hey! is this tik - ka ma - sa - la dish full of cash - ews?

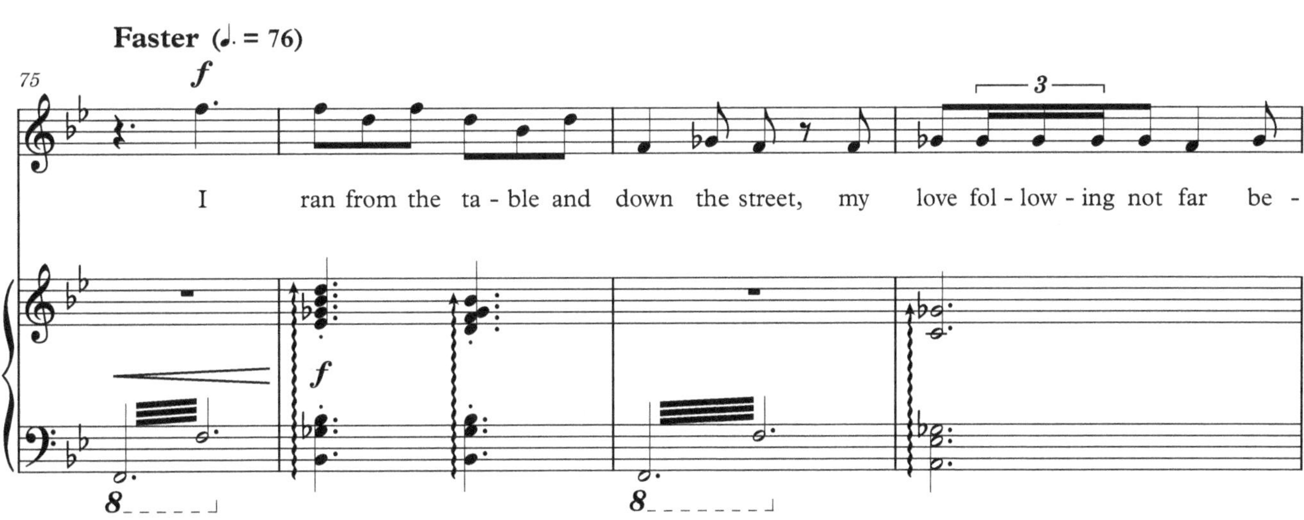
Faster (= 76)
75
f
3
I ran from the ta - ble and down the street, my love fol - low - ing not far be -
f
8
8

79
-hind. I told___ my - self not to make a mess, just as that
8

accel.
♩. = 88
rit.
82
bright red, hot spic - y tik - ka ma - sa - la came up - chuck - ing on - to my
ff

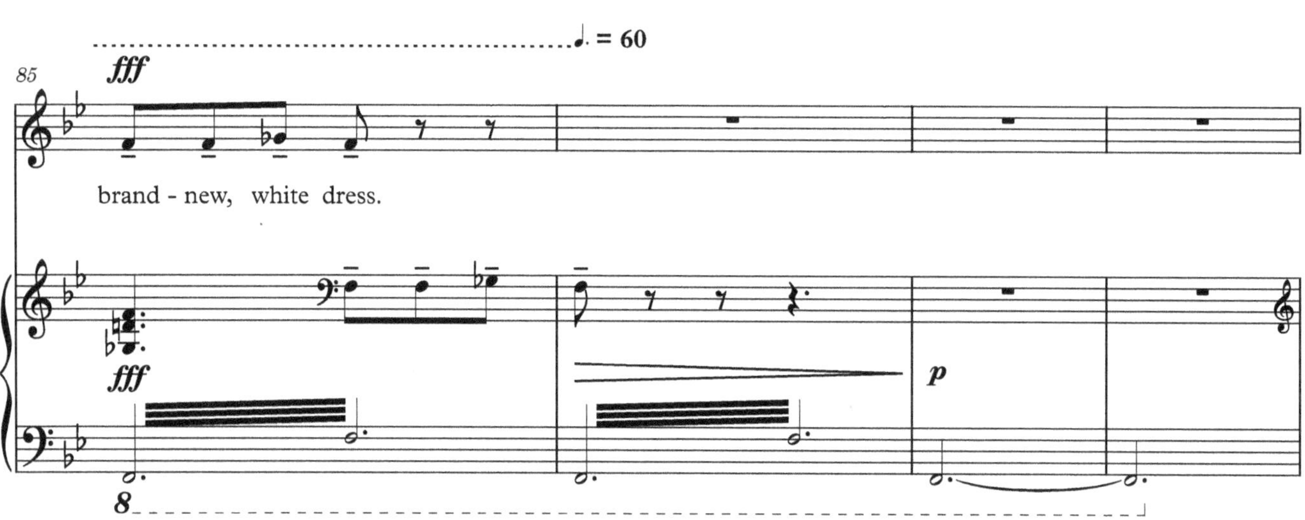
♩. = 60
85
fff
brand - new, white dress.
fff
p
8

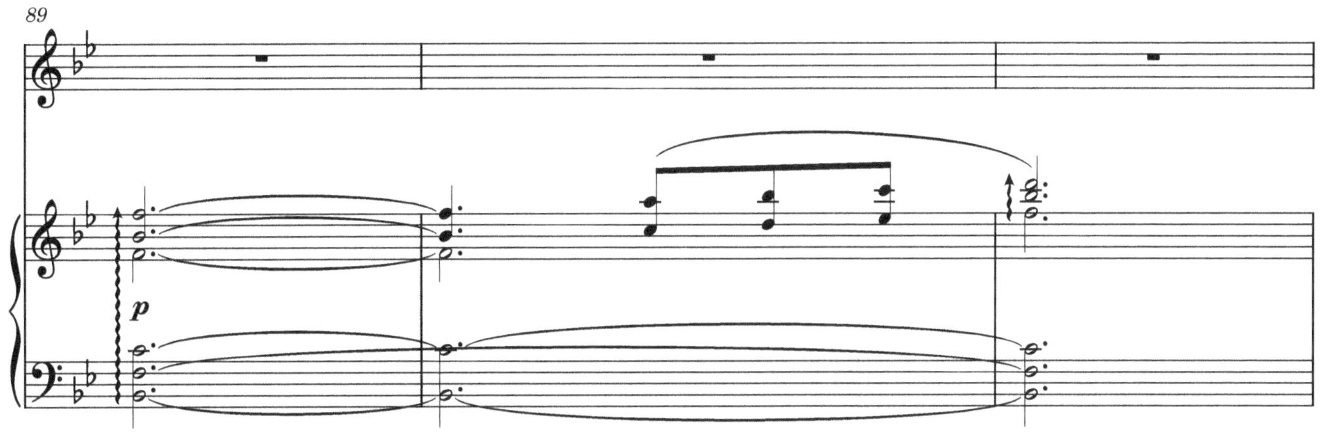
89
p

92
p
And my love, my

94
love, as I moved, I saw him watch it. His care for

97
me was in - stinct - ive, so he reached out his hands to

long, awkward pause
100
catch it. Love, love,

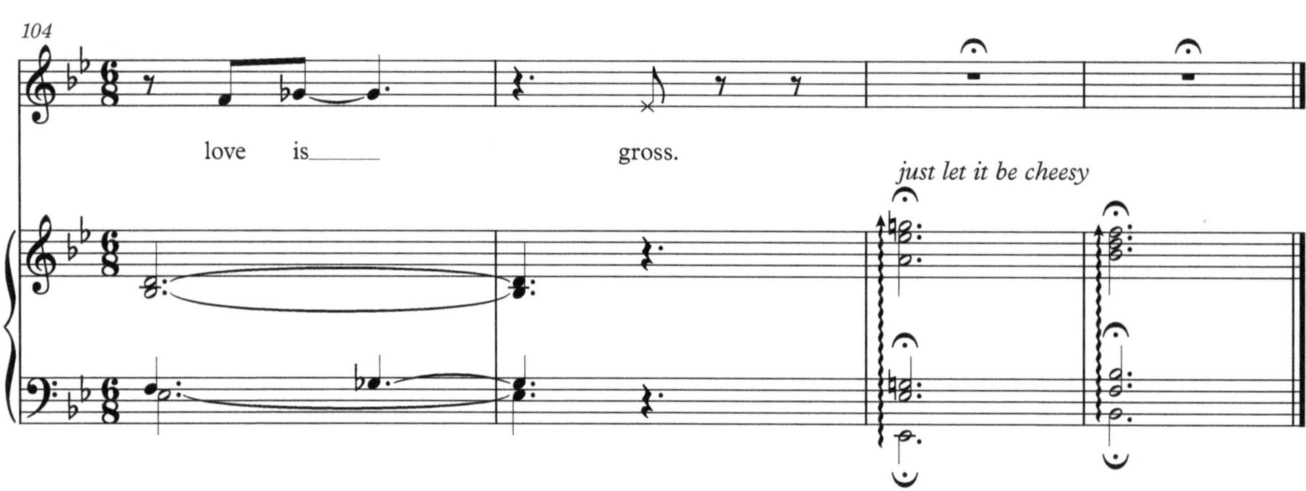
104
love is gross.
just let it be cheesy

composed for songSLAM NYC I 2017

Walking Past a window...

from *Songs of the Soul Beams*

Brittany Goodwin

FELIX JARRAR
(2017)

4
f
p
mf
God was there God was there I
5
p
8
walked past a win - dow on the next flor and through the door's frame in a
6
f
3
mf
8
bed I saw a man lay - ing in lim - - - bo

This page intentionally left blank to facilitate page turns

A little faster (♩ = 68)

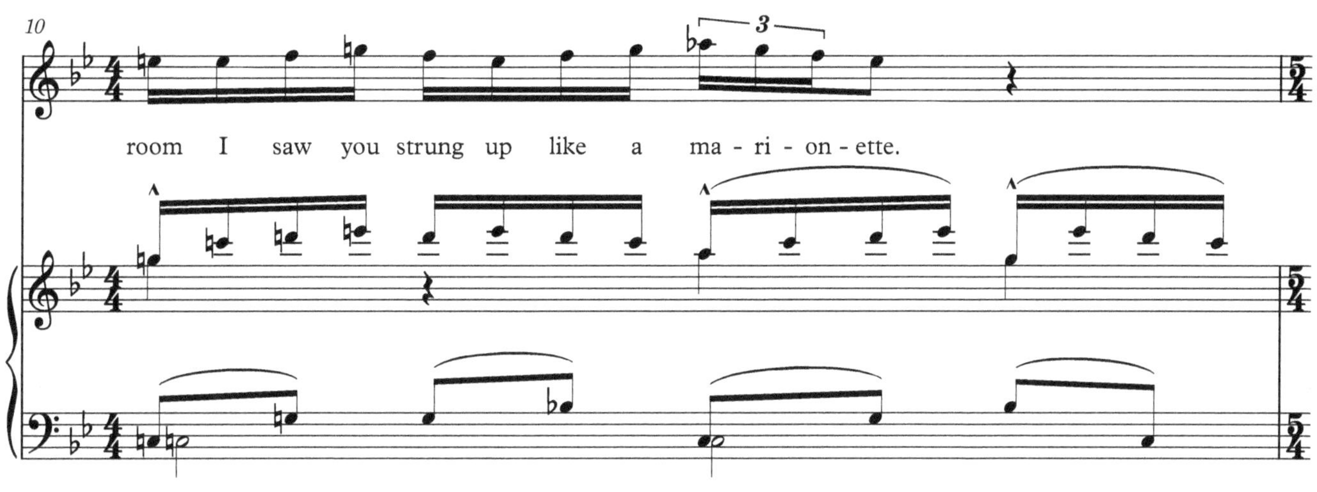
10
room I saw you strung up like a ma - ri - on - ette.

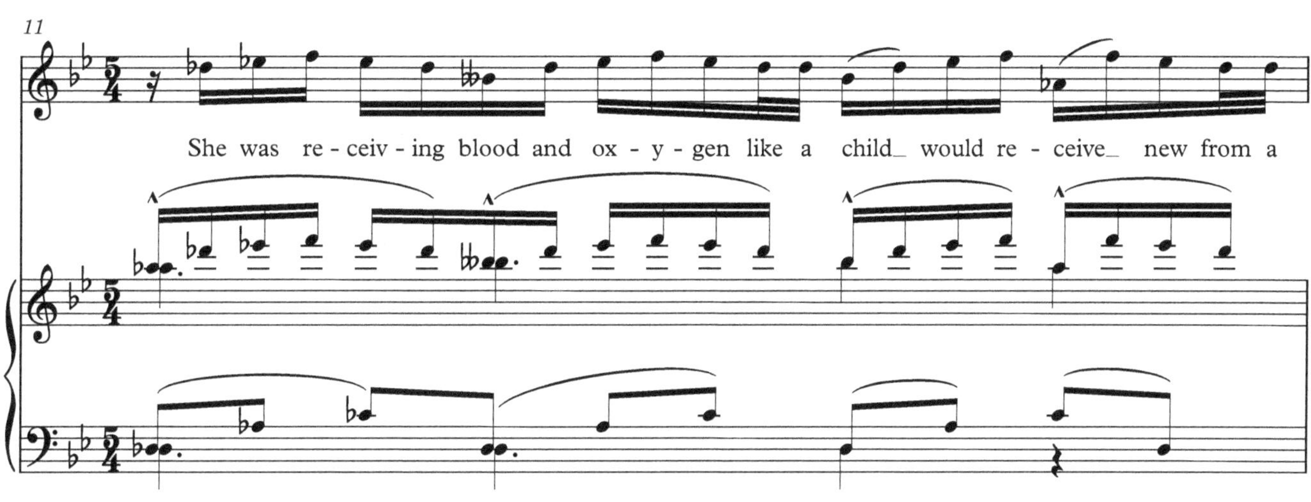
11
She was re - ceiv - ing blood and ox - y - gen like a child_ would re - ceive_ new from a

rit......
12
string and a tin can
I
mf
tr
mf

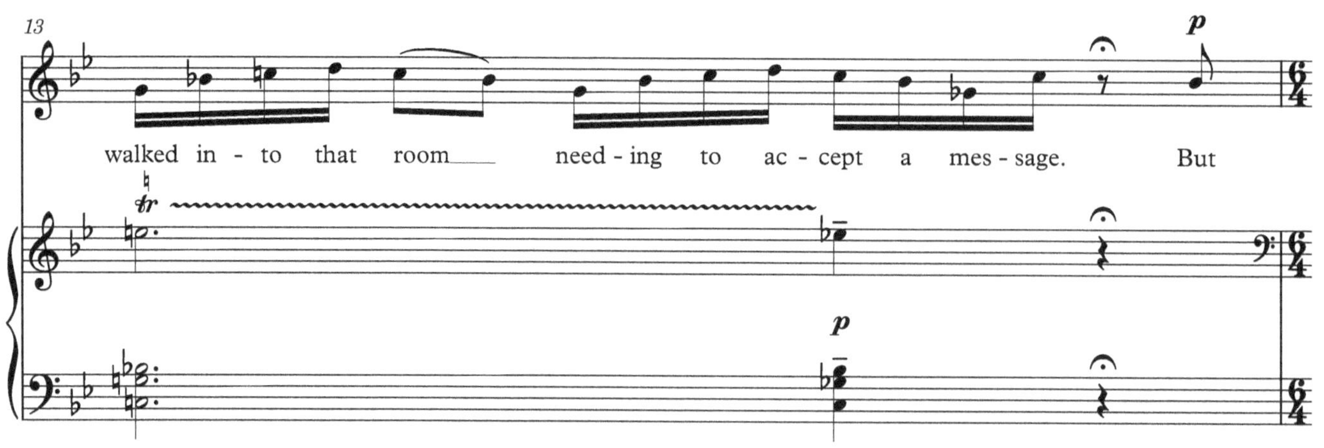
13
p
walked in - to that room
need - ing to ac - cept a mes - sage.
But
tr
p

Slow, languid (♩ = 52)
14
God was - n't there
God
was - n't there
pp
8

accel.
15
mf
I
ppp
mf

This page intentionally left blank to facilitate page turns

Slow, with motion ♩ = 60
16
3
looked up to the ceil - ing and won - dered where the che - ru - bim
19
f
p sub.
were. Where was the
p
20
3
tin - sel, the i - vy, the pa - per moon? Where
ff
pp
8

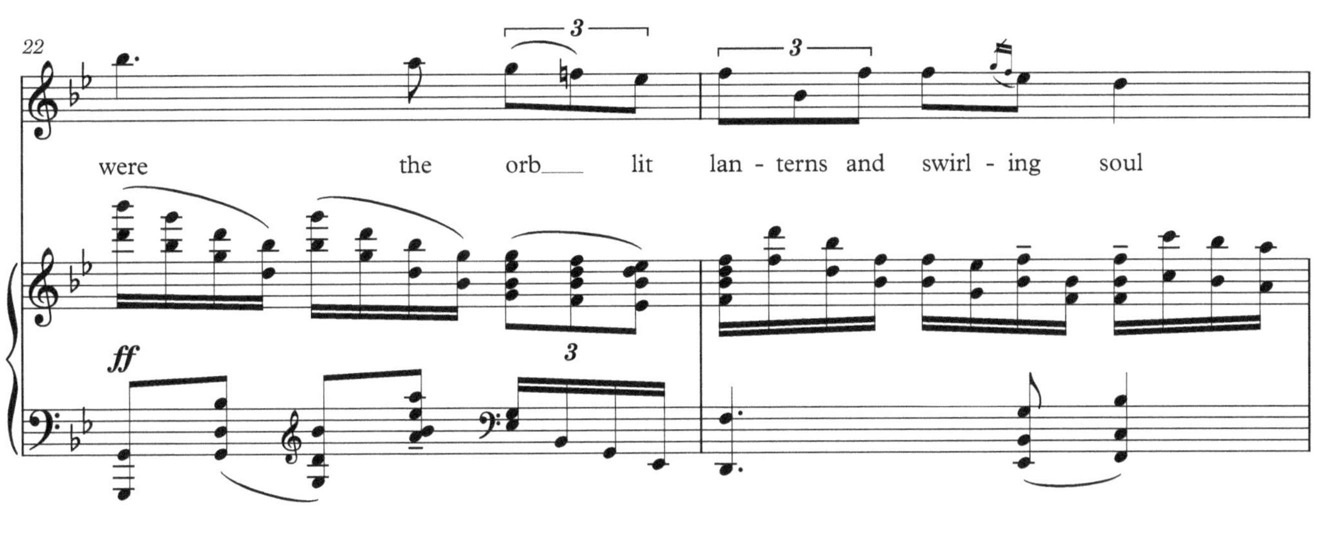
22
were the orb___ lit lan - terns and swirl - ing soul
3
3
ff
3

24
beams? I'm dis - cov - er ing there's a fee - ble par - a - pet be -
3

26
rit.
p
pp
- tween one's psy - che and the Earth. And that I am a co - ward.
3
3
tr
tr
p
pp

a tempo
29
mf
3
Van - i - ty, in beau - ty, ham - mocks it -
3
mf

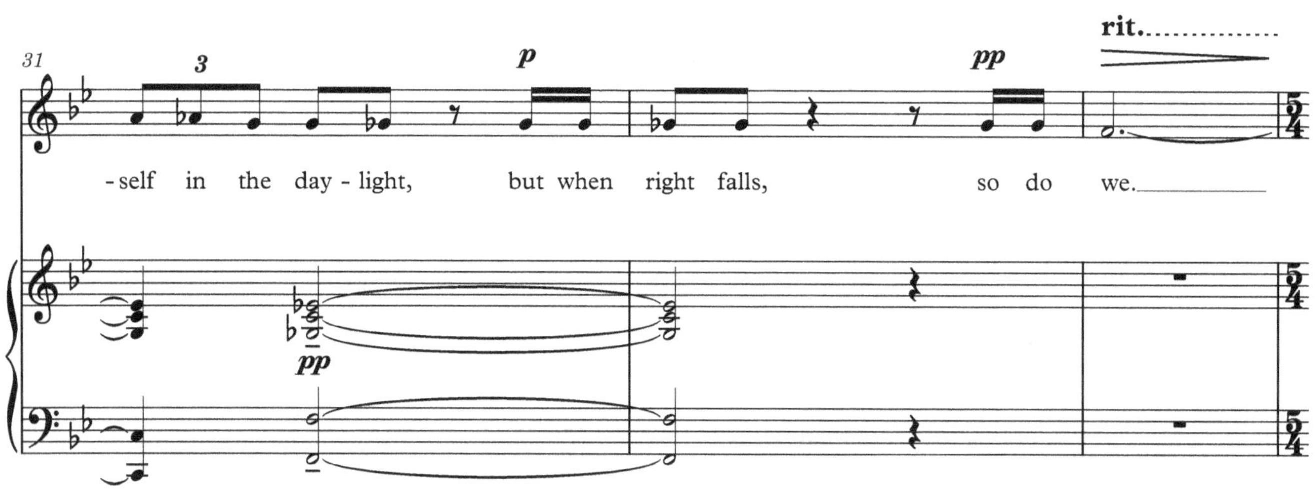
rit.
31
3
p
pp
- self in the day - light, but when right falls, so do we.
pp

a tempo
rit.
34
ppp
p
pp

for Vivien Shotwell
composed for songSLAM Toronto 2019

Al claro de luna

from *Sueños desde el abismo*

Delmira Agustini

LAURENCE JOBIDON
(2018)

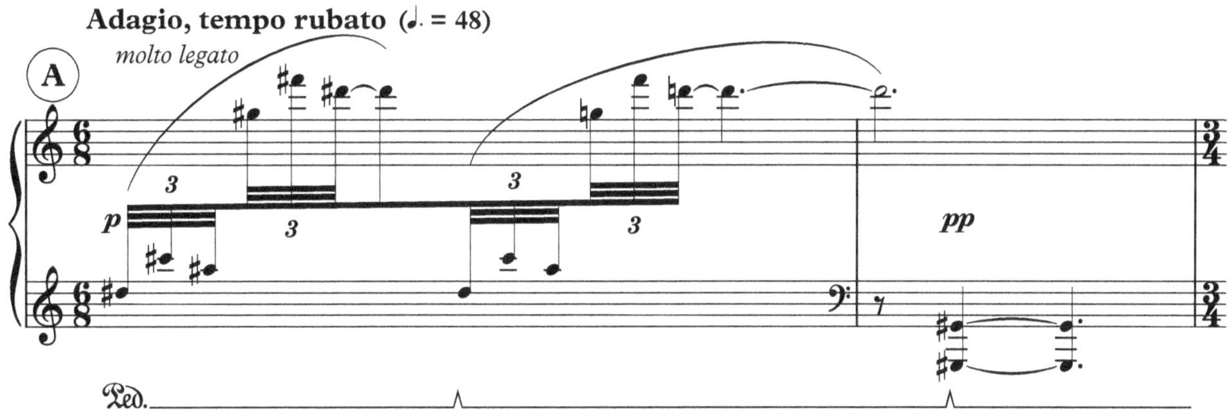

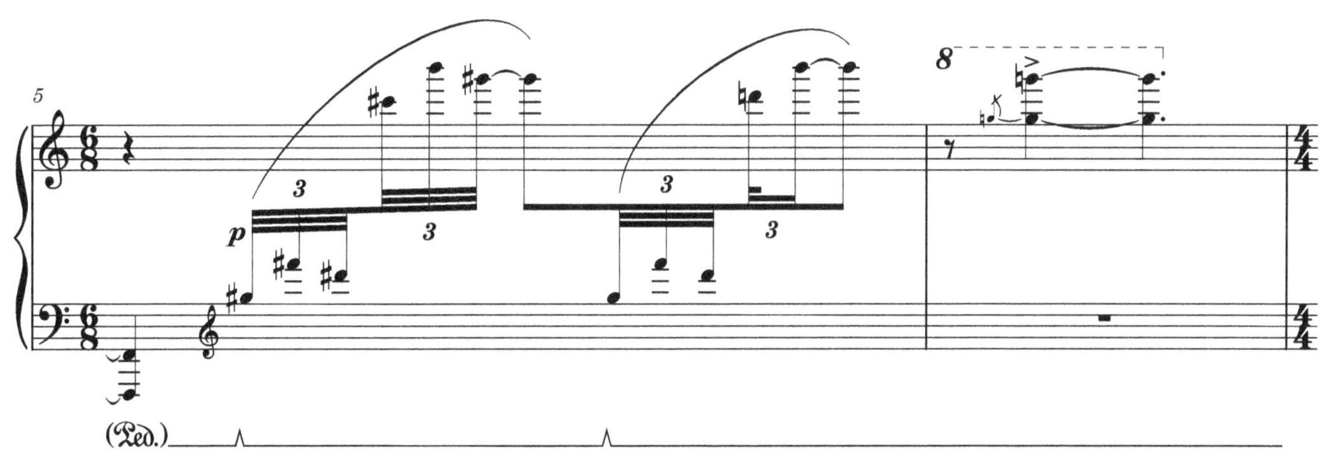

7
pp
3
3

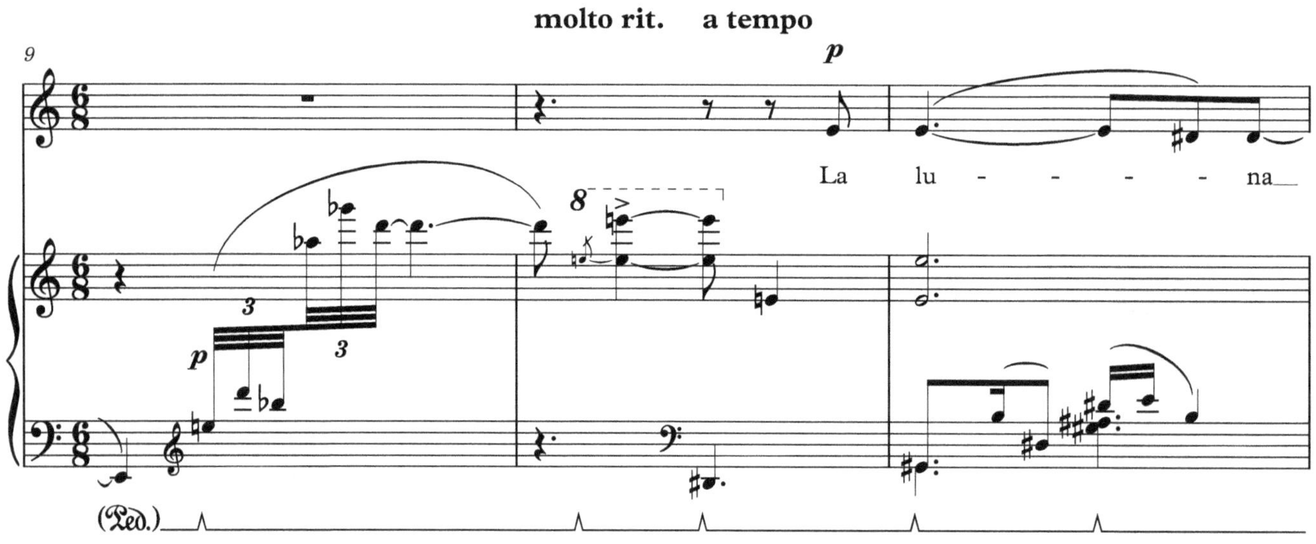
molto rit.
a tempo
9
p
La lu - - - - - na
8
3
3
p
(Ped.)

12
2
es pá - li - da y tris - te, la

15
2
mp
lu - - - - - - - na es ex - san - - güe y yer -
mp

18
mf
4
- - ta. La me - - - dia lu - na fi - gú - ra - se -
cresc.
mf

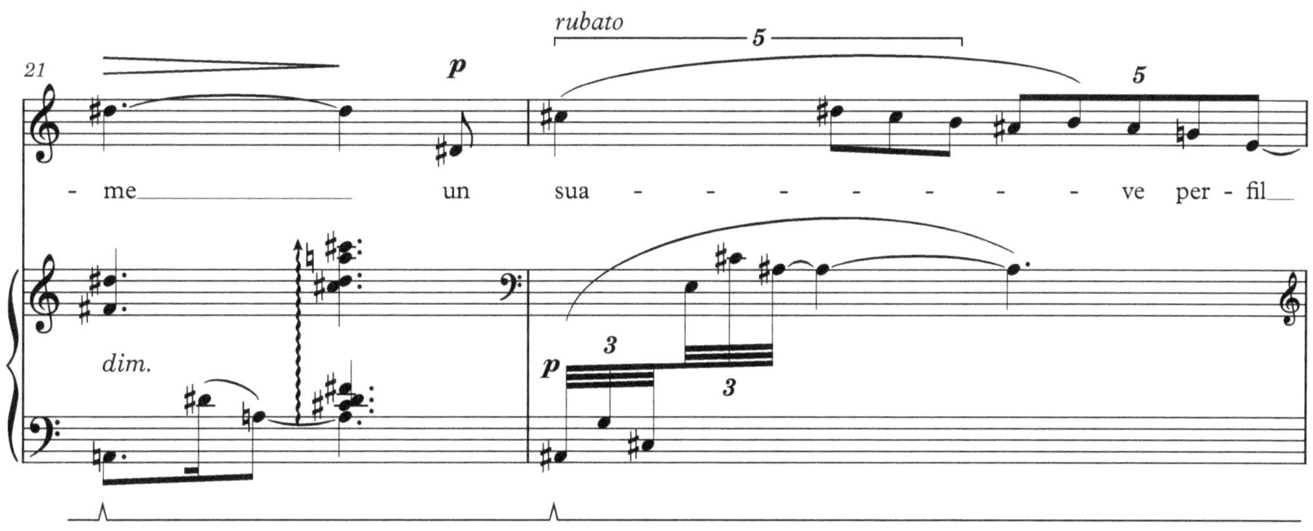
21
rubato
5
p
5
- me un sua - - - - - - ve per - fil
dim.
p
3
3

23
f
de muer - ta...
mf 3
3
f
Ped.

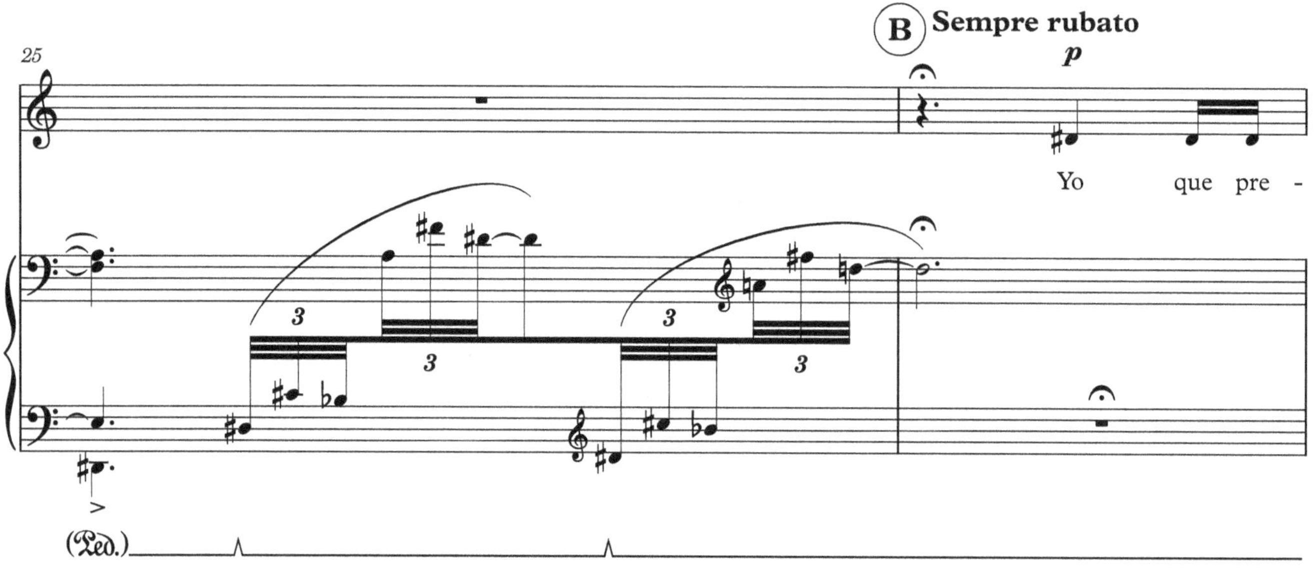
B Sempre rubato
p
25
Yo que pre -
3
3
3
3
(Ped.)

27
- fie - ro a la in - si - gne pa - li - dez en - ca - re - ci - da de to - das las per - las
pp

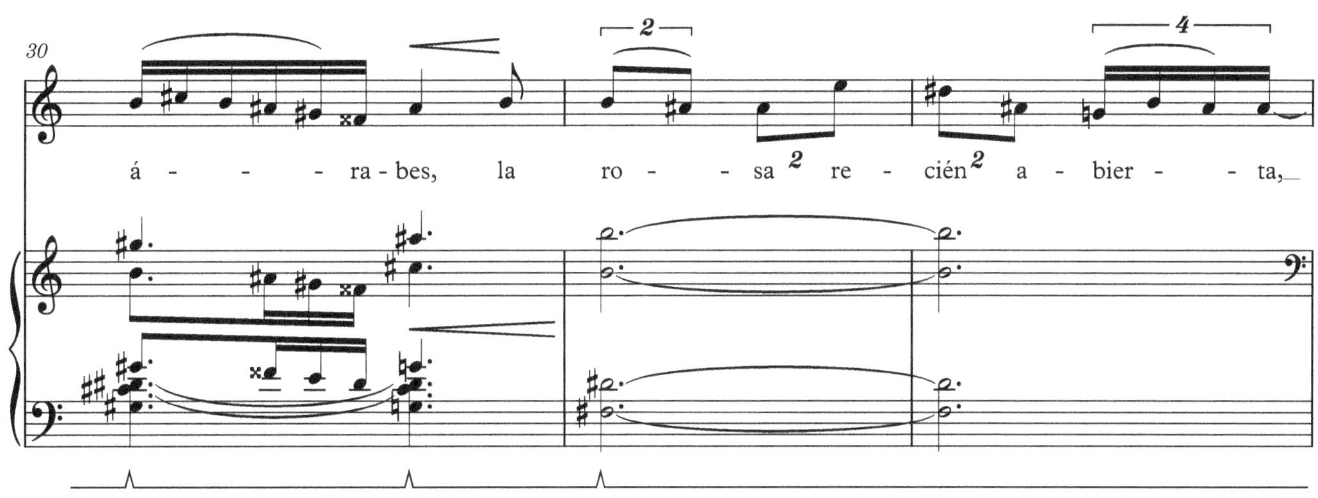

Poco meno mosso

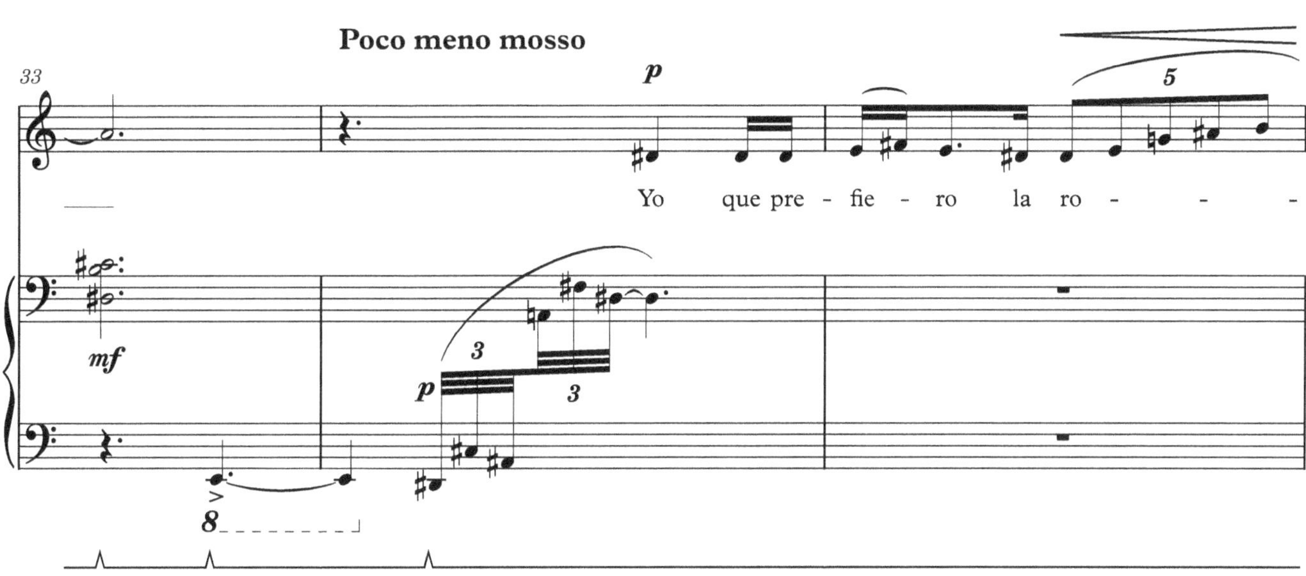

Tempo primo

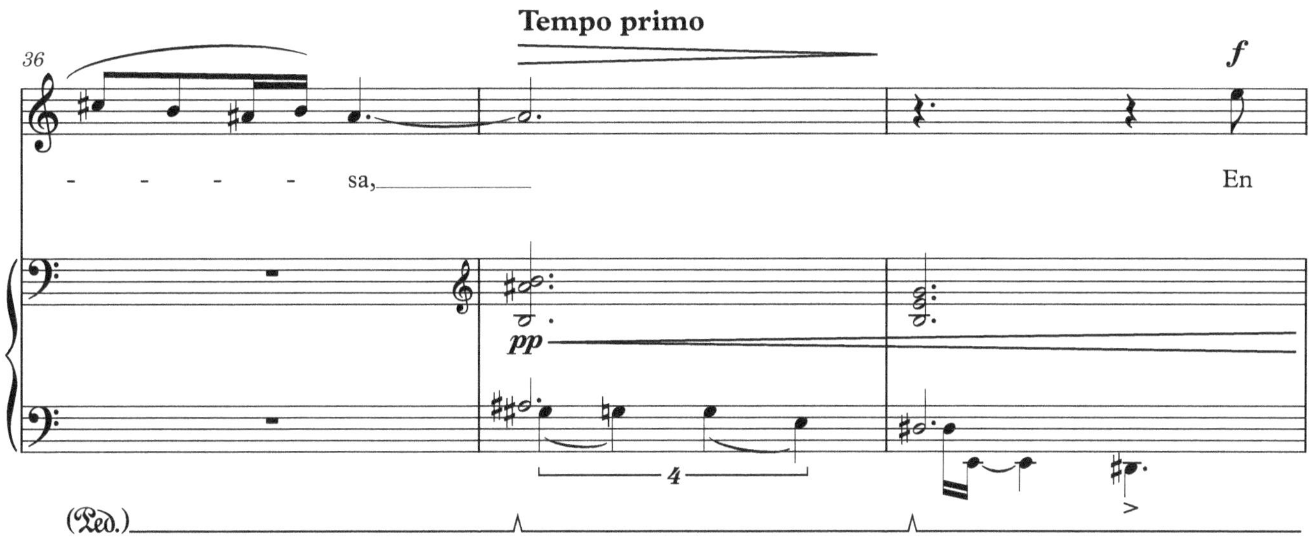

C
un rin - cón del ter - ru - ño con el co - lor de la
2
f

42
vi - da, a - do - ro es - a lu - na pá -
2
2

45
Poco meno mosso
p
- li - da, a - do - ro es - a faz
3
3
p

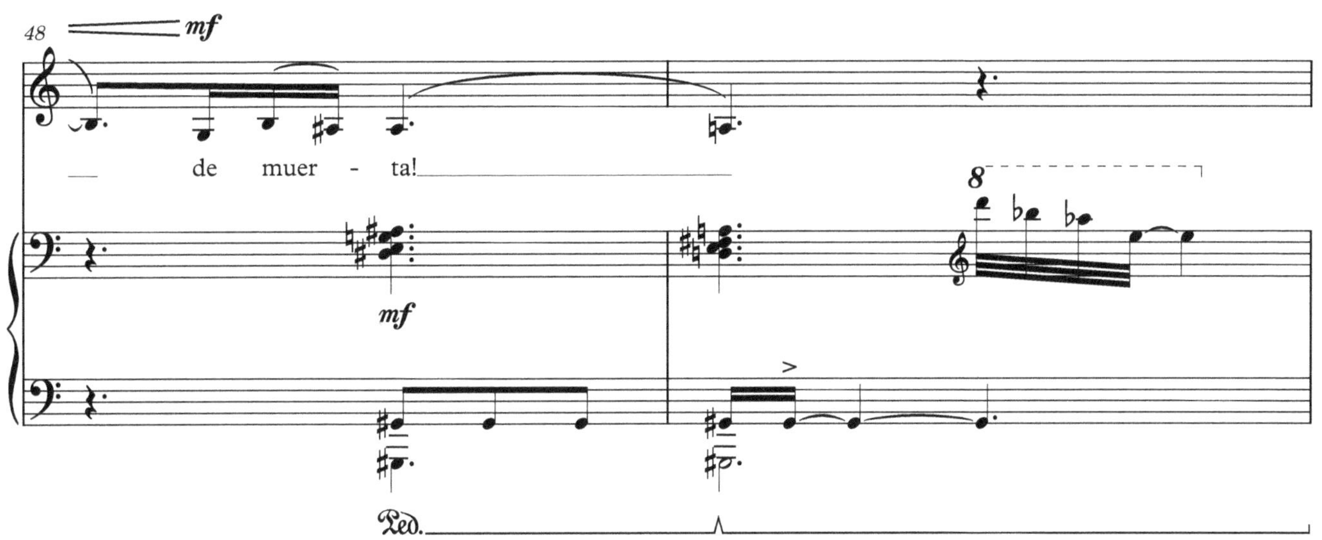
48
mf
de muer - ta!
8
Ped.

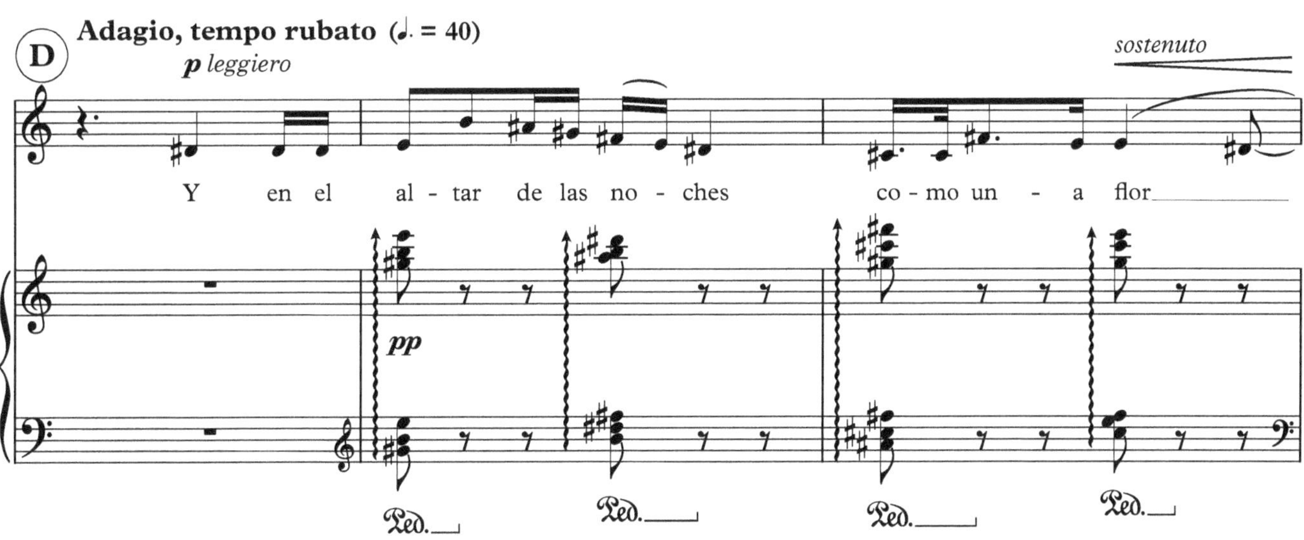
D
Adagio, tempo rubato (♩. = 40)
p leggiero
sostenuto
Y en el al - tar de las no - ches co - mo un - a flor
pp
Ped.

53
mf
rall.
f
en - cen - di - da y e - - bria d'ex - tra - ños per - fu - mes, mi
Ped.

Poco meno mosso

Agitato (♩. = c. 52)

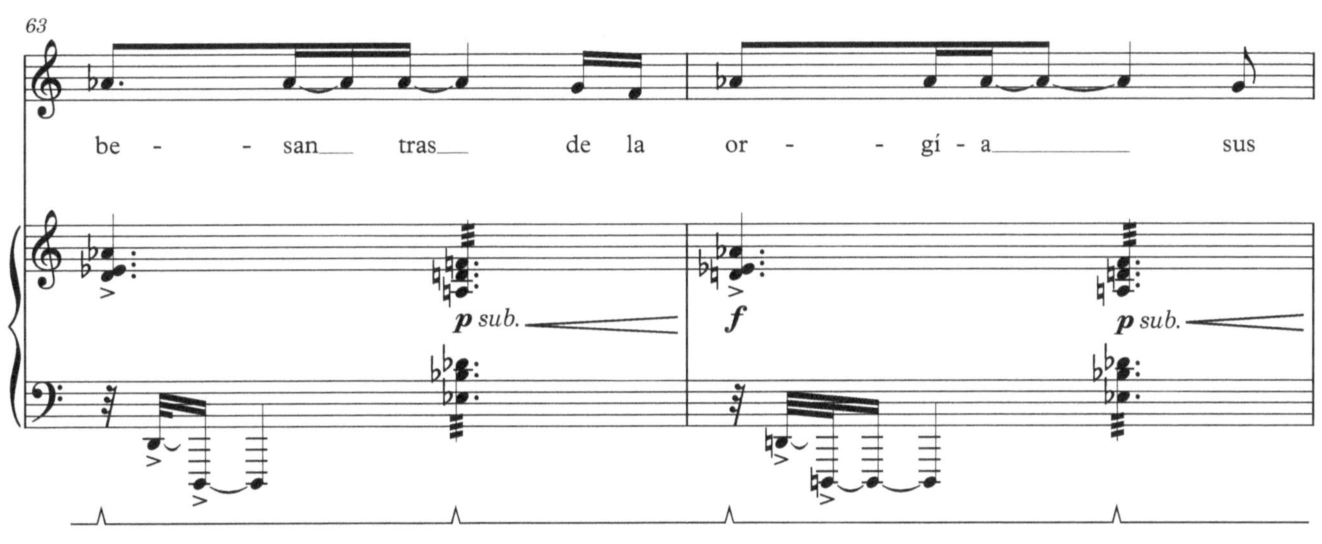
63
be - - san tras de la or - - gí - a sus
p sub.
f
p sub.

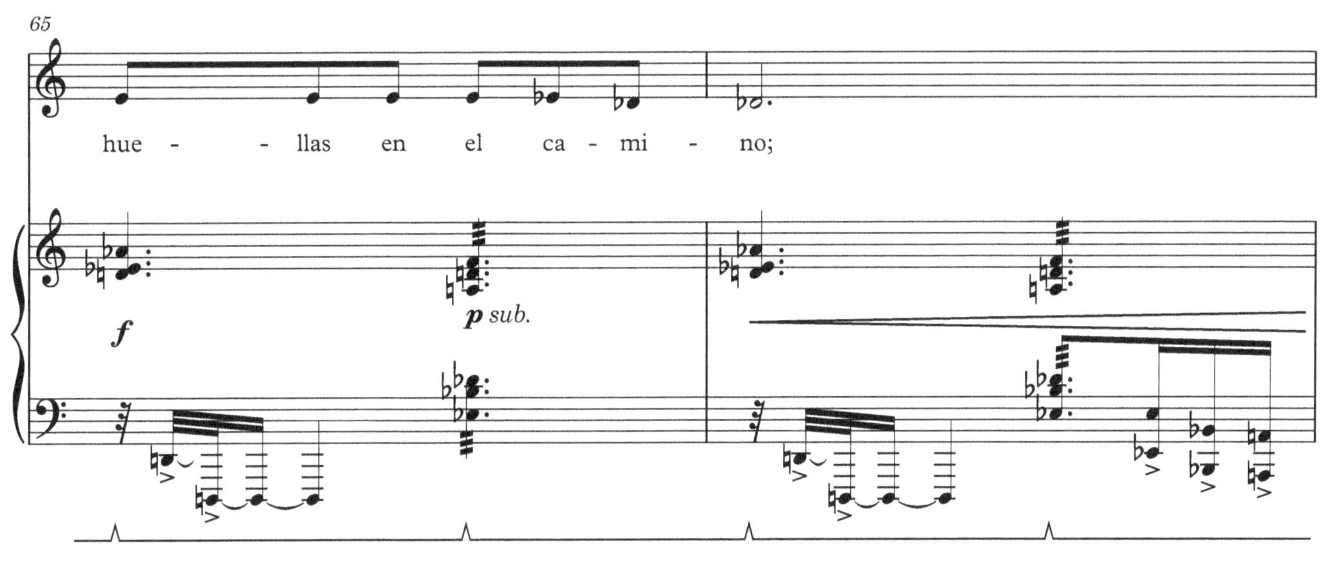
65
hue - - llas en el ca - mi - no;
f
p sub.

67
(ff)
Lo - cos que mue - ren be - san -
ff

69
- do su i - ma - gen en la - gos yer - tos...
yo

71
mp
sé...
yo
mp

rall.
73
p
sé...
Por -

F
Adagio, tempo rubato (♩. = 40)
f
-que e - lla es luz de in - o -
p

78
-cen - cia por - que a es - a luz mis -

81
mp dolce
-te - - - - - ri - o - sa a - lum - - bran las

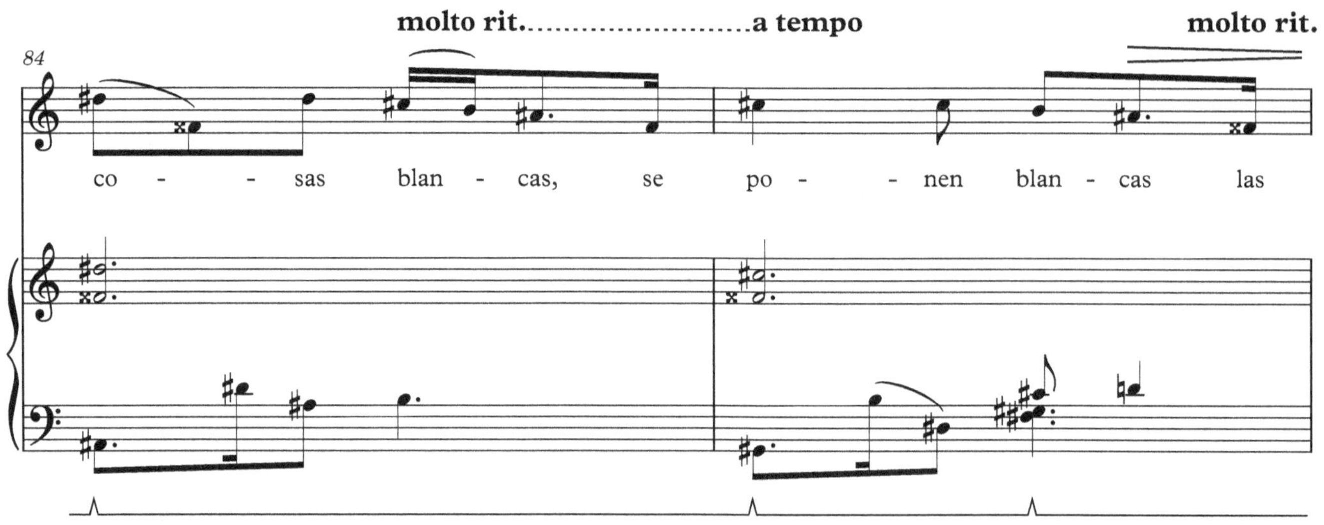
molto rit.
a tempo
molto rit.
84
co - - sas blan - cas, se po - - nen blan - cas las

a tempo
molto rit.
86
co - - sas, y has - ta las al - mas mas

a tempo
88
mp
ne - - gras to - man cla - ro - res in -
mp

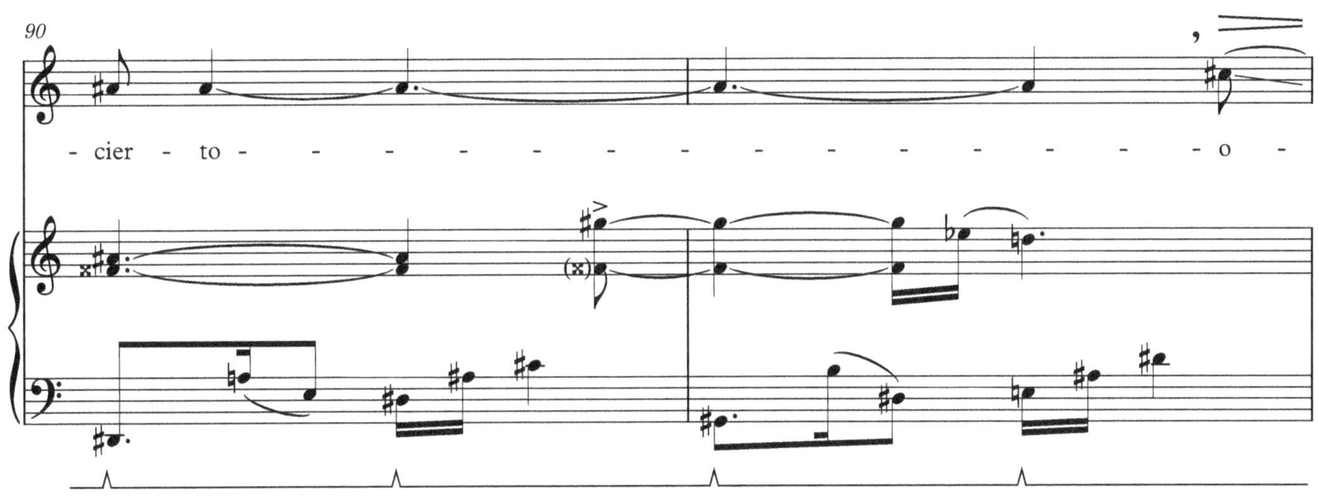
90
- cier - to - - - - - - - - - - - - - - o -

pp
92
- - - - - - - - - os

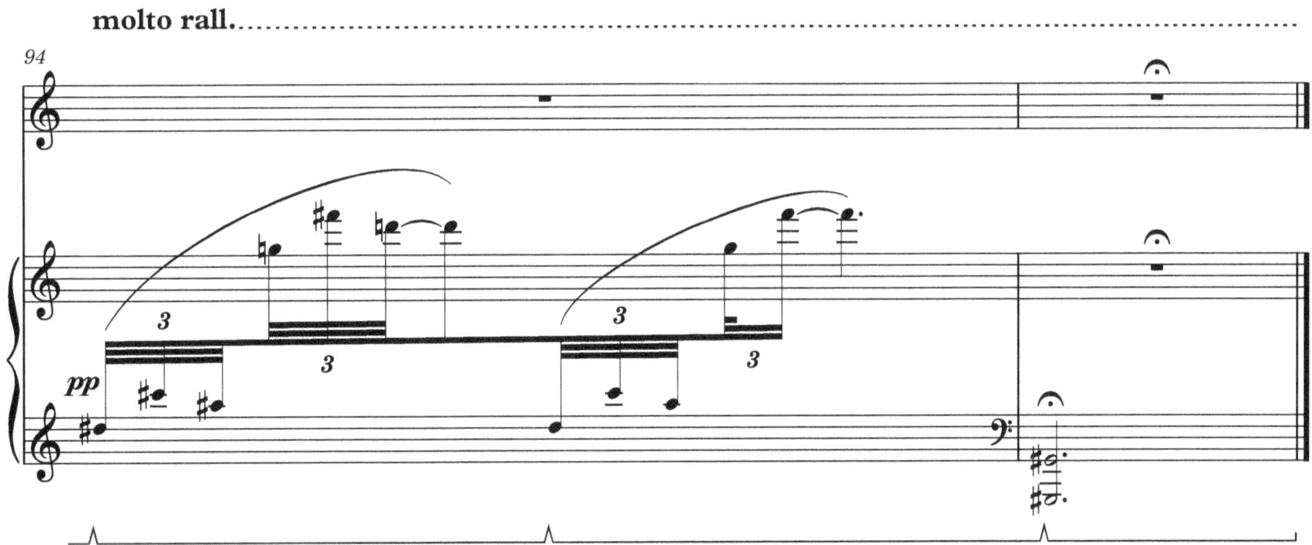
molto rall.
94
pp

This page intentionally left blank to facilitate page turns

for Katie
composed for songSLAM Minneapolis 2019

Today, There Is a Spring in Me!

Words and Music by
ISAAC LOVDAHL
(2018)

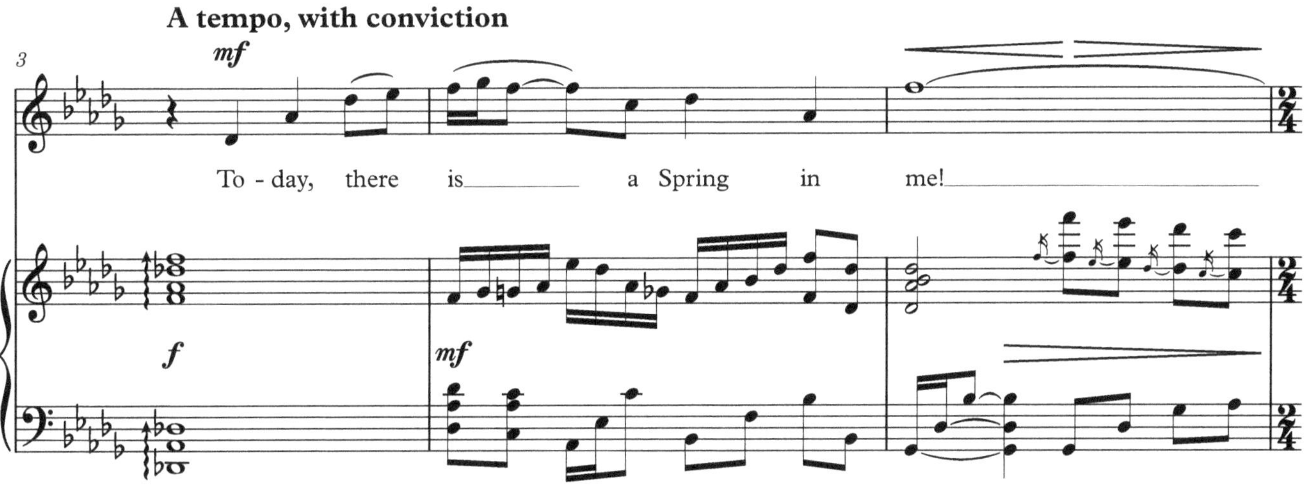

Fludly (♩ = c. 72)
9
me!
mf

11
mf
In my heart, I feel the trem - bling buds of

13
3
al - most blos - somed flow - ers.

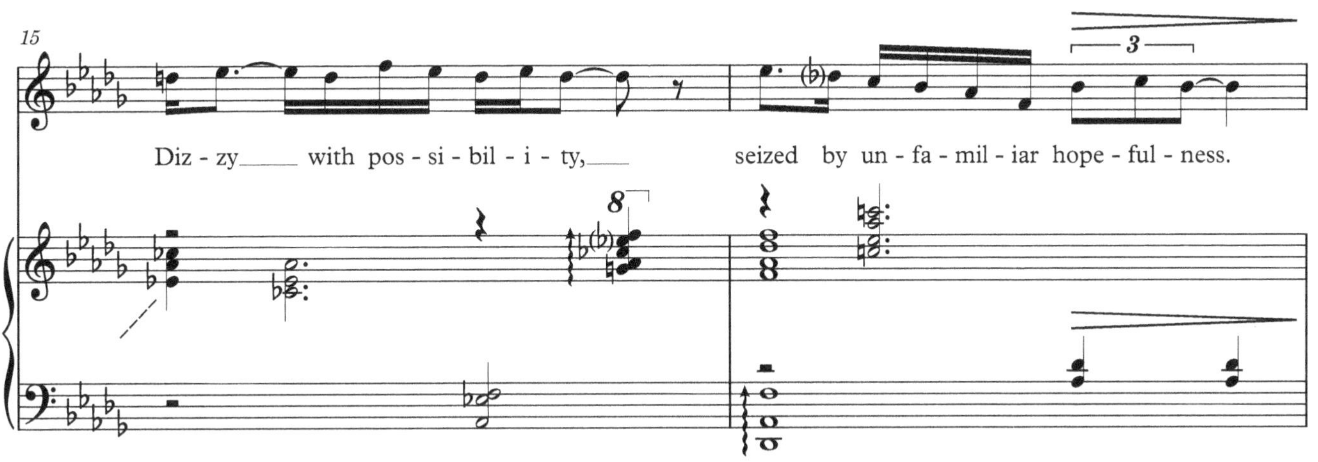
15
Diz - zy with pos - si - bil - i - ty, seized by un - fa - mil - iar hope - ful - ness.
8
3

Slightly slower
17
mp
To - day, I am not an is - land. I am an ar - chi -
mp

20
f rubato
- pel - - a - go, a - bound - - ing. Teem - ing with
3
3
f rubato

Lively (♩. = c. 56)
22
mf
life.
This is the
mf

24
glo - ri - ous con - se - quence of you...

26
of you.
Com - men - su - rate col - ors do

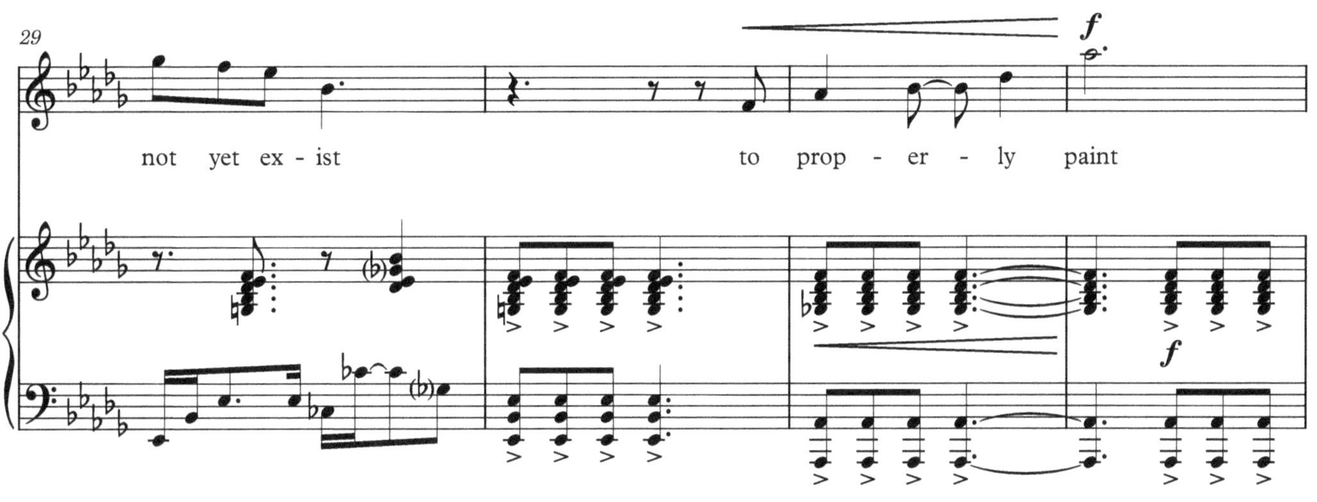
29
f
not yet ex - ist
to prop - er - ly paint
f

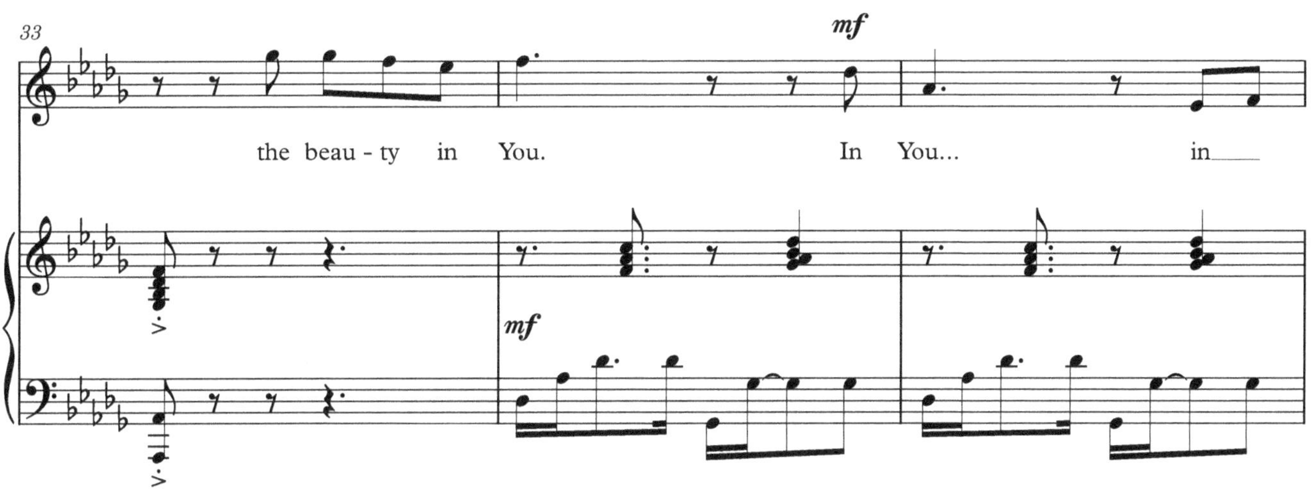
33
mf
the beau - ty in You.
In You...
in
mf

As before (♩ = c. 72)
36
mp
You...
in You
I find my -
mp

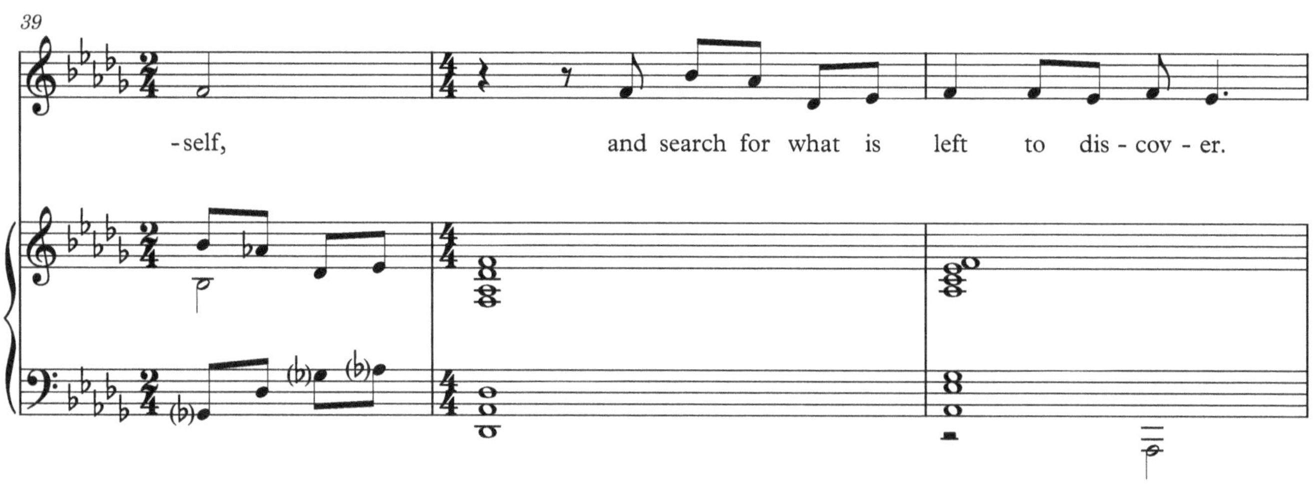
39
-self,
and search for what is left to dis - cov - er.

42
mf
To - day, there is a Spring in me...
mf

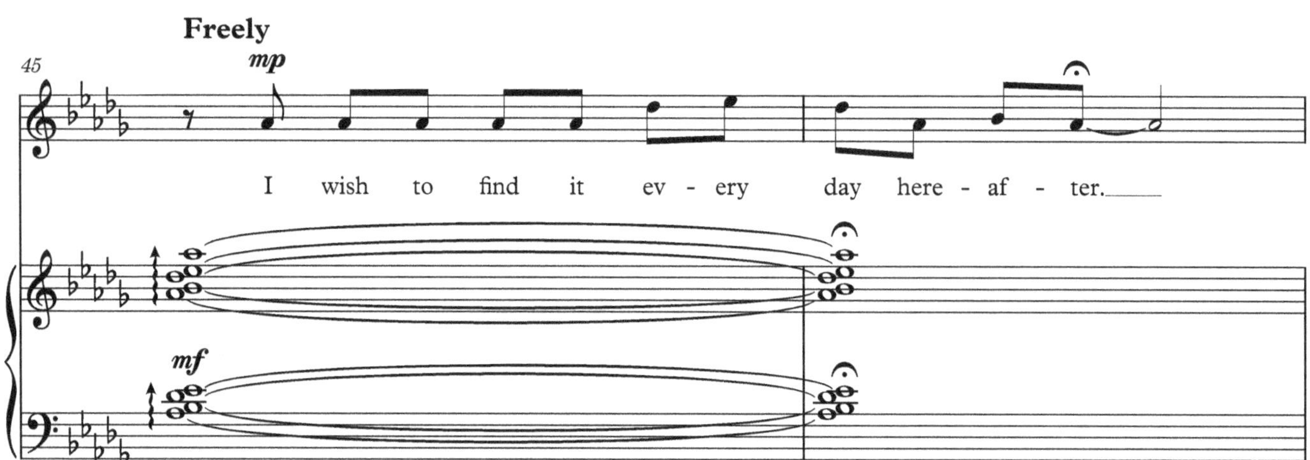
Freely
mp
45
I wish to find it ev - ery day here - af - ter.
mf

47
mf
tratt.
From dead wood comes new life, and balm - y mu - sic for my
mf
tratt.

♩ = c. 84
50
Soul.
(♭)
(♭)

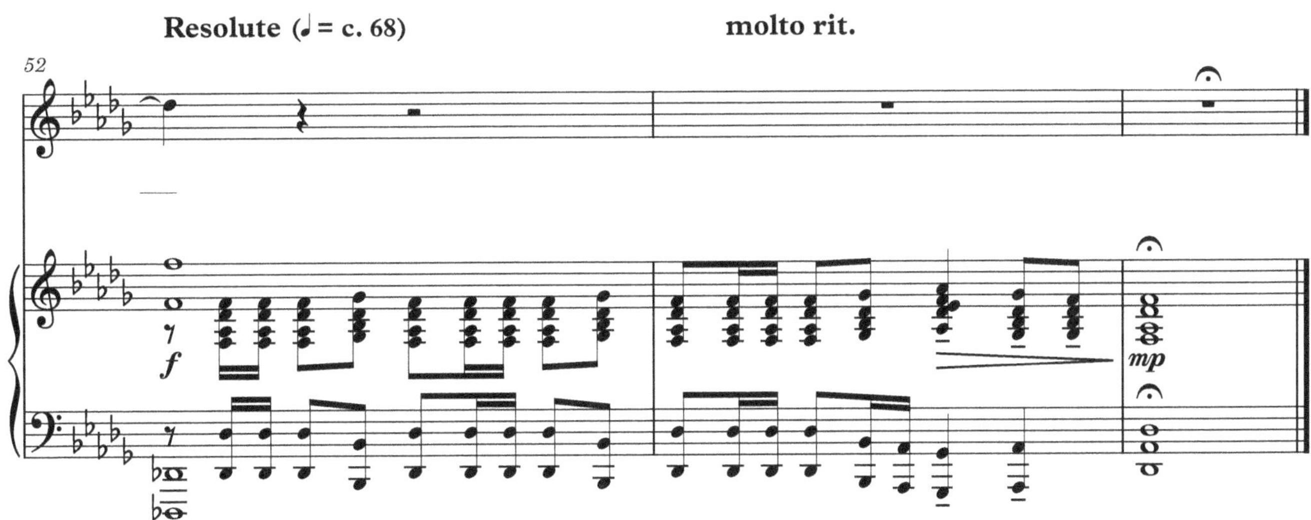
Resolute (♩ = c. 68)
molto rit.
52
f
mp

for Riley Cardona and Matt Olson,
and the inaugural songSLAM Minneapolis 2018

Crepuscule

E.E. Cummings

LIAM MOORE
(2017)

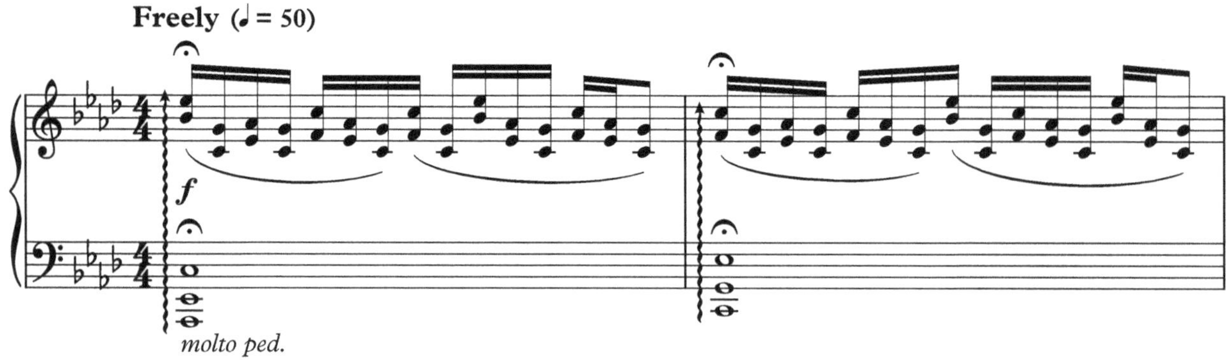

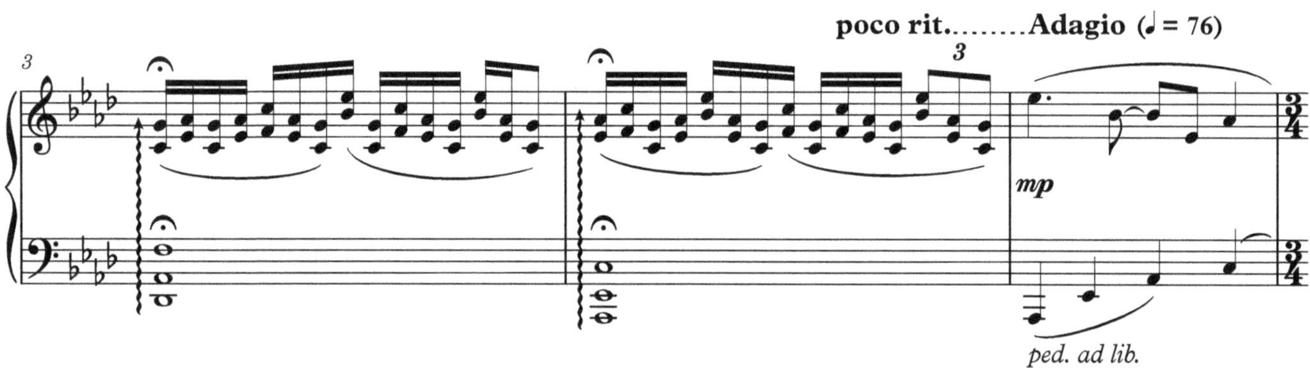

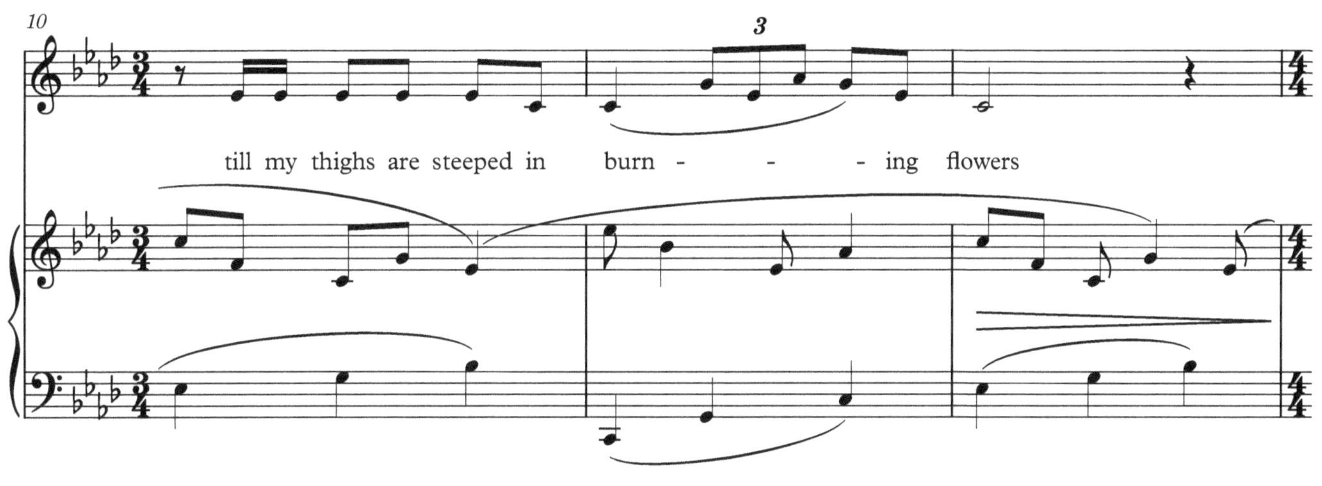
10
till my thighs are steeped in burn - - - ing flowers

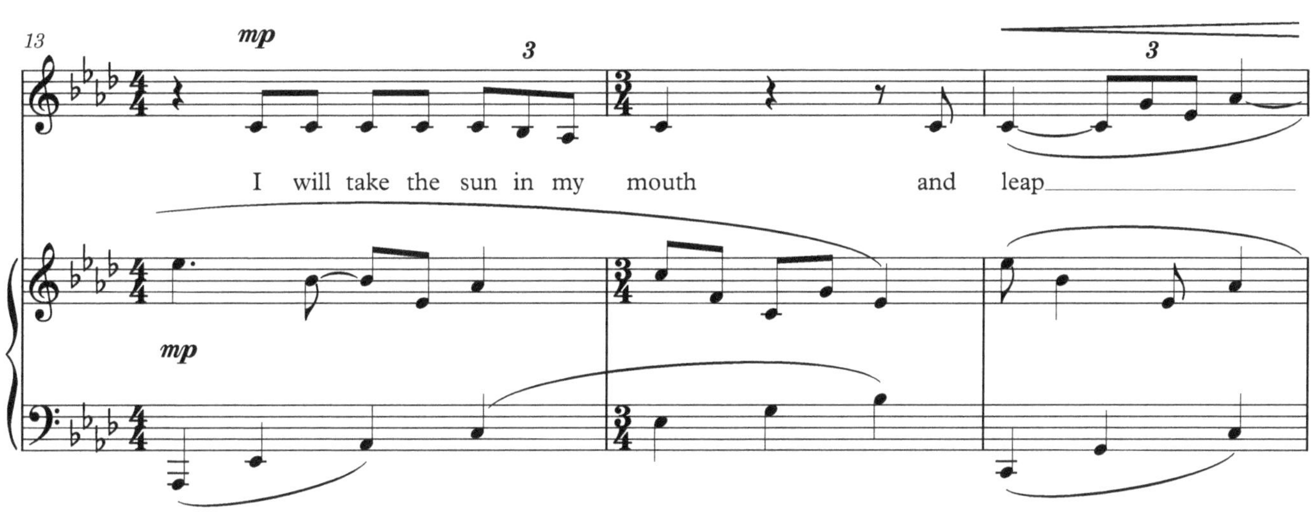
13
mp
I will take the sun in my mouth and leap
mp

16
mf
in - to the ripe air

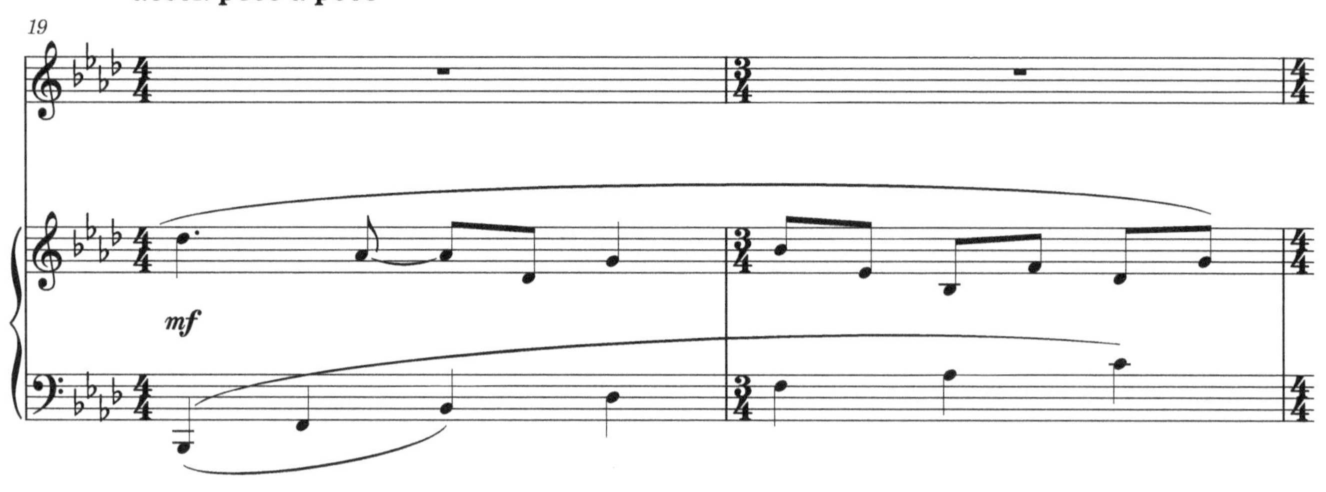
accel. poco a poco
19
mf

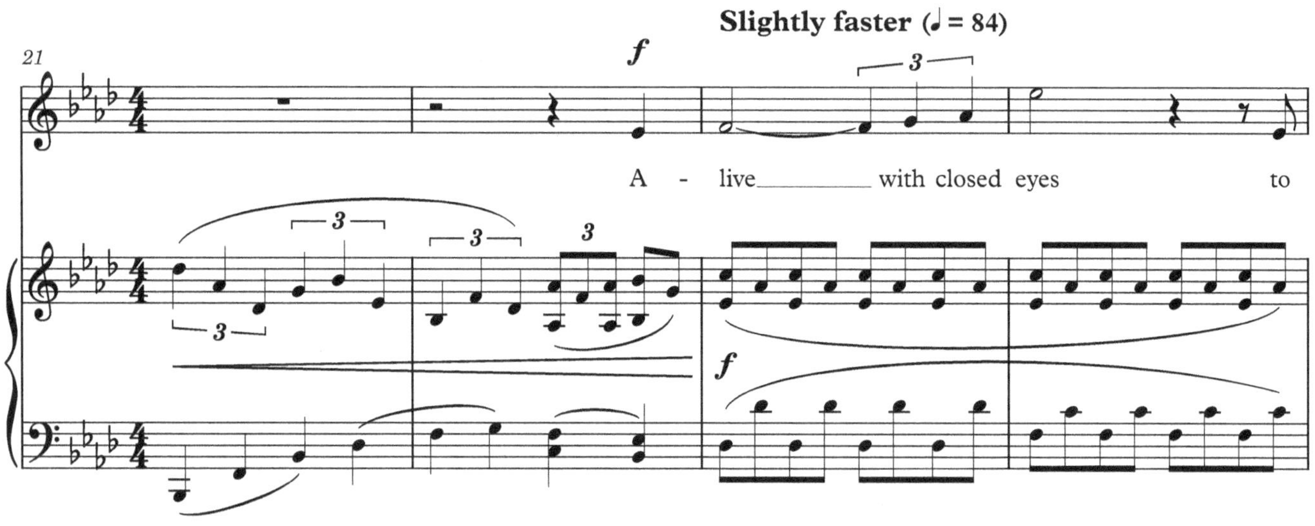
Slightly faster (♩ = 84)
21
f
A - live with closed eyes to
3
f

25
dash a - gainst dark - - ness in the sleep -
3

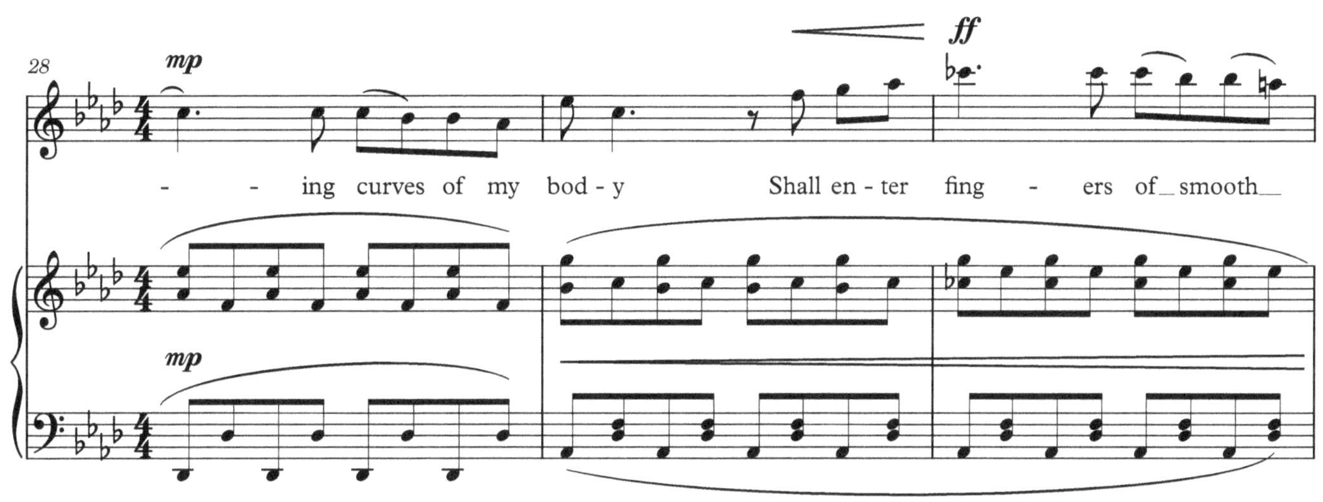
mp
ff
- - ing curves of my bod - y Shall en - ter fing - ers of smooth
mp

accel.

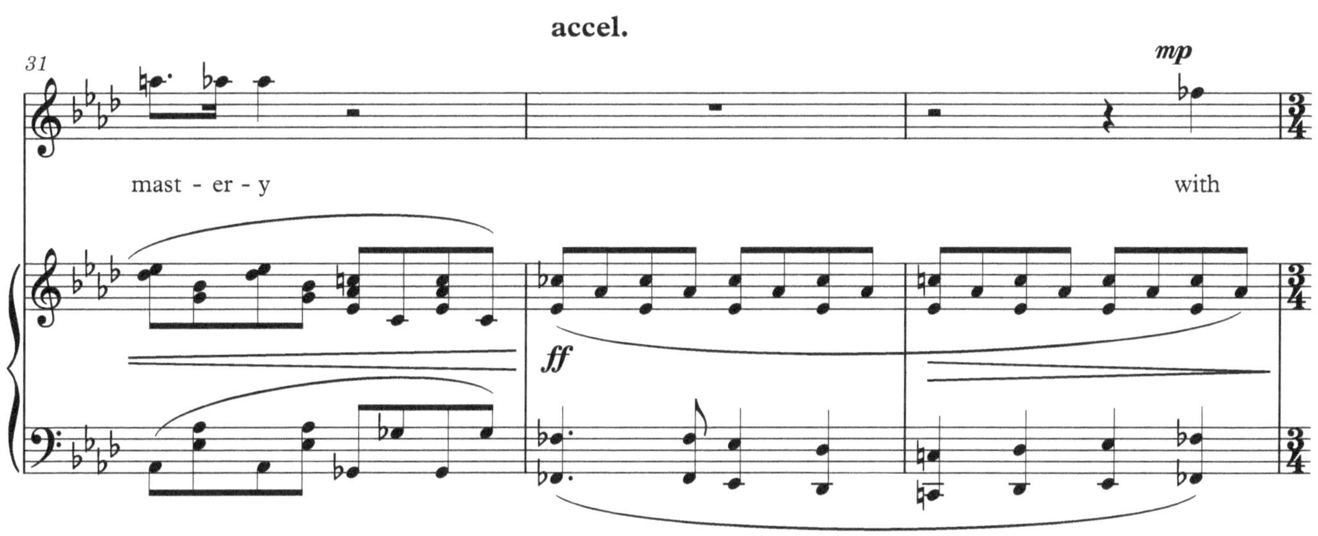
mp
mast - er - y with
ff

Faster, waltz-like (♩ = 98)
chaste - ness of sea - - - - girls
mp leggiero, meno pedale

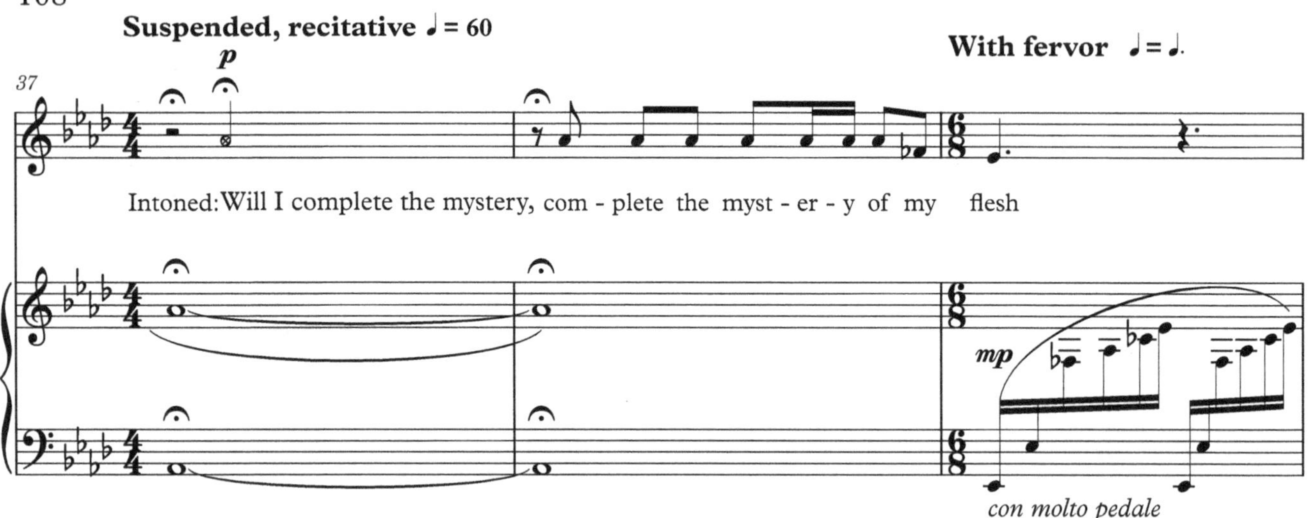

40

mf

43

mf

f

I will rise________ Af - ter a thou - - sand

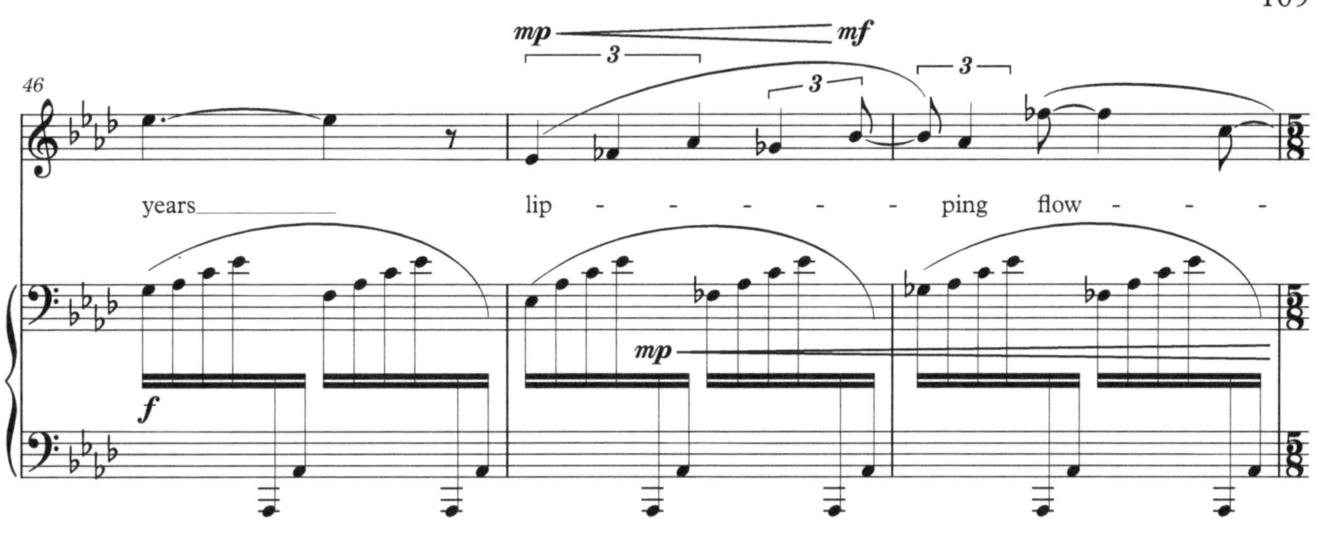

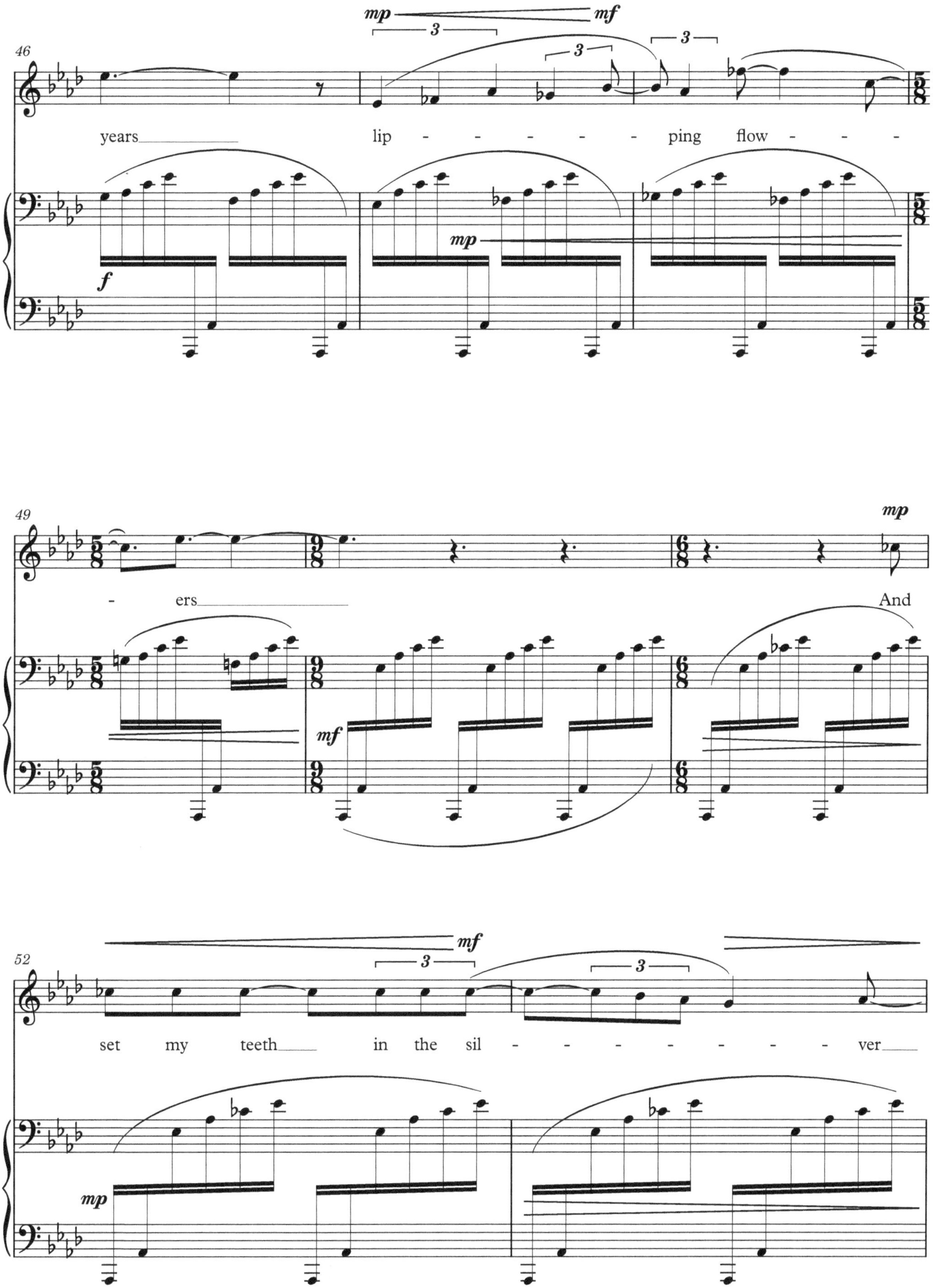

46
mp
mf
years
lip - - - - - - ping flow - - - -
f
mp
49
mp
- ers
And
mf
52
mf
set my teeth in the sil - - - - - - - ver
mp

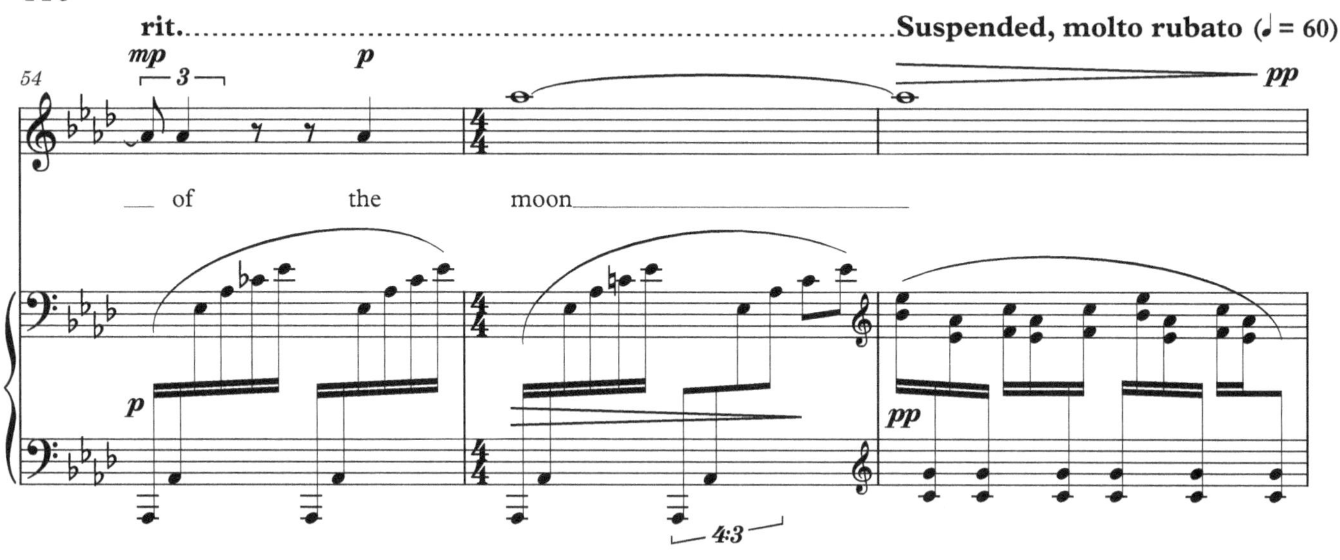

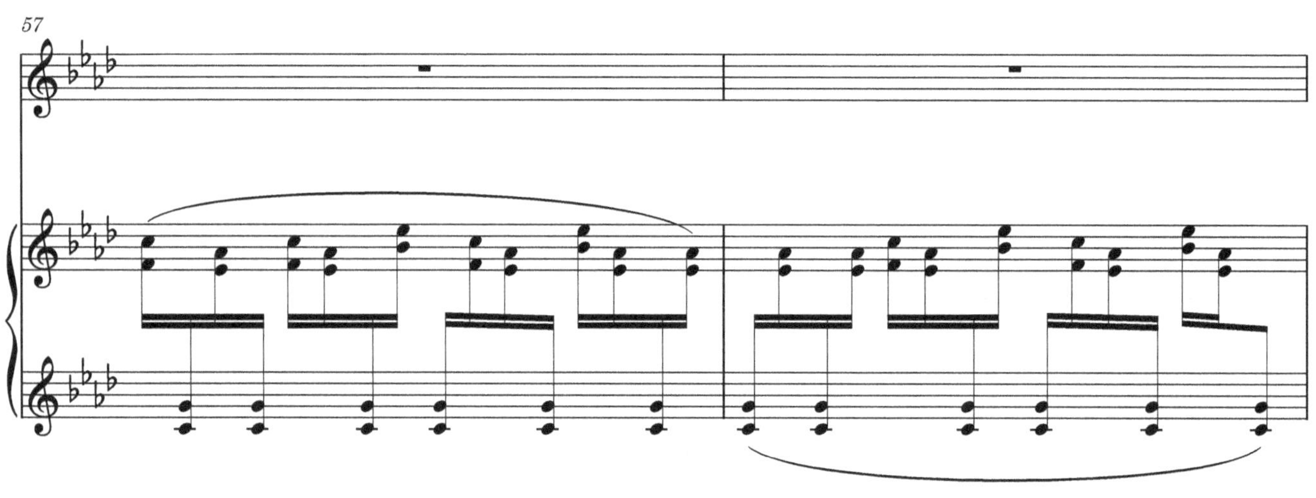

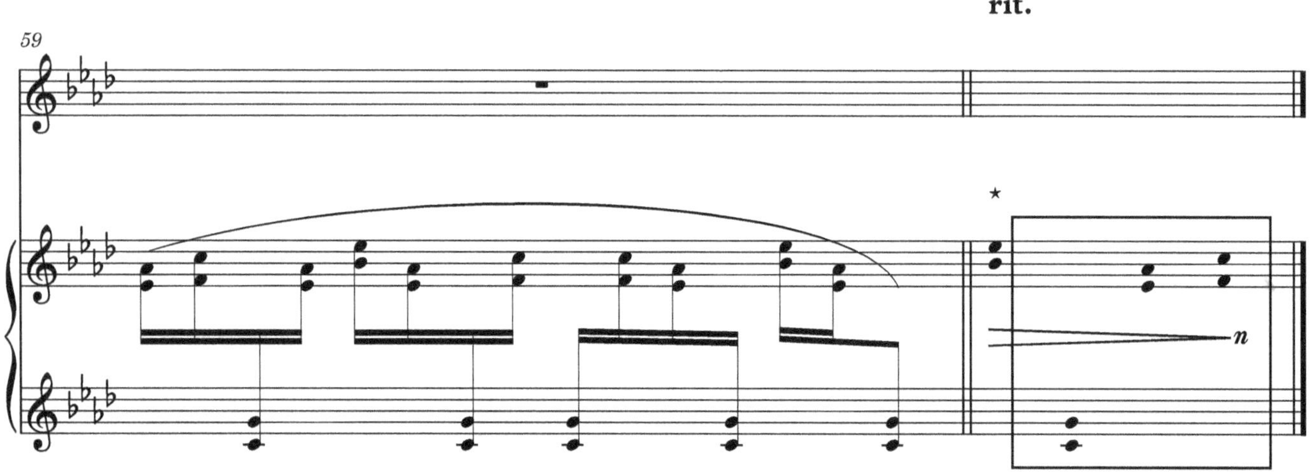

* Continue briefly (2-4 more measures) with these boxed sonorities in a similar pattern to mm. 56-59, notes breaking away from their dyads, and sounding independently, *rit.* and *dim. al fine.*

composed for songSLAM NYC I 2017

at that time i could not breathe like the others

Words and Music:
HALEY OLSON
(2017)

12
tr
f
p
sfz
p
p

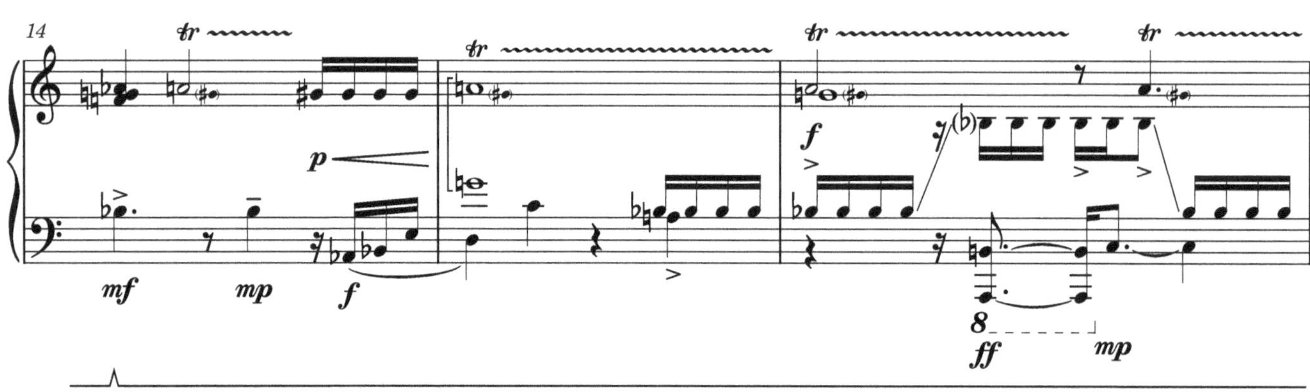
14
tr
tr
tr
tr
p
f
mf
mp
f
8
ff
mp

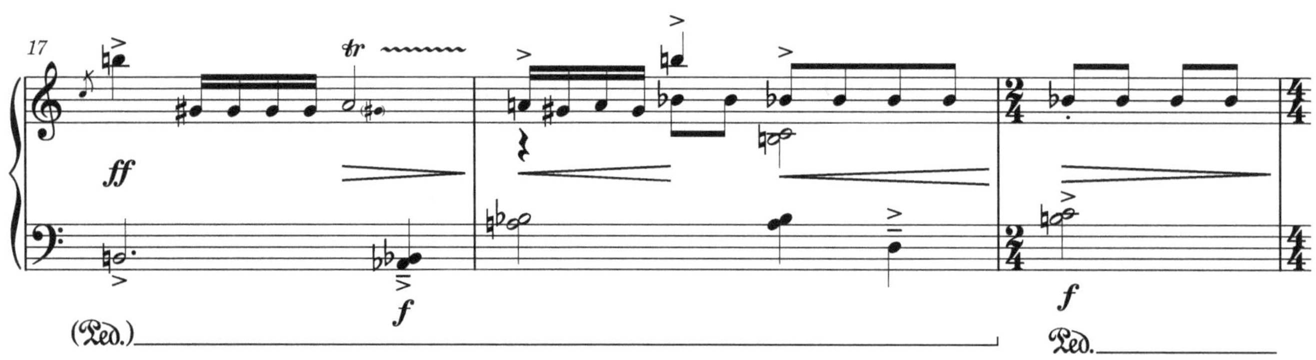
17
tr
ff
f
f
(Ped.)
Ped.

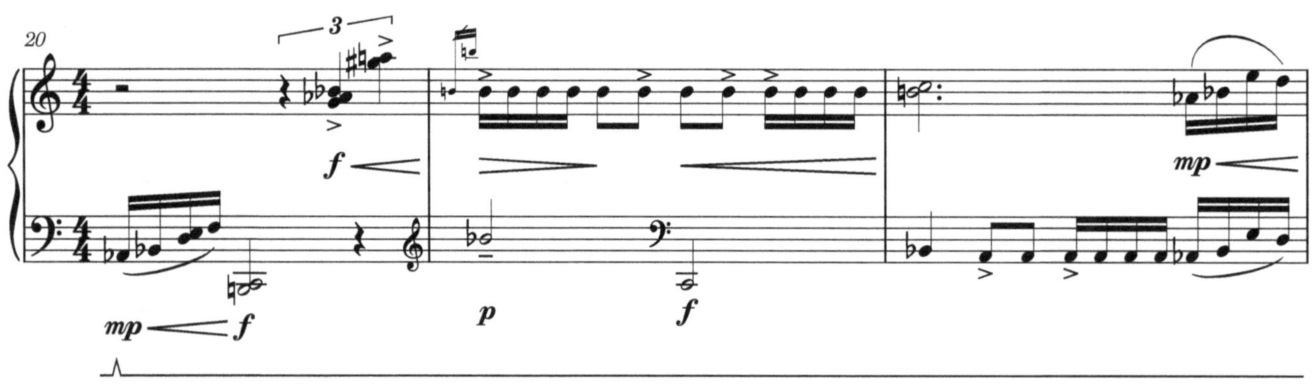
20
3
f
mp
mp
f
p
f

23
f
at this time, i could not breathe like the
mf
f
mp
mf
(Ped.)
Ped.

26
oth - ers per - haps it was oth - ers
mf
f
mp
ff
(Ped.)
Ped.

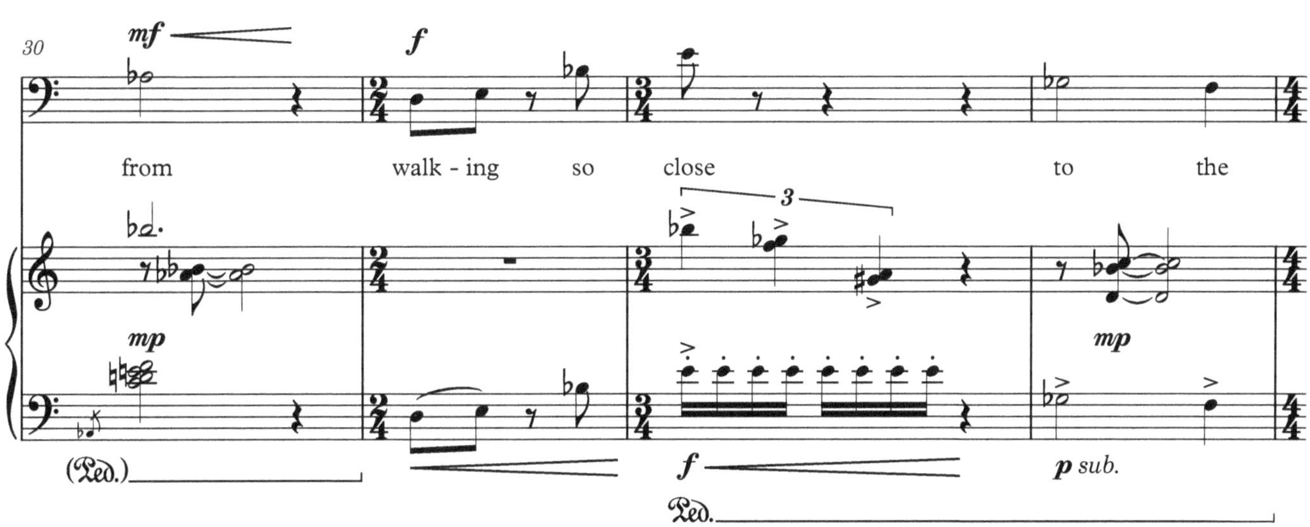
30
mf
f
from walk - ing so close to the
3
mp
mp
(Ped.)
f
p sub.
Ped.

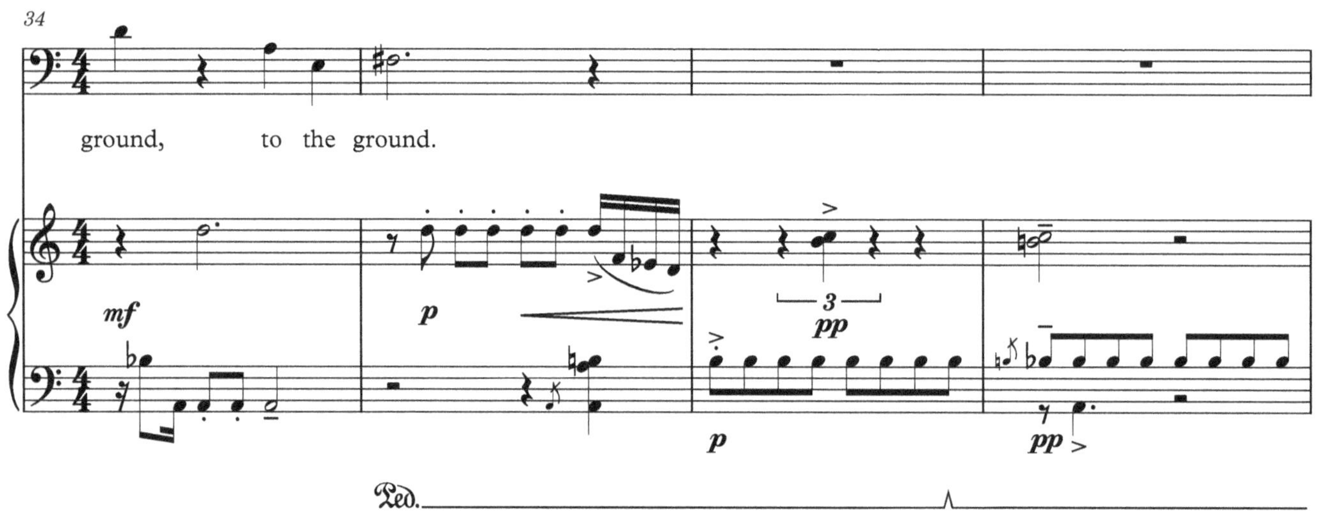
34
ground, to the ground.
mf
p
3
pp
p
pp
Ped.

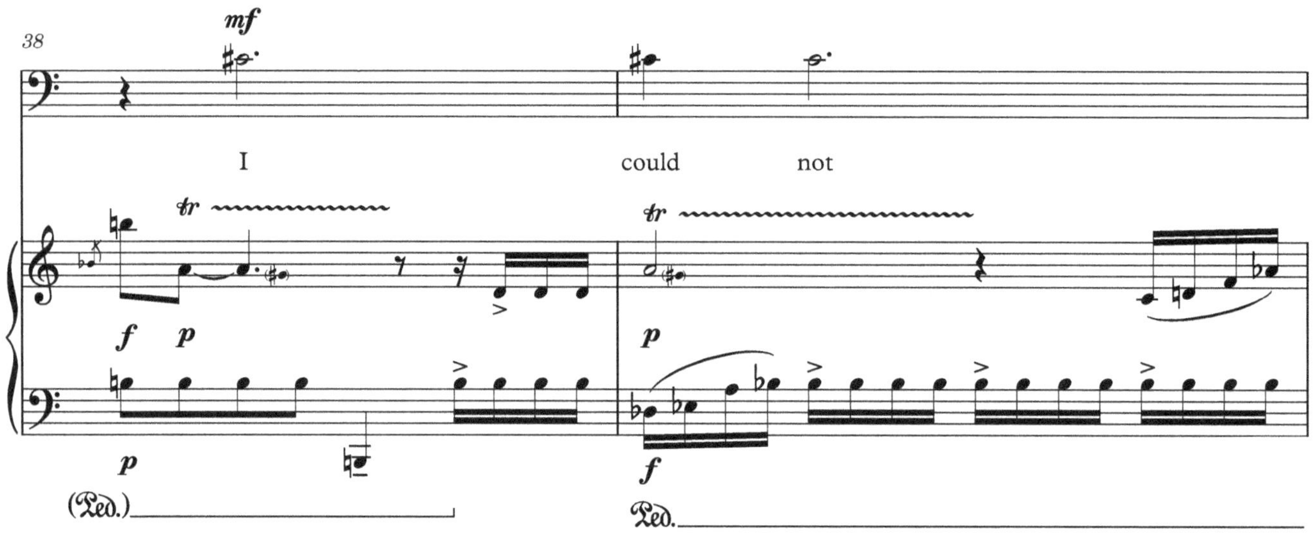
38
mf
I could not
tr
f p
p
p
f
(Ped.)
Ped.

40
breathe
mp
f

43
mf
f
breaths al - ways came in gasps
mp
f
mp
f
mp
Ped.
Ped.
46
cresc.
as though a rope was
f
(Ped.)
rit. a tempo
49
f
mf
pull - ing at my lungs.
mf
f
mp
p
mp
Ped.
Ped.

51
p
(Ped.)
8
Ped.

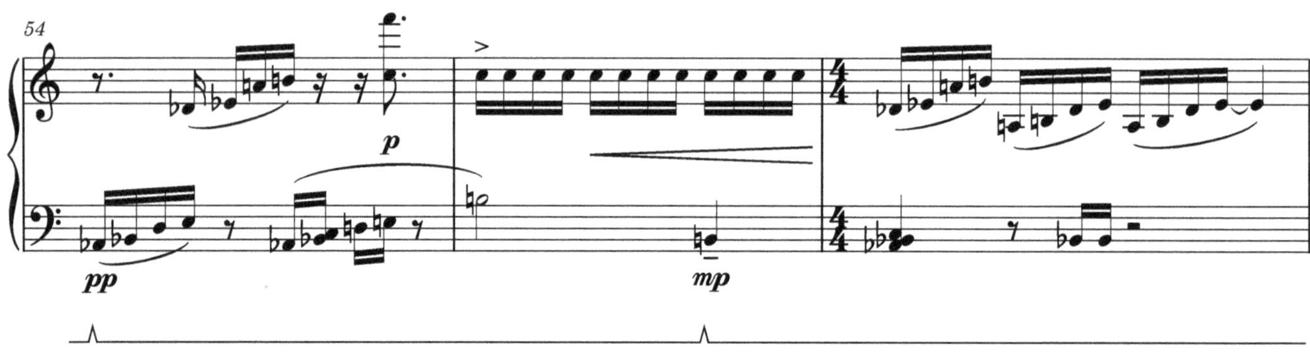
54
p
pp
mp

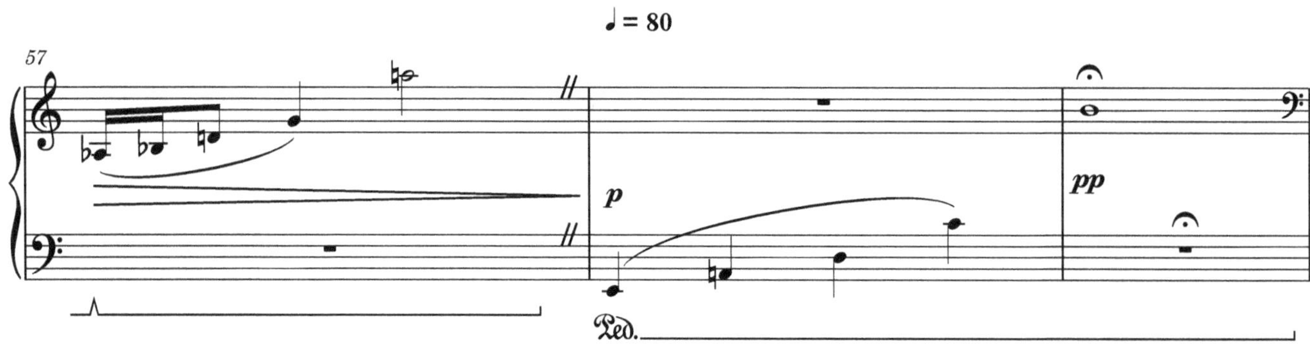
♩ = 80
57
p
pp
Ped.

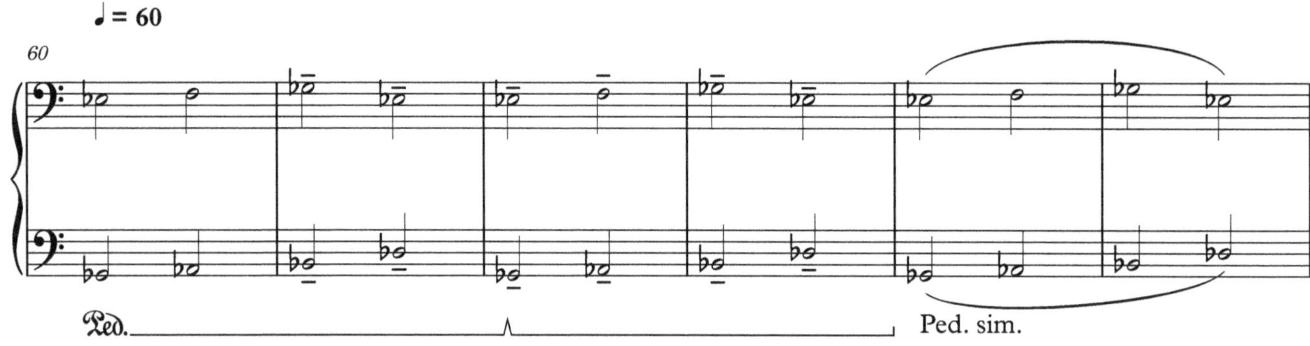
♩ = 60
60
Ped.
Ped. sim.

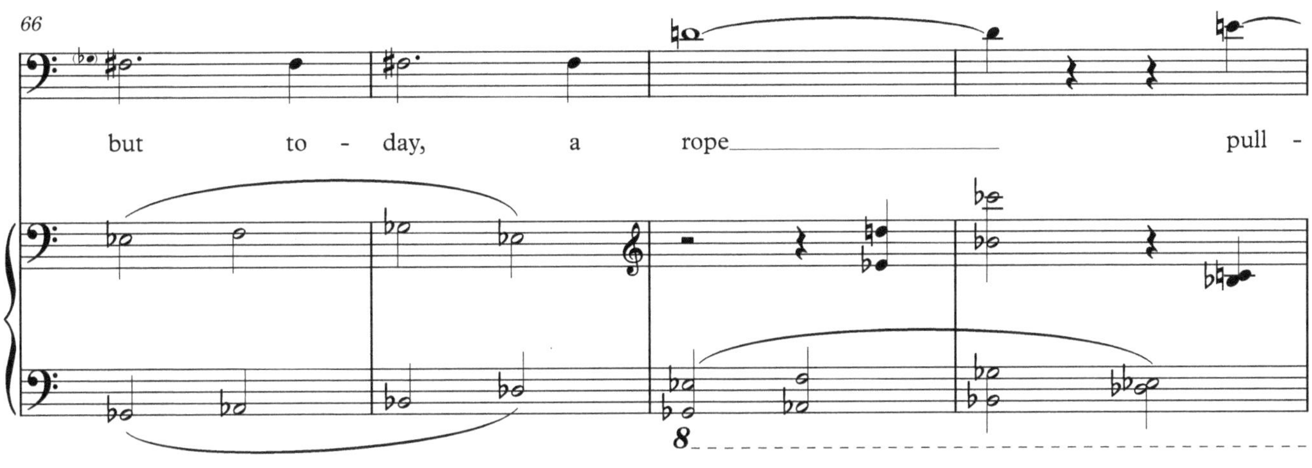
66
but to - day, a rope pull -
8

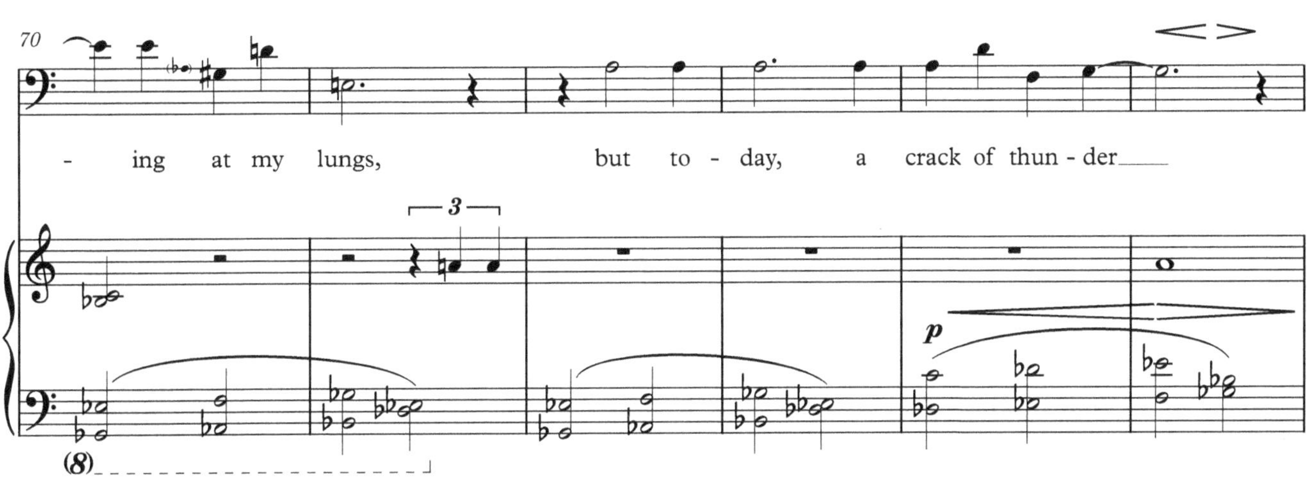
70
- ing at my lungs, but to - day, a crack of thun - der
3
p
(8)

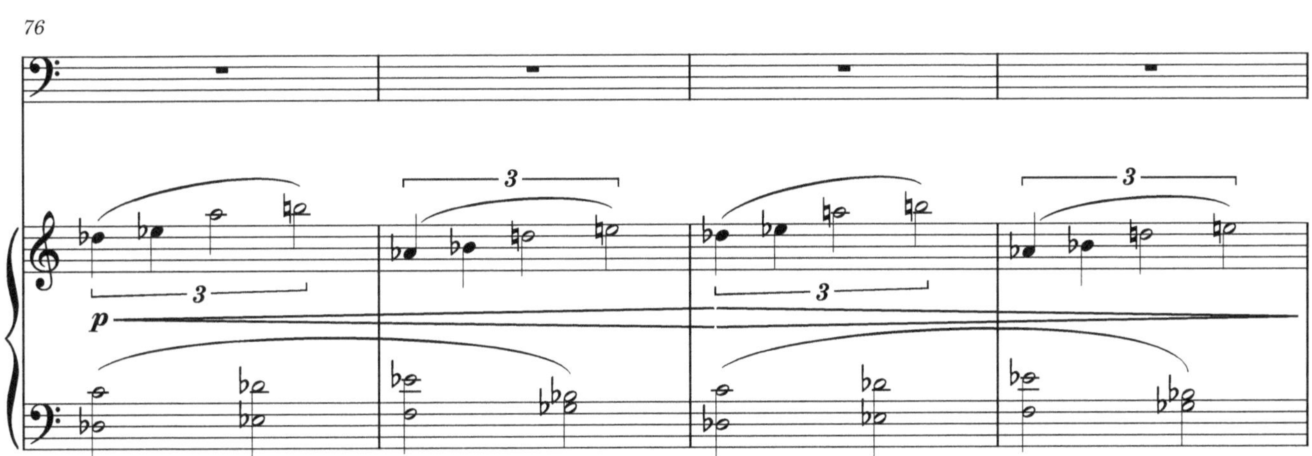
76
3
3
3
3
p

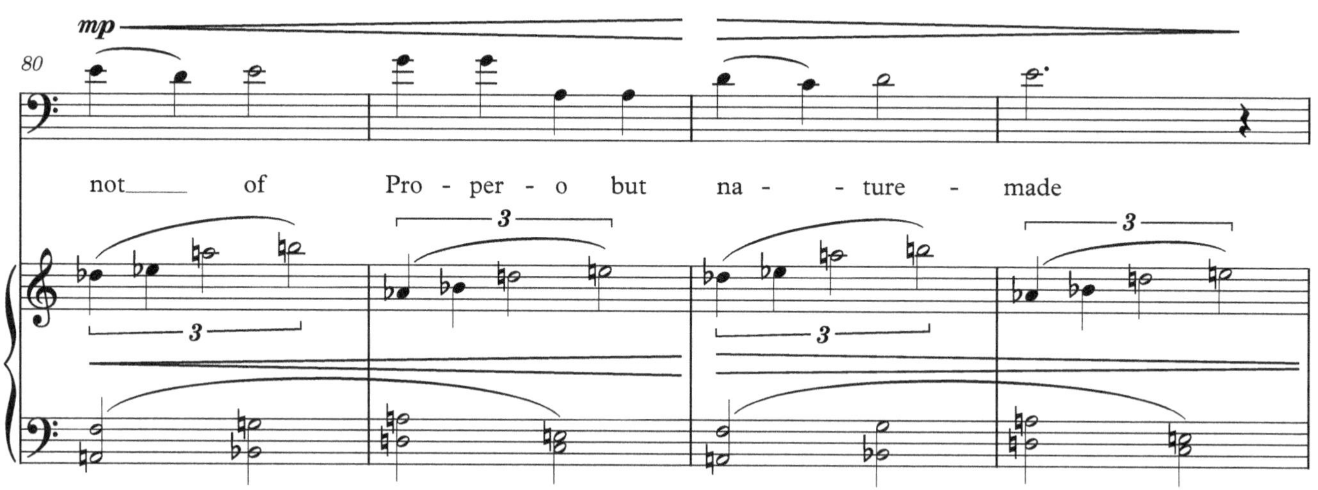
mp
80
not
of
Pro - per - o
but
na - - ture - made
3
3
3
3

p
84
shook
the
isle,
shook
the
isle
3
3
3
3
mp

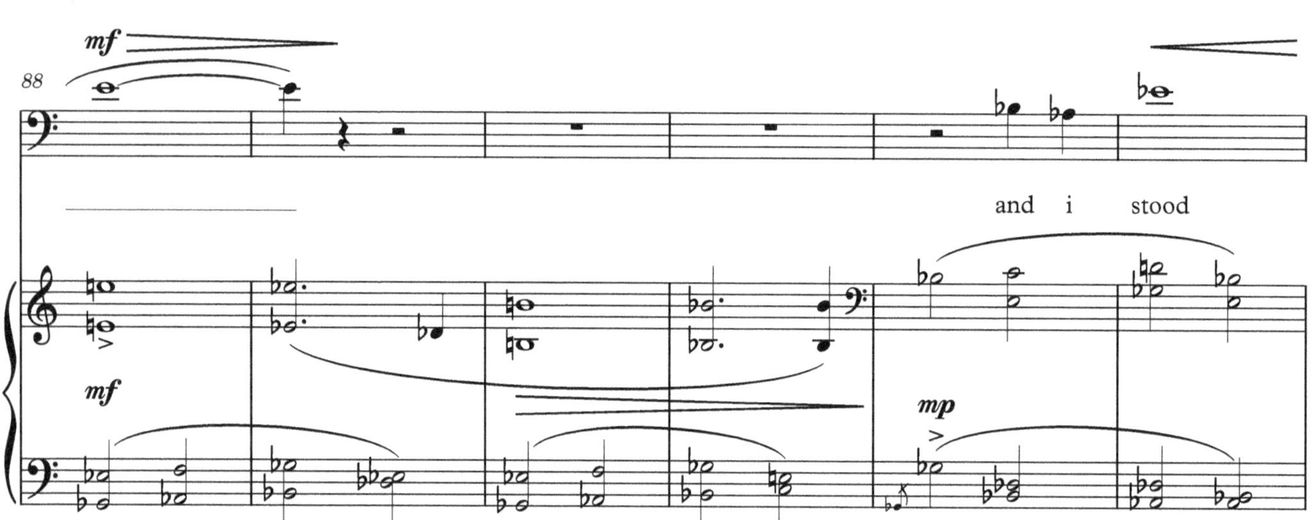
mf
88
and
i
stood
mf
mp

94
mf
to watch the sea swal - - low the
f
mp
p
Ped.
97
3
rocks
breath - ing in the sea -
mp
p
p
99
f
- wa - - ter with huge gulps
mf
ff

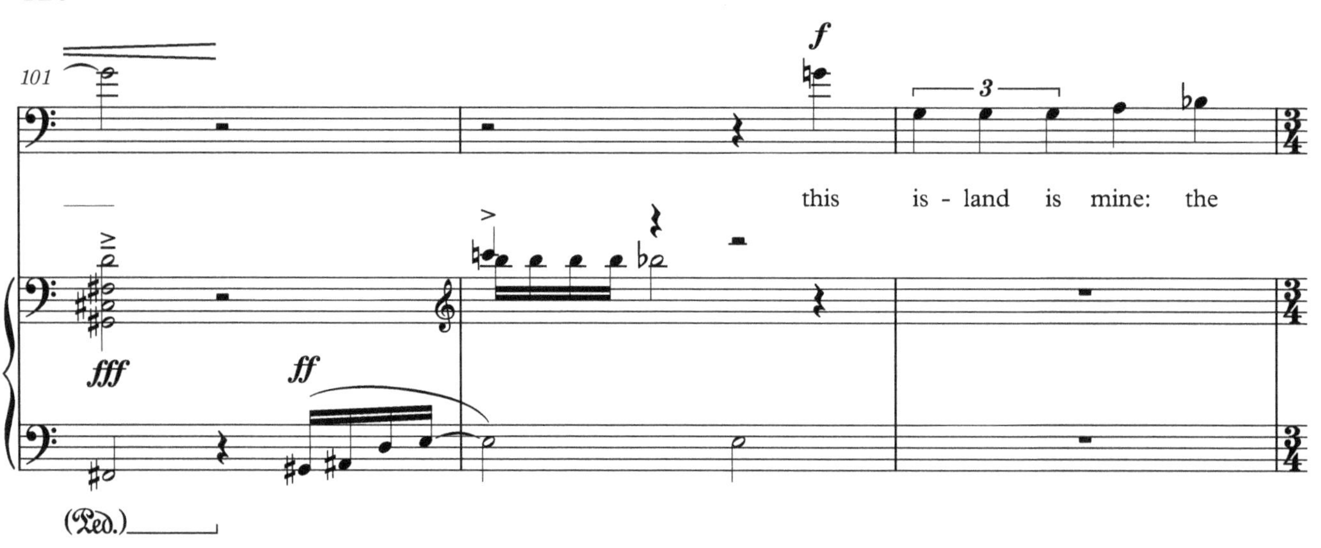
101
3
this is - land is mine: the
fff
ff
(Ped.)

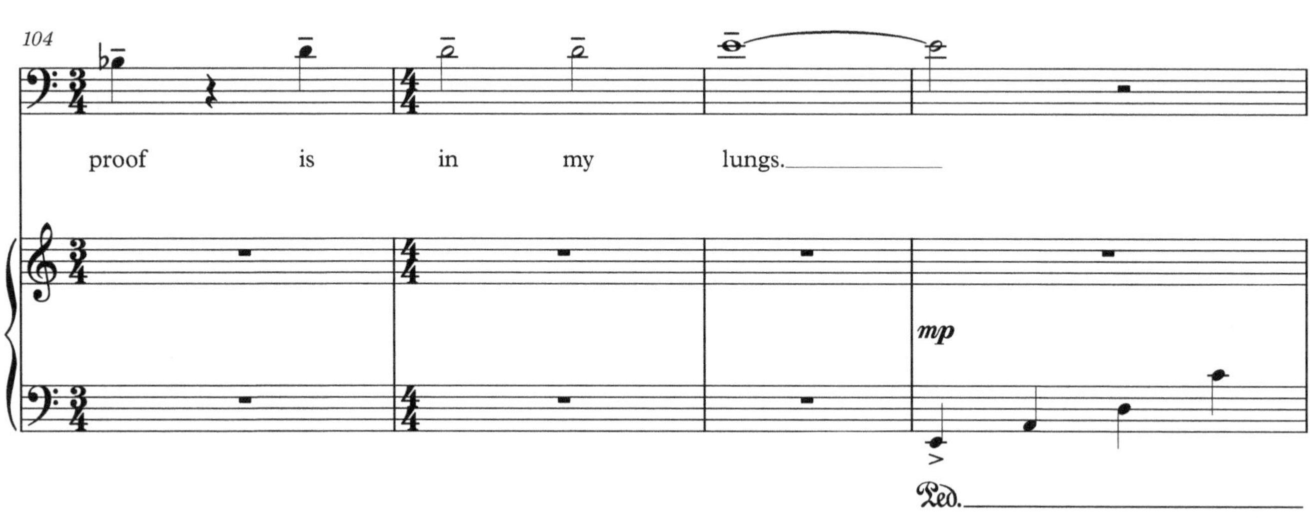
104
proof is in my lungs.
mp
Ped.

108
p
sfz
p
(Ped.)

111
tr
mp
mf

114
p
3
p
mf

accel.
rit...
117
p
(Ped.)
Ped.

120
pp
3
ppp
(Ped.)

composed for songSLAM NYC III 2019

Big Sky

from *Idaho Songs*

Jordan Bowman, Madelein Bowman, and Nathan Scalise

NATHAN SCALISE
(2019)

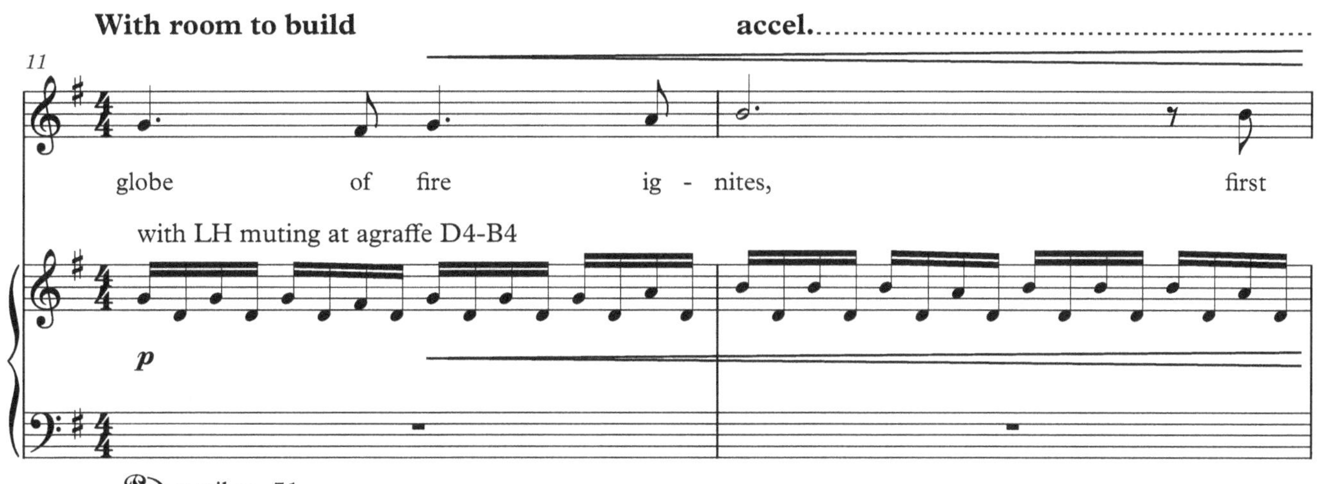
With room to build
accel.
11
globe of fire ig - nites, first
with LH muting at agraffe D4-B4
p
Ped. until m. 51

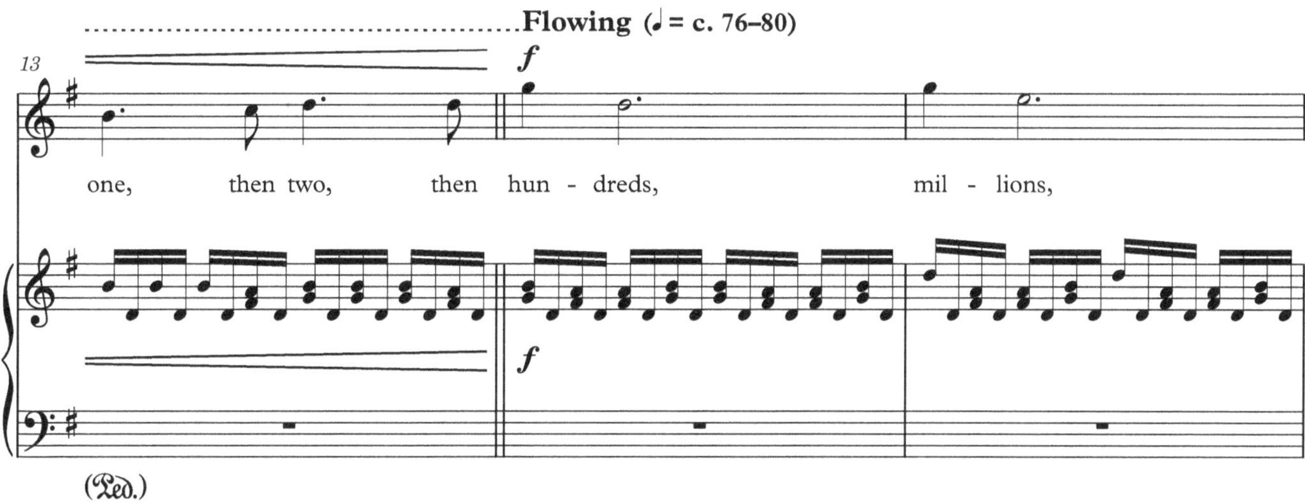
Flowing (♩ = c. 76–80)
13
f
one, then two, then hun - dreds, mil - lions,
f
(Ped.)

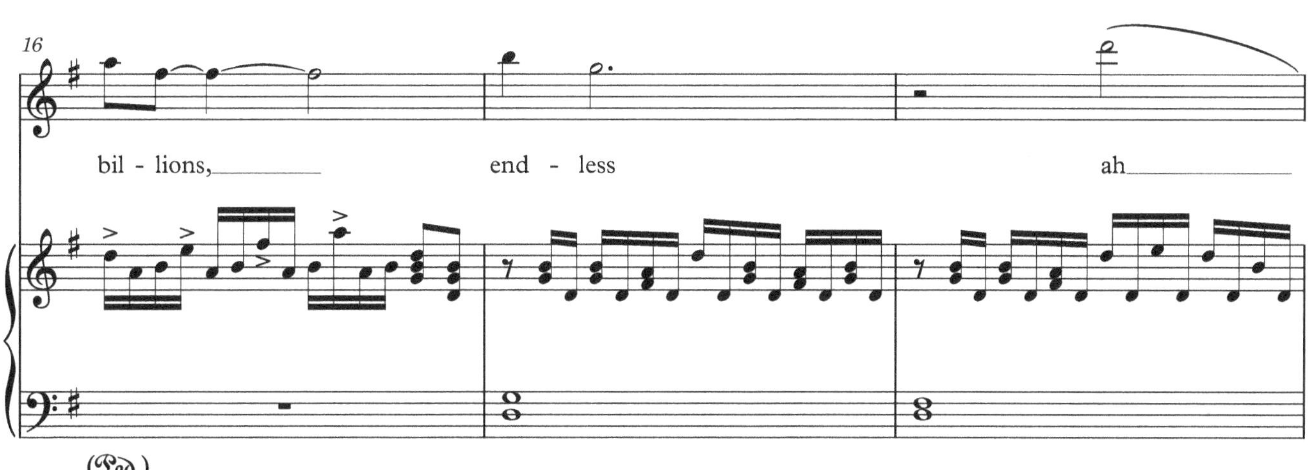
16
bil - lions,
end - less
ah
(Ped.)

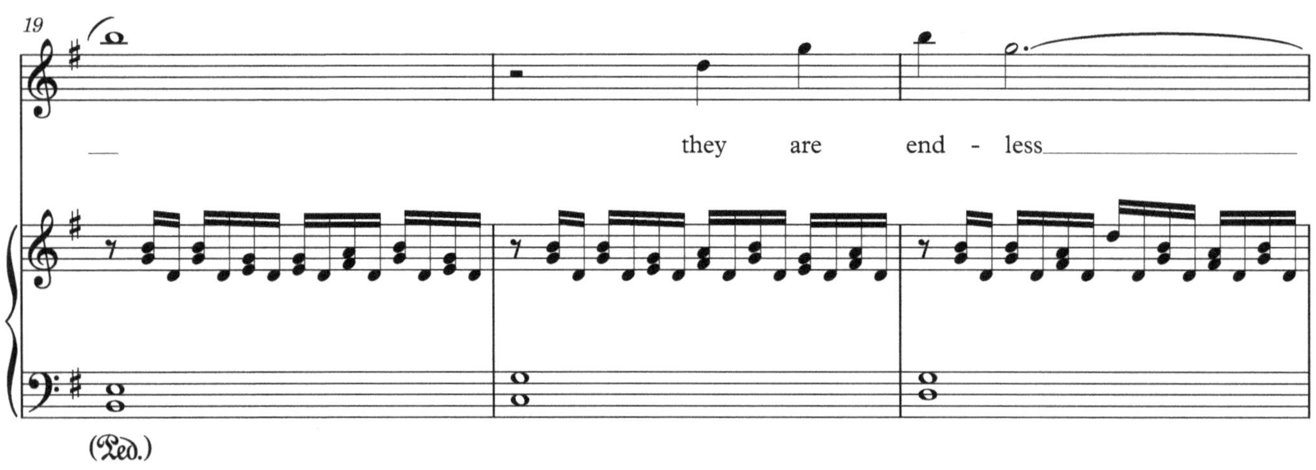
19
they are end - less
(Ped.)

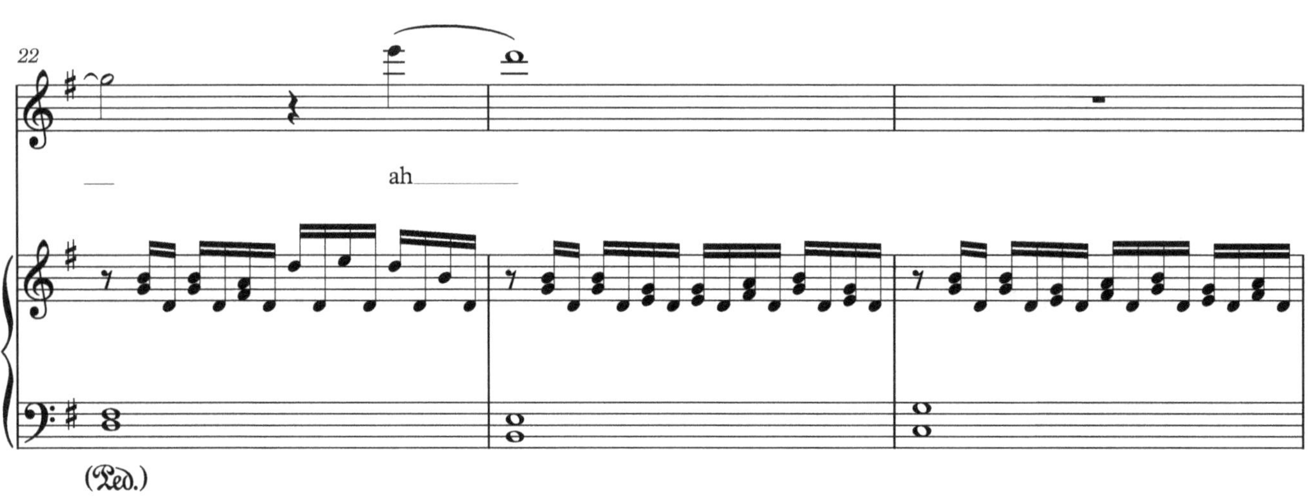
22
ah
(Ped.)

25
mf
Milk - y Way cha - ses god - dess Moon a - cross the
mf
(Ped.)

27
f
mf
vast sea of stars.
She bla - zes the heav - ens
sim.
(Ped.)

30
f
and makes night just as day!
(Ped.)

33
rit.
(Ped.)

Spacious, gentle (♩ = c. 66)
36
mp
He says "Moon, come to
use LH to mute all chords
(Ped.)

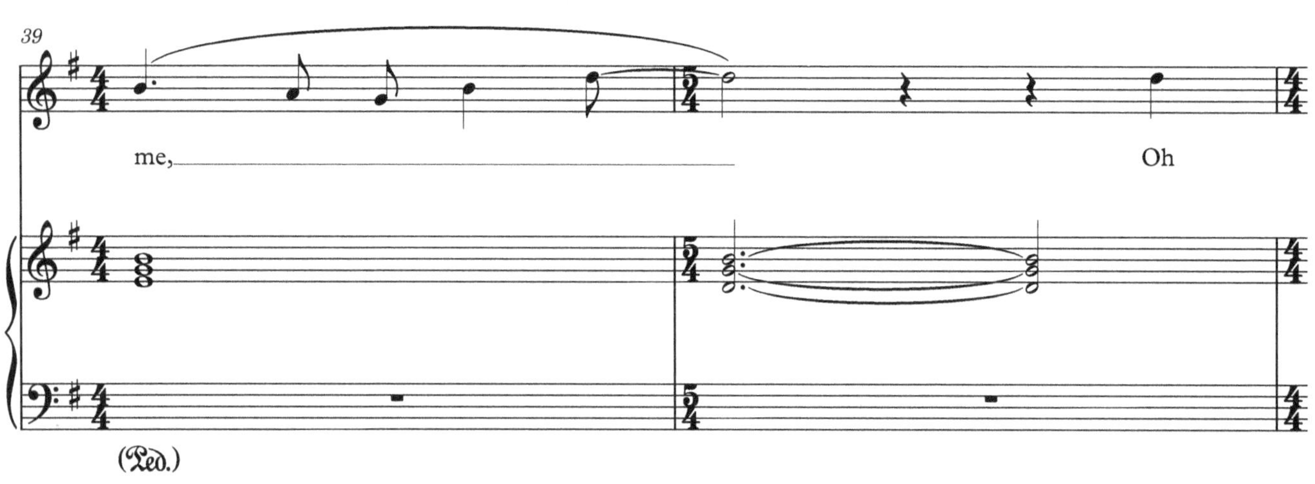
39
me, Oh
(Ped.)

41
Moon, be with me!
(Ped.)

44
These are your stars! This is our
(Ped.)

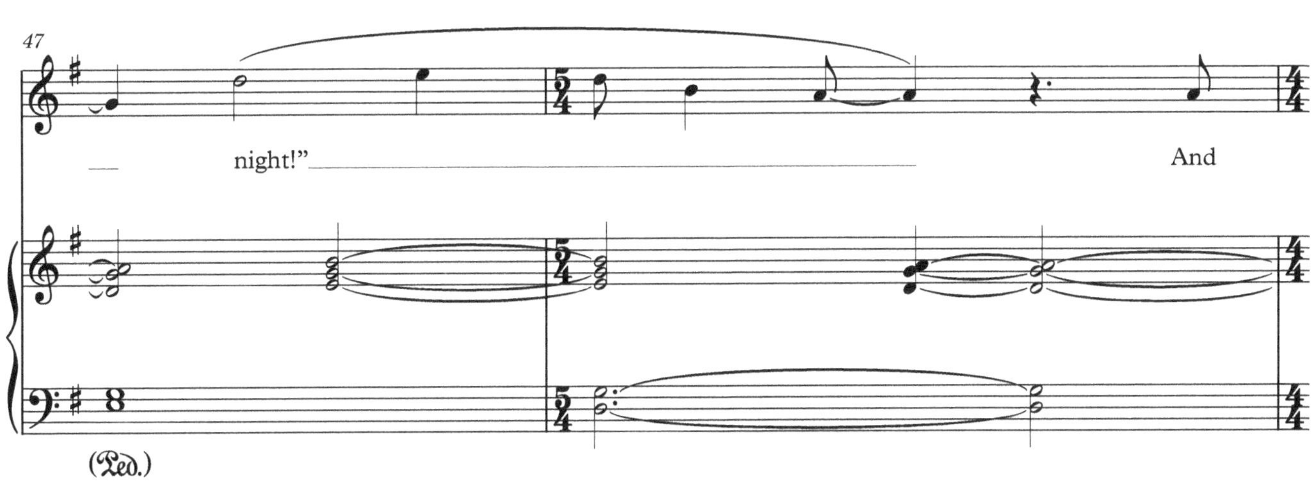
47
night!" And
(Ped.)

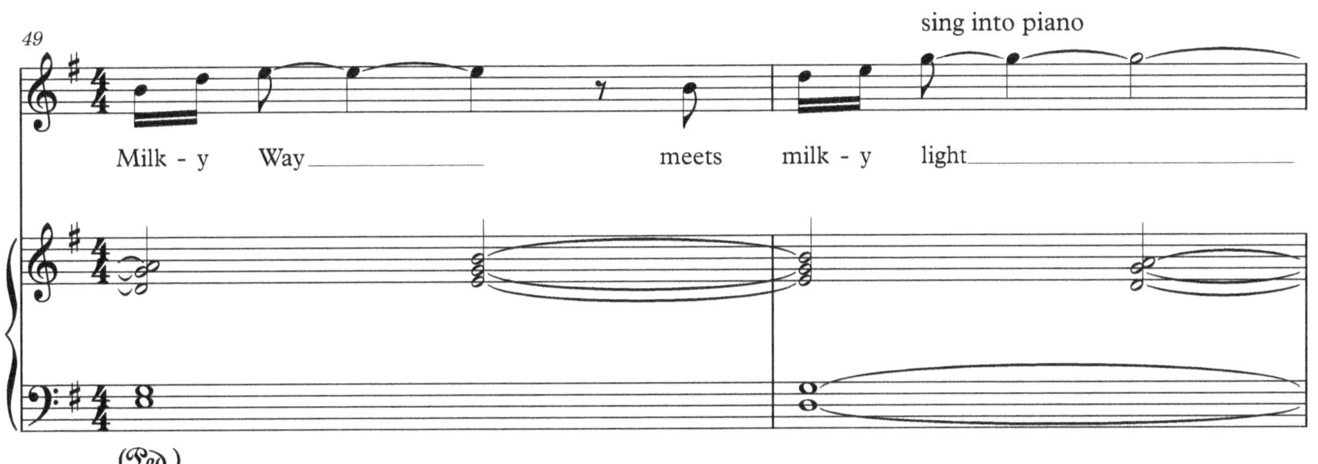
49
sing into piano
Milk - y Way meets milk - y light
(Ped.)

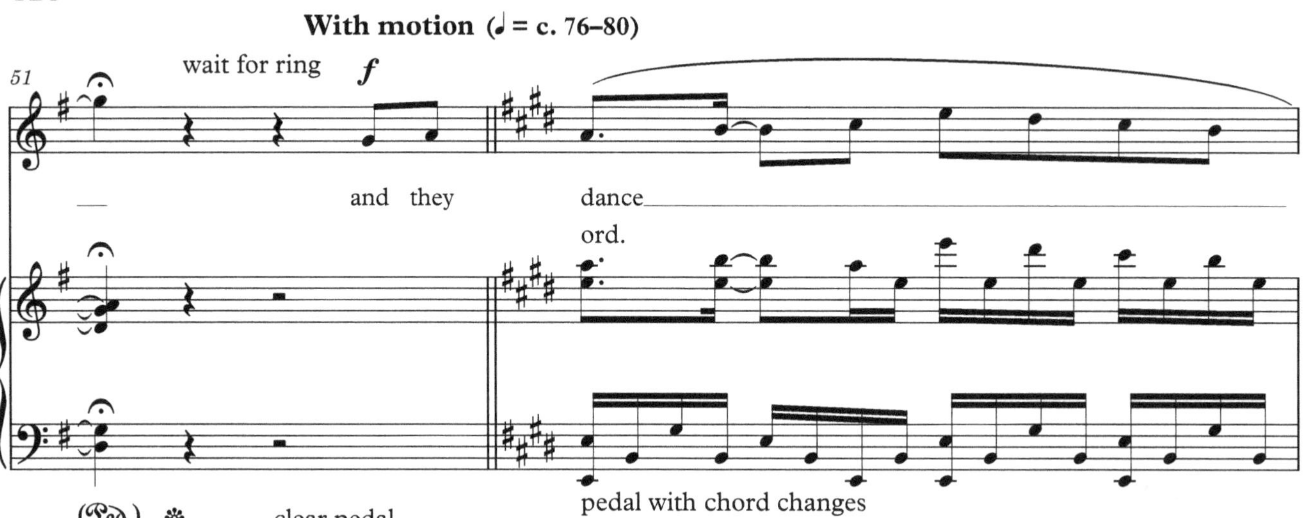
With motion (♩ = c. 76–80)
51
wait for ring
and they
dance
ord.
(Ped.)
clear pedal
before anacrusis
pedal with chord changes

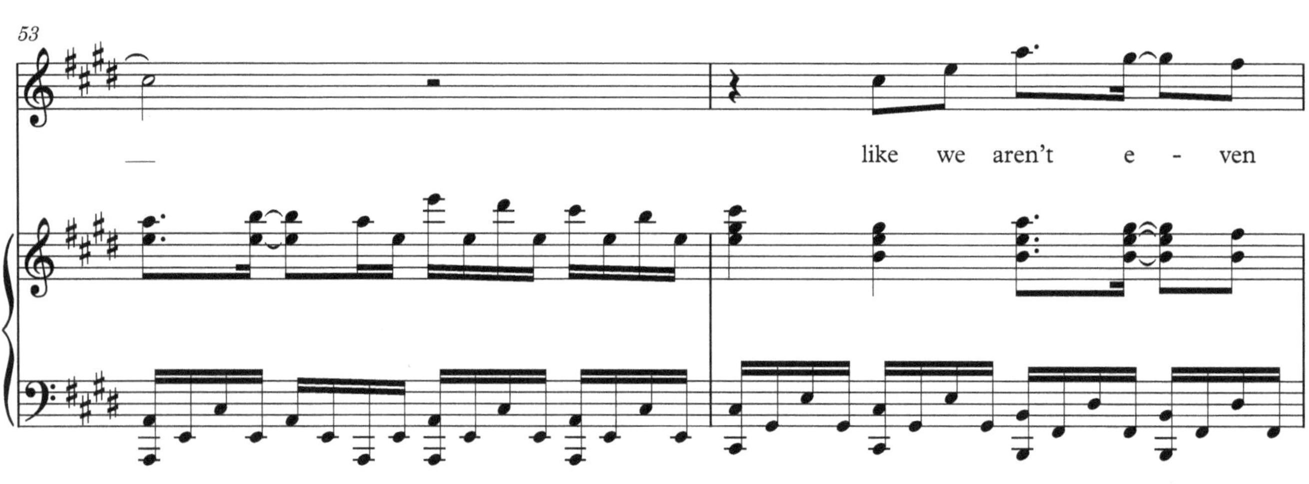
53
like we aren't e - ven

55
watch - ing
And we

57
dance

59
like they aren't e - ven there!
Ped. hold pedal through end

61
LH muting B3-G#4
mp
(Ped.)

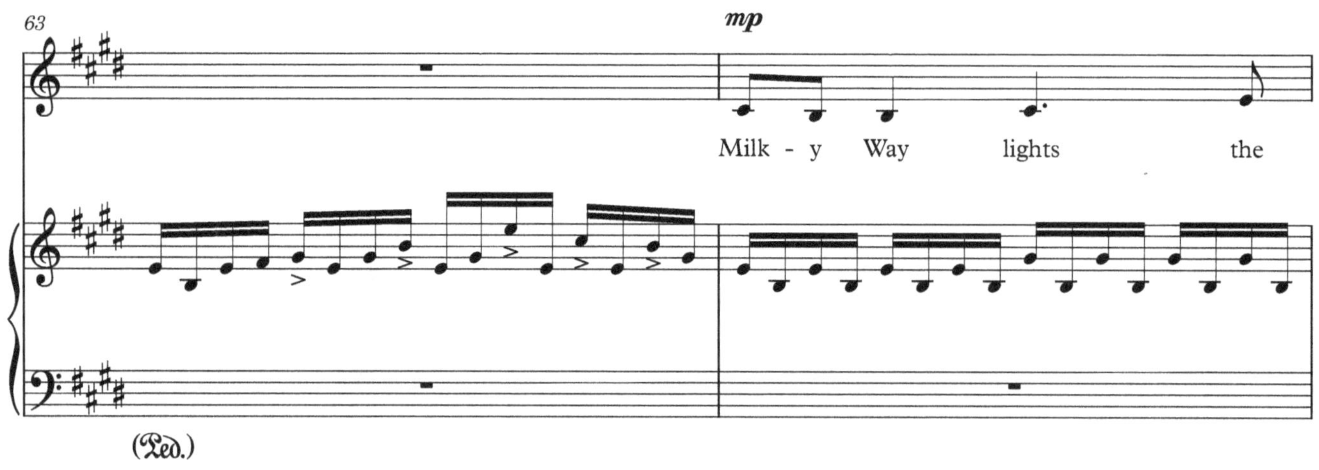
63
mp
Milk - y Way lights the
(Ped.)

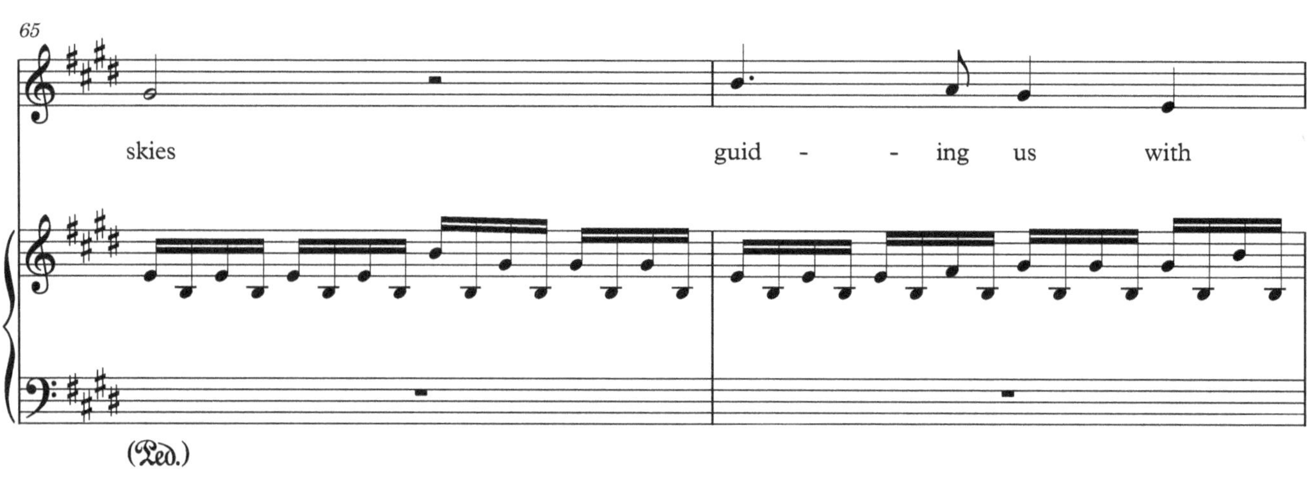
65
skies
guid - - ing us with
(Ped.)

67
bright star - ry beams
(Ped.)

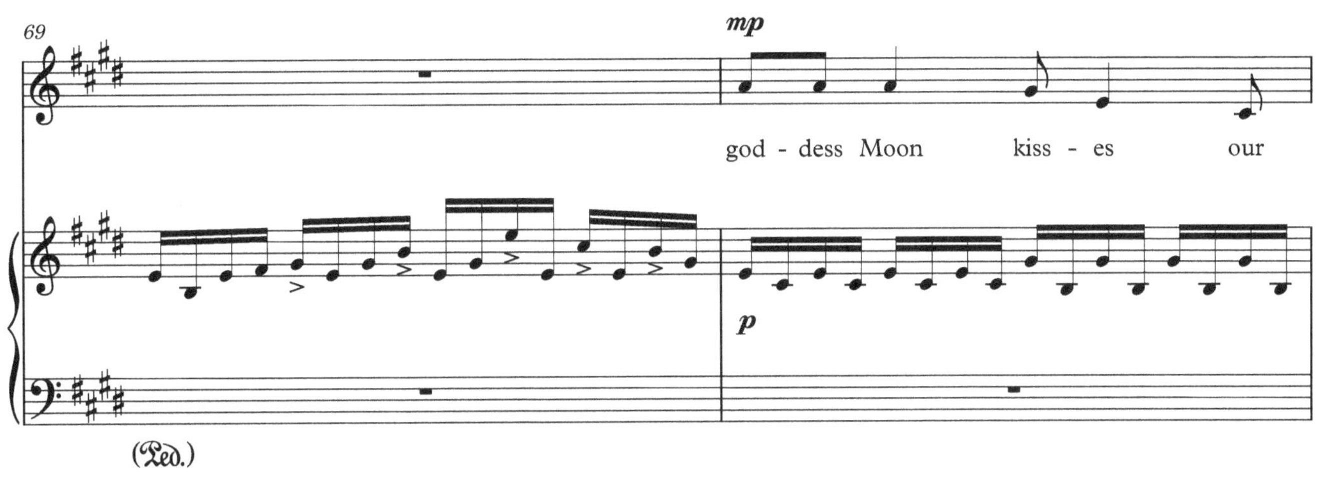
69
mp
god - dess Moon kiss - es our
p
(Ped.)

71
eyes
send - ing us to
(Ped.)

73
p
sweet, coun - try dreams
pp
(Ped.)

composed for spevSLAM Slovenia 2019

Ko te ni

Jakob Barbo

TILEN SLAKAN
(2019)

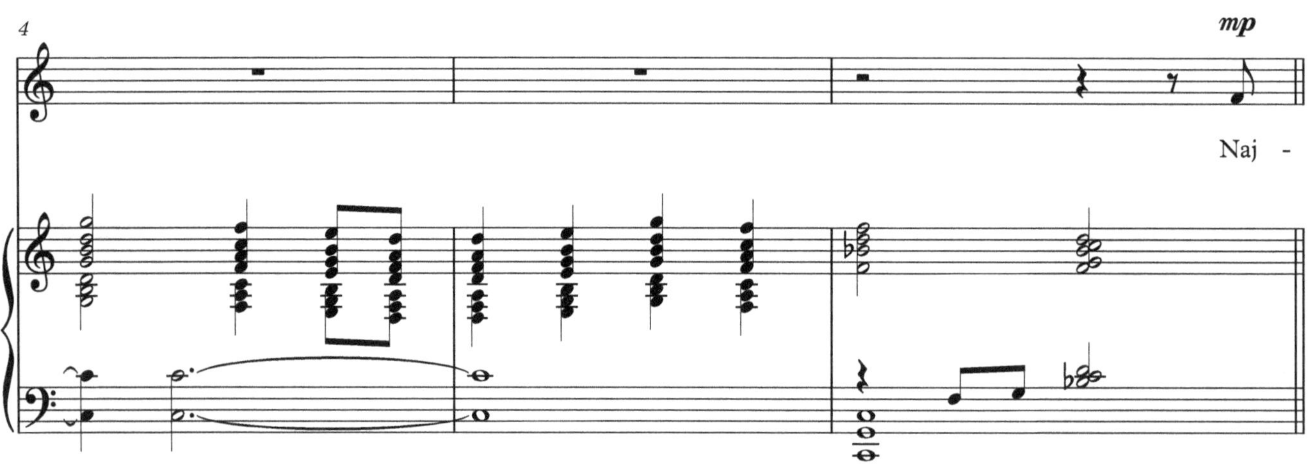

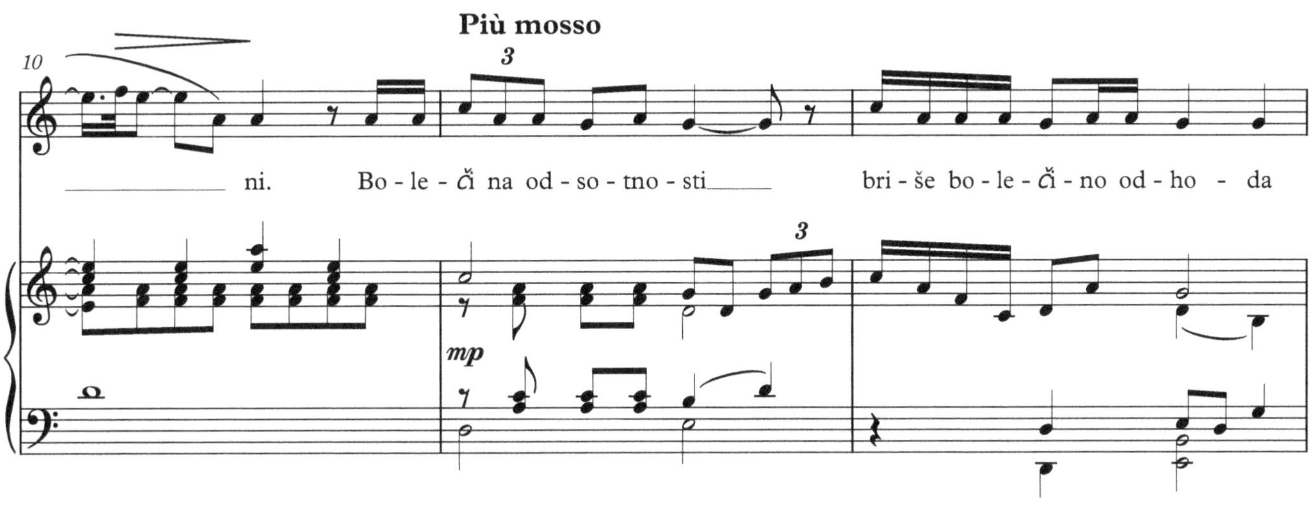
Più mosso
10
ni. Bo - le - či na od - so - tno - sti bri - še bo - le - či - no od - ho - da
mp

rit.
13
mf
in ra - dost pri - ho - da nek - je...

A tempo
16
p
mp
da - - leč... vsa - ko dru - go ra - dost.
p

molto rit.

20
3
3

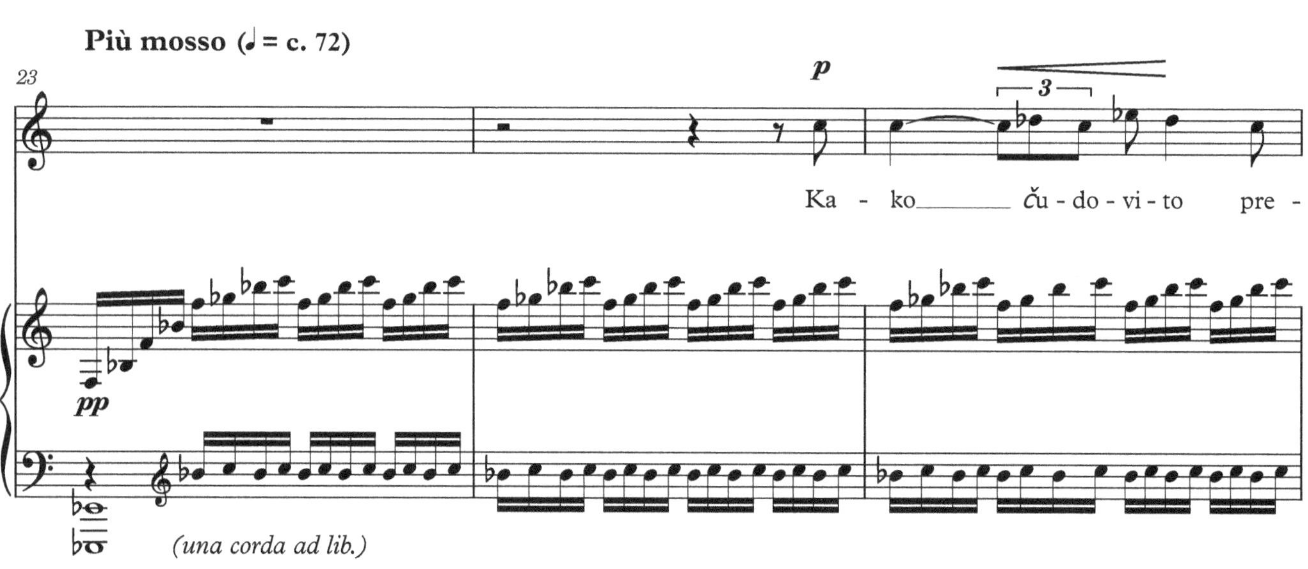
Più mosso (♩ = c. 72)
23
p
3
Ka - ko ču - do - vi - to pre -
pp
(una corda ad lib.)

26
mp
-ba - - da slu - - tnja vr - ni - - - tve,

This page intentionally left blank to facilitate page turns

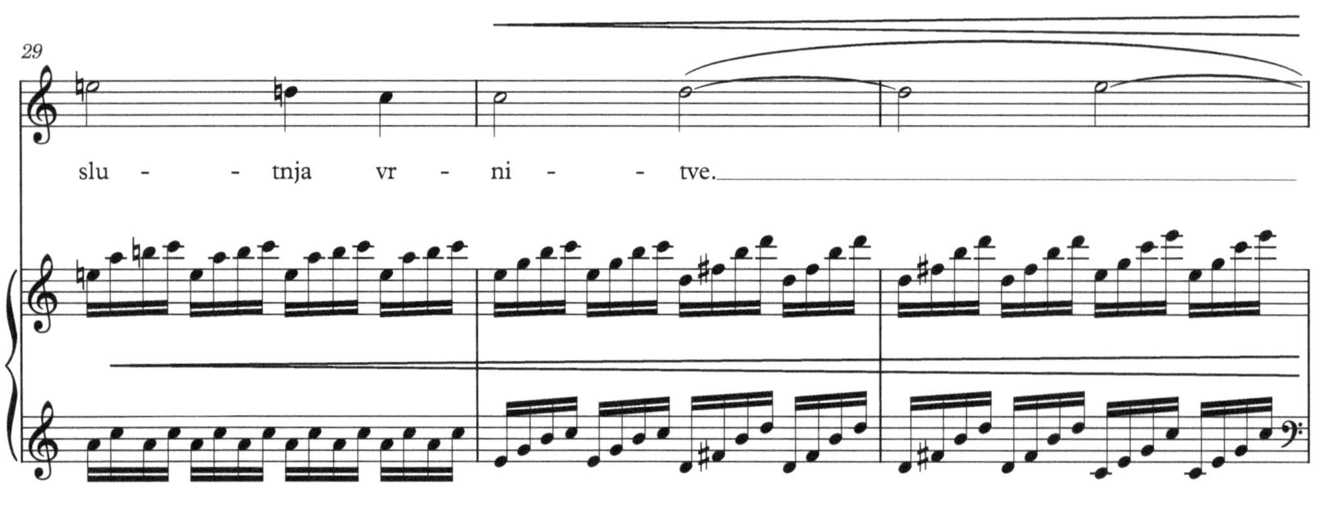
29
slu - - tnja vr - ni - - tve.

32
mf
mp
Ka - ko ču - do - vi - - to pre-

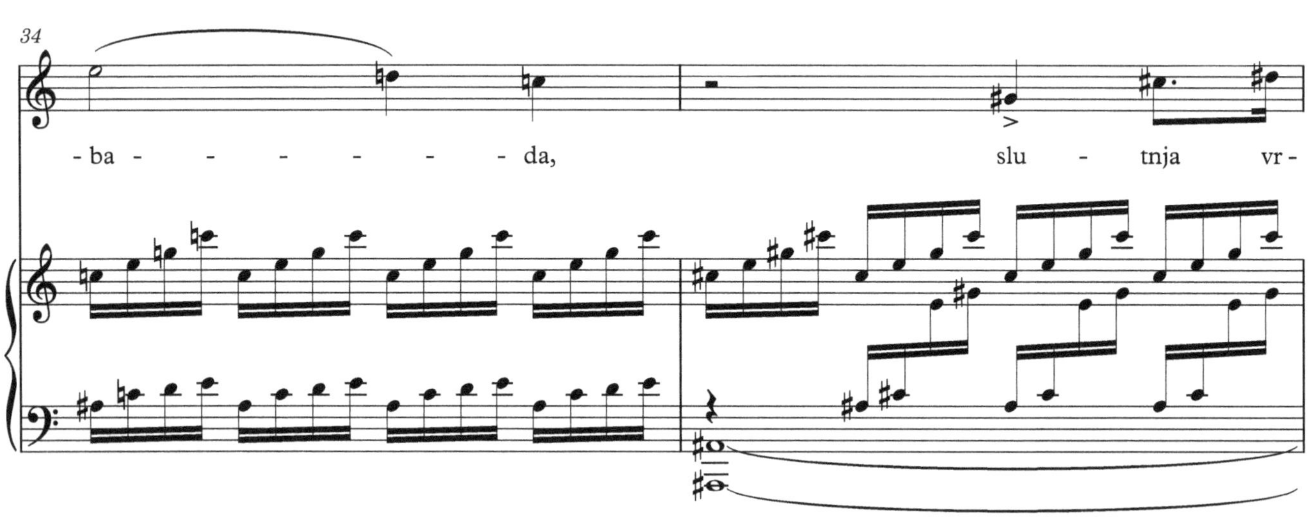
34
- ba - - - - - da, slu - tnja vr-

36
-ni - - tve, vse bolj in bolj, vse bolj in bolj vse bolj in bolj vse bolj in bolj od

rit.
39
3
nog do gla - ve, od gla - ve do pet, do

Široko (Broadly) (♩ = 64)
41
ff
vzdih (sigh)
f
3
pet... Oh! Naj - lep - ši so dne - vi, ko te
3
f
3

Più mosso
mp
ni.
Le dne - vi, ko si, so mi lep - ši. Le
mp
dne - vi, ko si, so mi lep - - - - ši. So mi
rit.
mf
Široko (♩ = 64)
f
rit.
lep - ši...!
f
ff

composed for songSLAM Ann Arbor 2017

Invictus

William Ernest Henley

EVAN L. SNYDER
(2017)

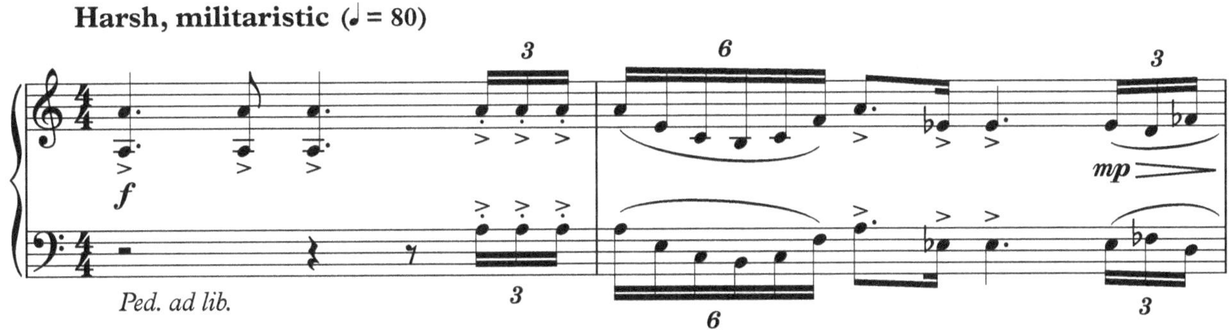

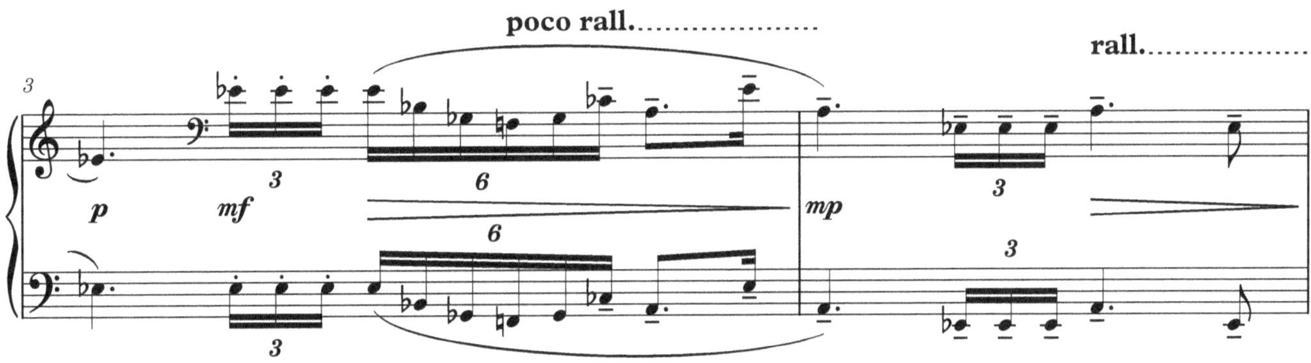

⋆ only include doubling at the octave if the piano's lowest A is unclear (or out of tune)

Freely, flowing (♩ = 54)

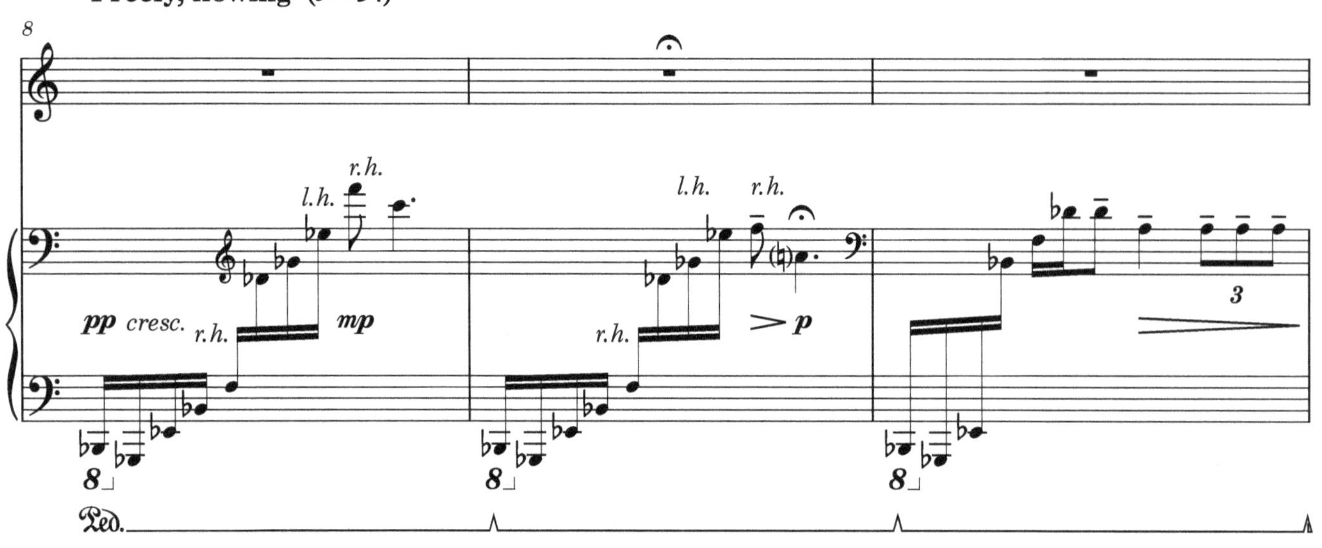

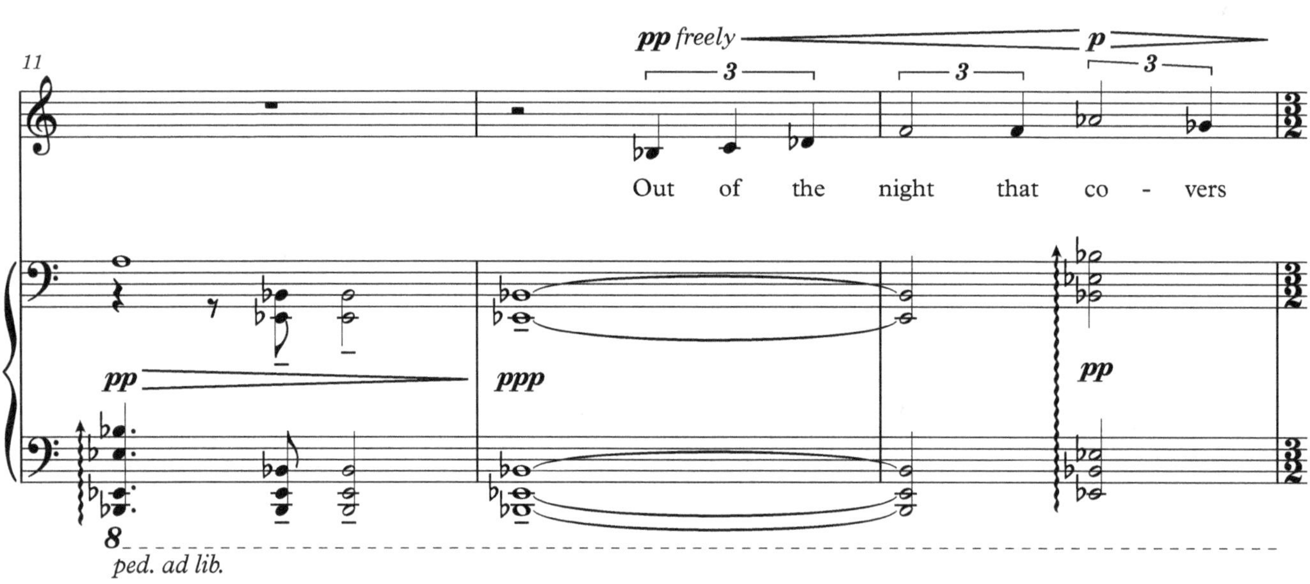

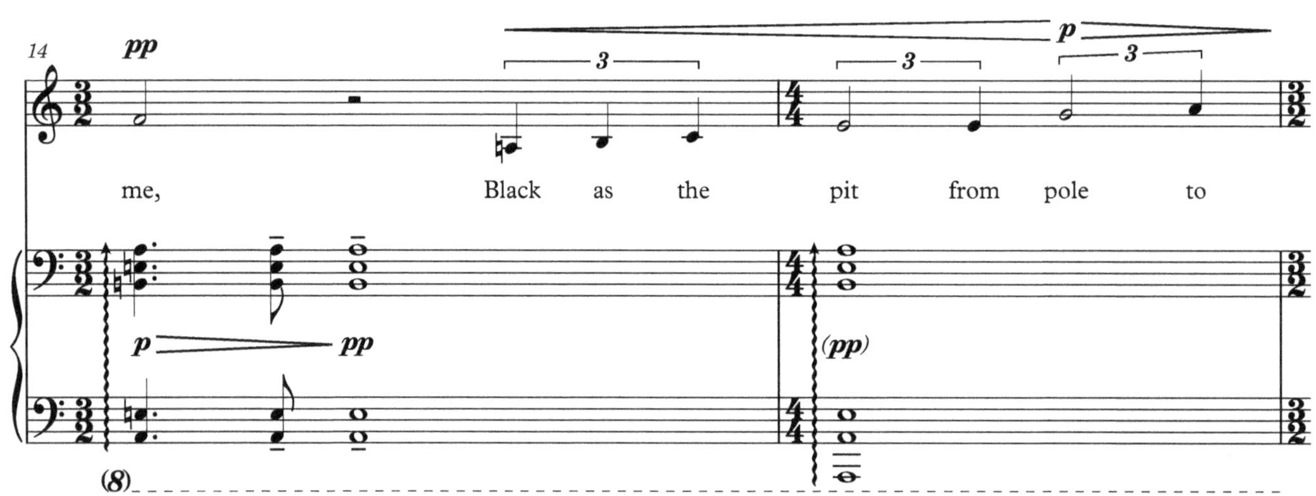

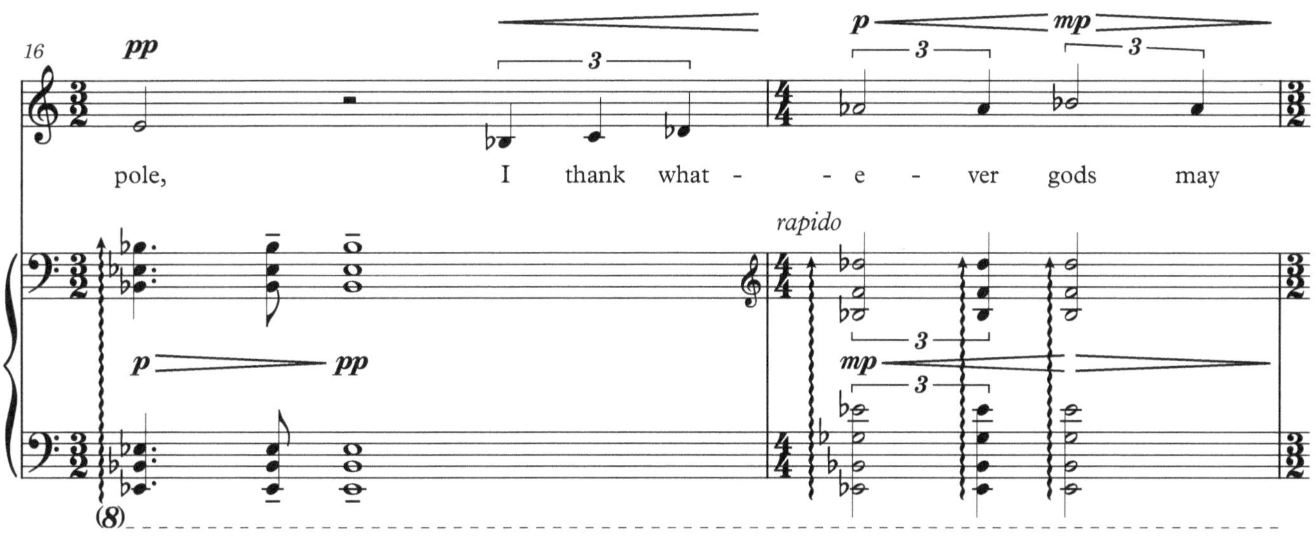
16
pp
p
mp
pole, I thank what - - e - ver gods may
rapido
p
pp
mp
(8)

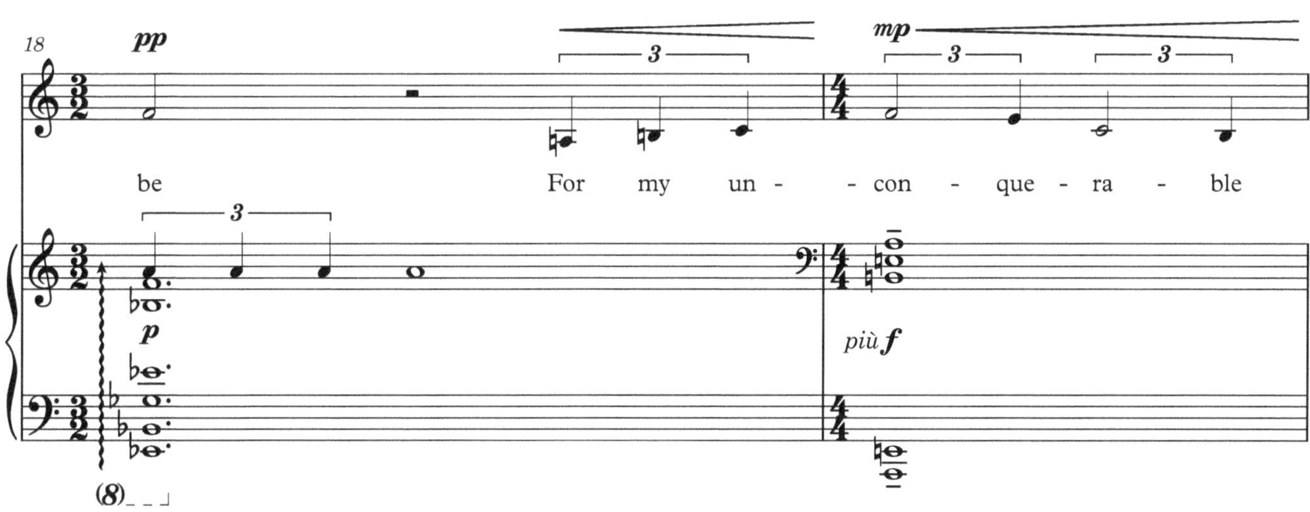
18
pp
mp
be For my un - - con - que - ra - ble
p
più f
(8)

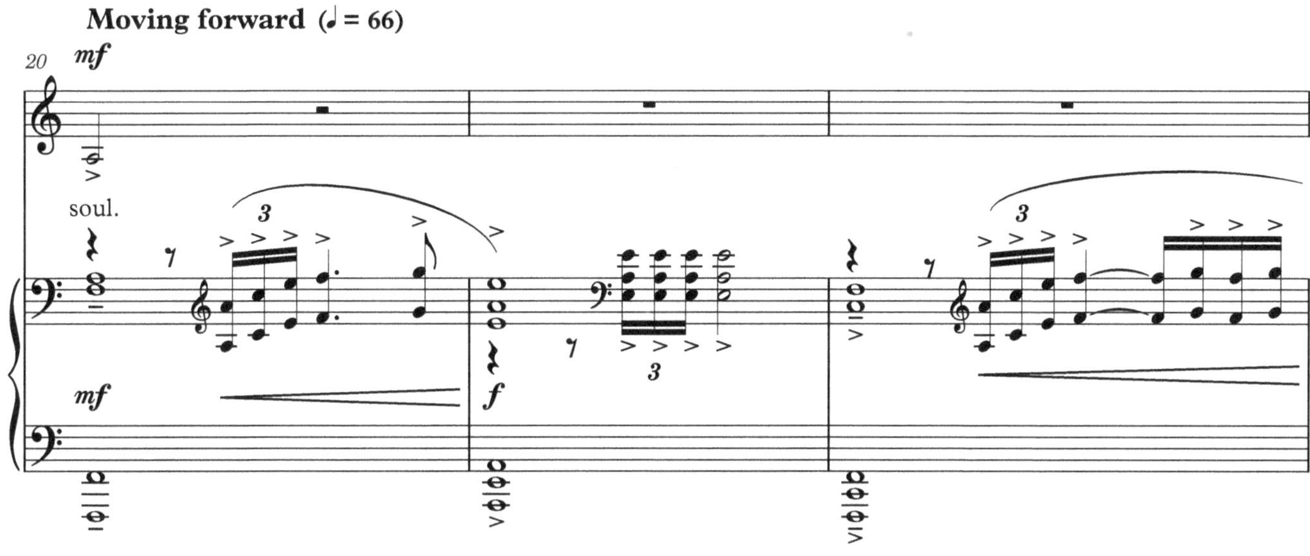
Moving forward (♩ = 66)
20
mf
soul.
mf
f

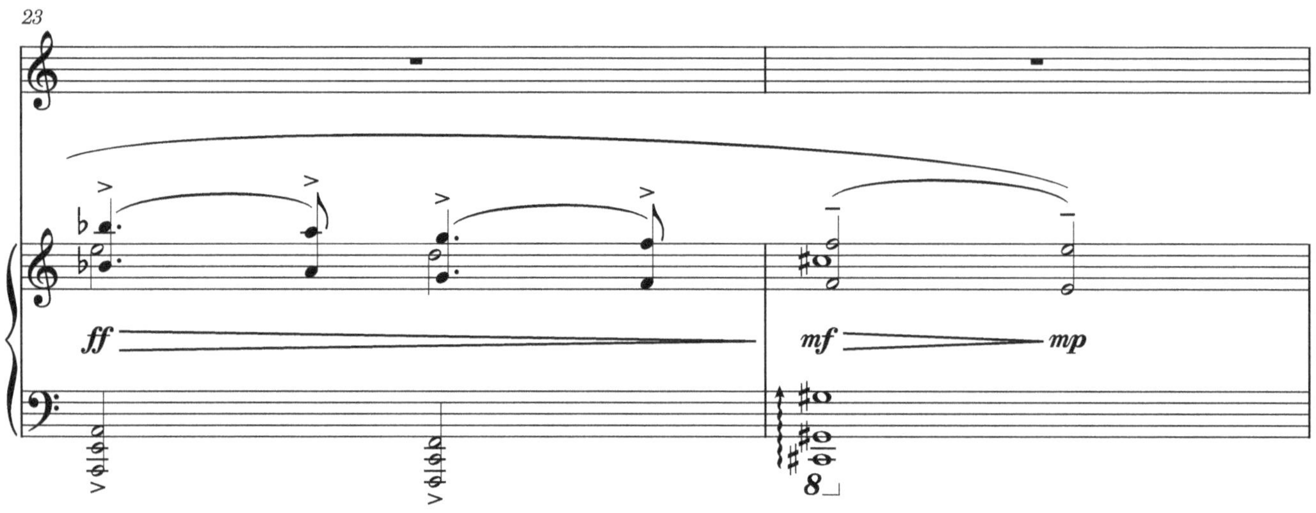
23
ff
mf
mp
8

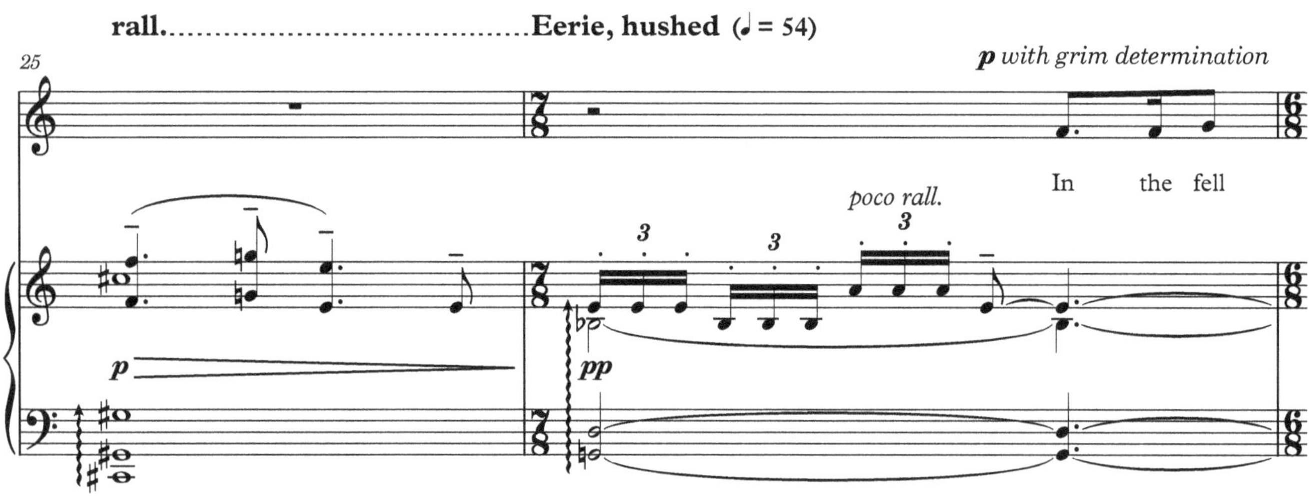
rall. Eerie, hushed (♩ = 54)
25
p with grim determination
In the fell
poco rall.
3
p
pp

27
clutch of cir - cum - stance
I have not
poco rall.
3
pp

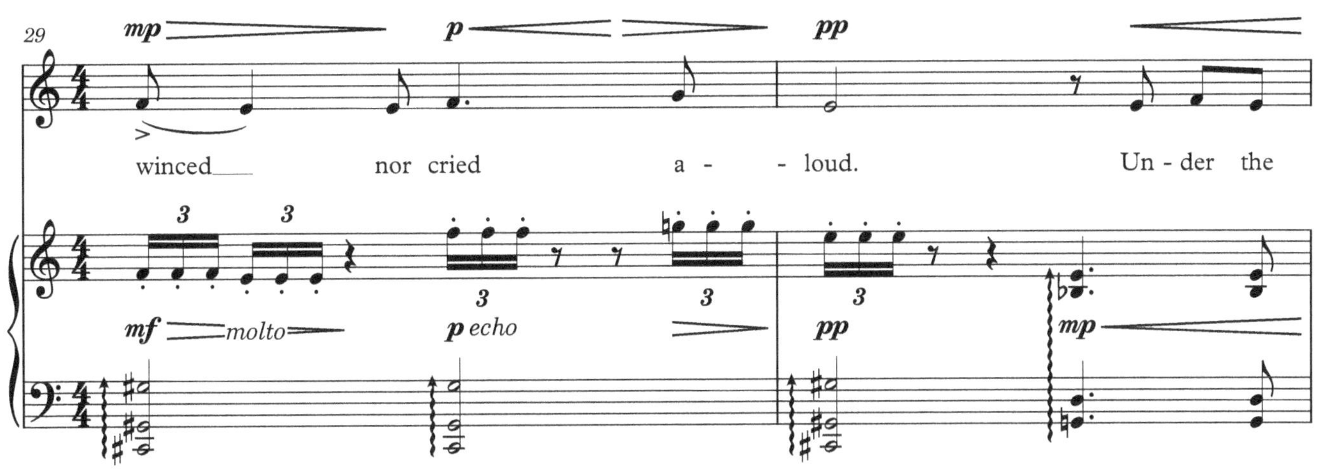
29
mp
p
pp
winced___ nor cried a - - loud. Un - der the
mf molto
p echo
pp
mp

31
mp
mf
poco rall.................Freely, slower
pp
blud - geon - ings of chance
My head is
mf colla voce f
mp
pp

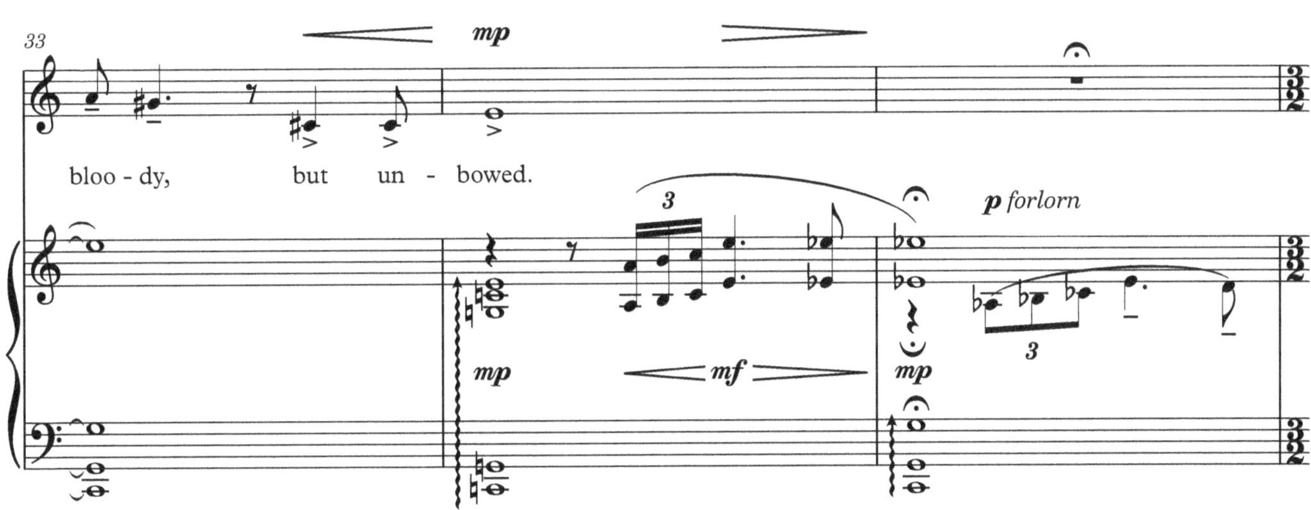
33
mp
bloo - dy, but un - bowed.
p forlorn
mp
mf
mp

Steady, trudgingly (𝅗𝅥 = 50)
36
mp
mf
mp
Be - yond this place of wrath and tears
8
p
38
p
mp
p
Looms but the Hor - ror of the shade,
8
mp
p
40
mp
mf
And yet the me - nace of the years
mp
mf non dim.

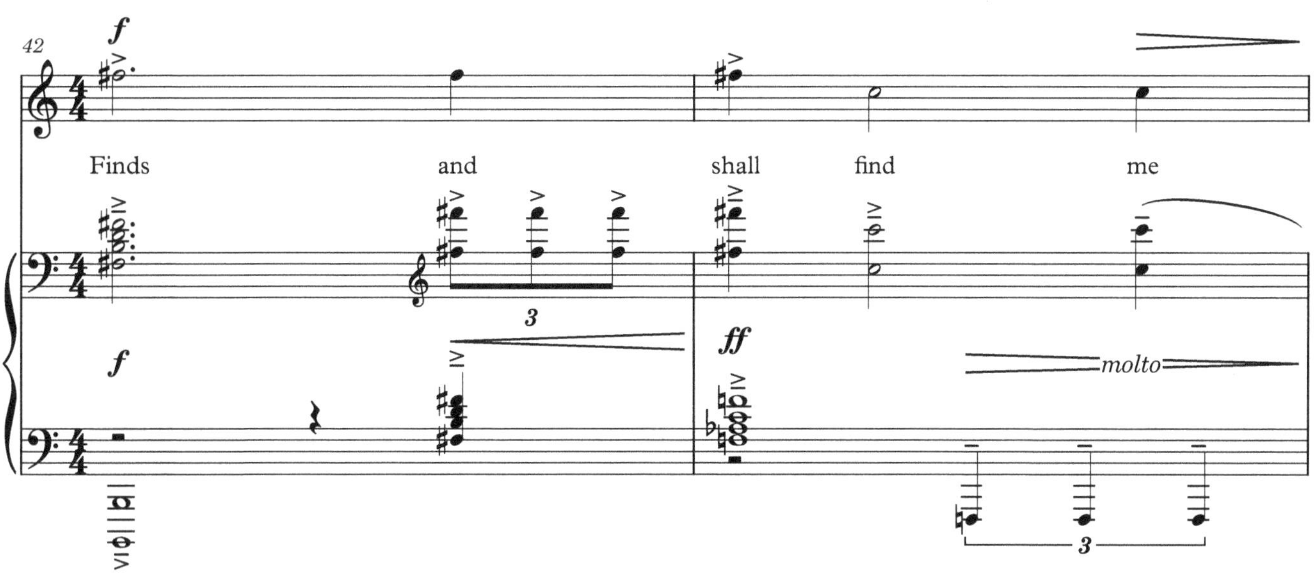

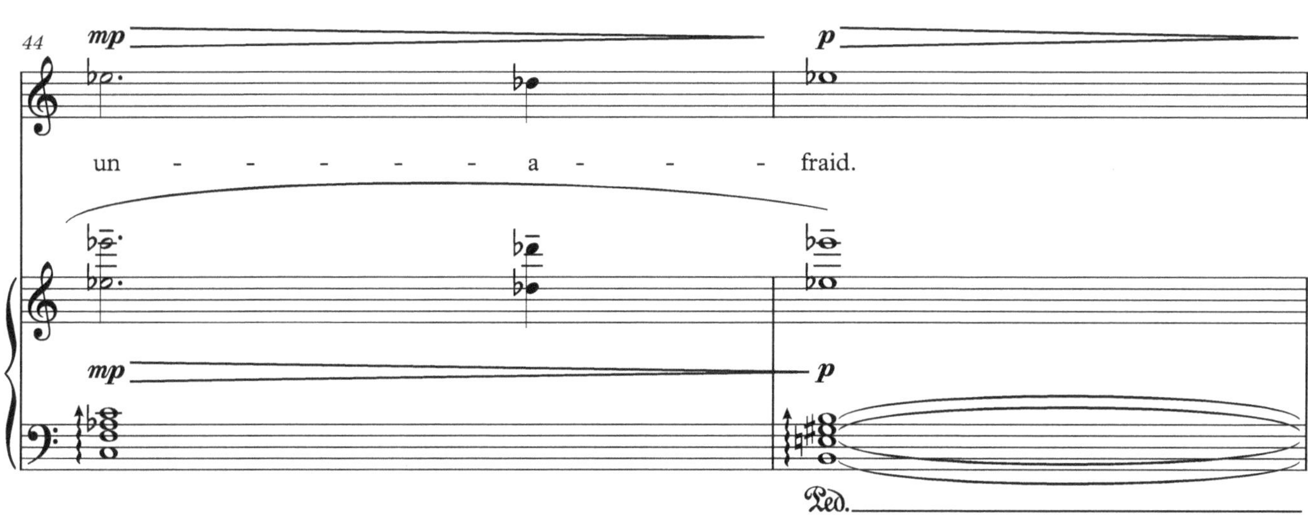

Somewhat relaxed (𝅗𝅥 = 44)

poco rall.

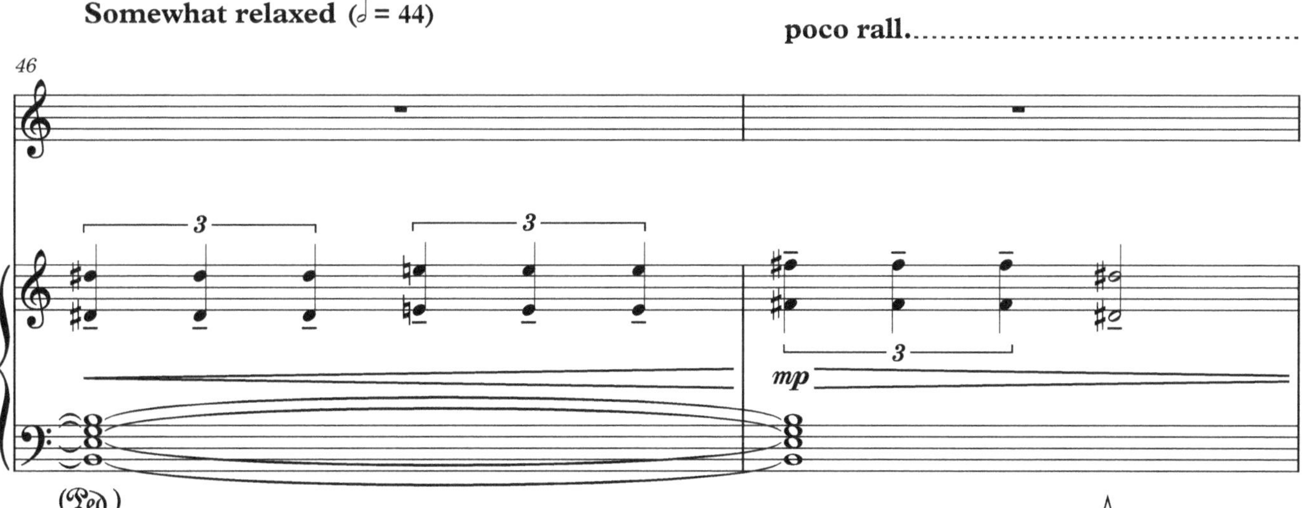

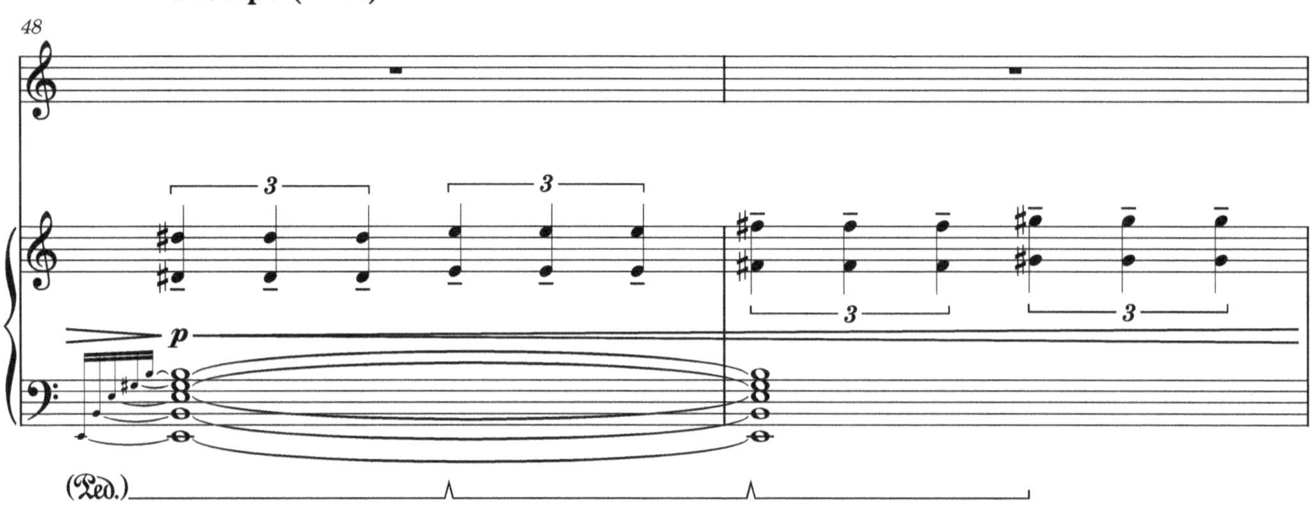

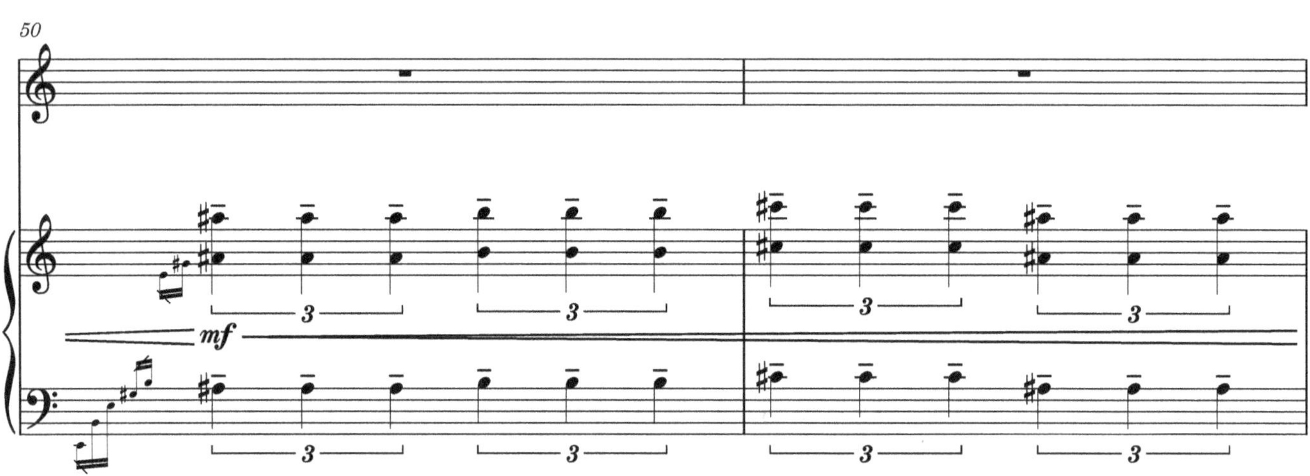

molto rall.

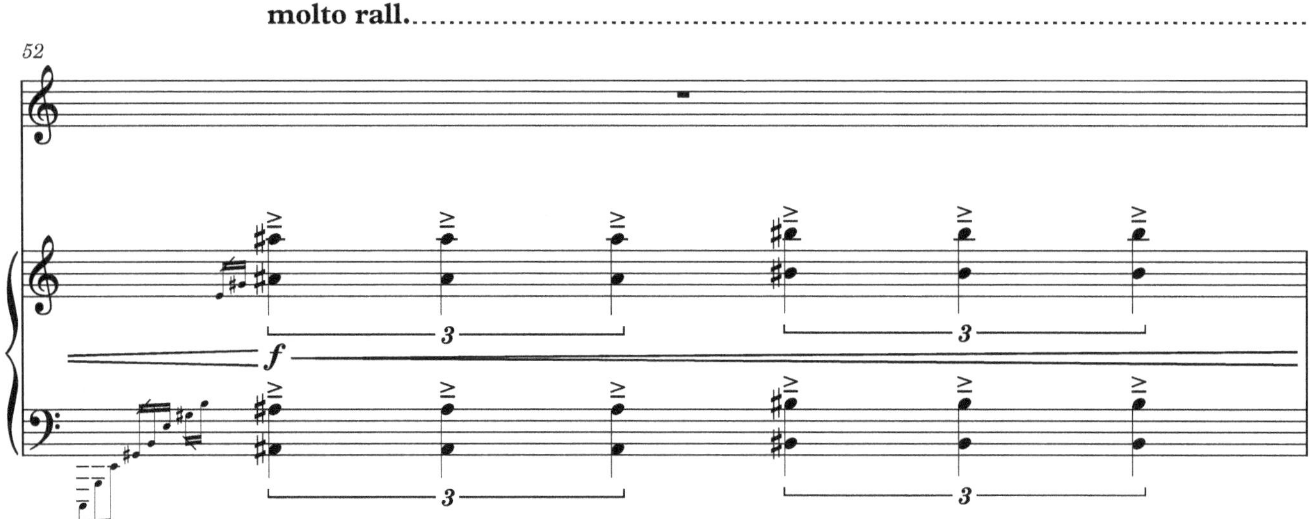

53
ff
Molto maestoso (𝅗𝅥 = 54)
54
f
It mat - ters not how strait the
fff
p
Ped.
56
gate,
How charged with
fff
(Ped.)

58
pun - - ish - ments the scroll,
p
(Ped.)
freely
ff
60
I am the mas - ter of my fate,
fff sempre colla voce
ff
fff
molto rall.
meno f
I am the
ffff
64
fff
cap - tain of my soul.
ff
fff
ffff

composed for songSLAM NYC II 2017

Oh Hell No

Maggie Smith

DENNIS TOBENSKI
(2017)

10
3
Cas - - - - - ual - ly
a
f.
8
3

13
p
OH
p

16
ff
HELL
NO.
ff

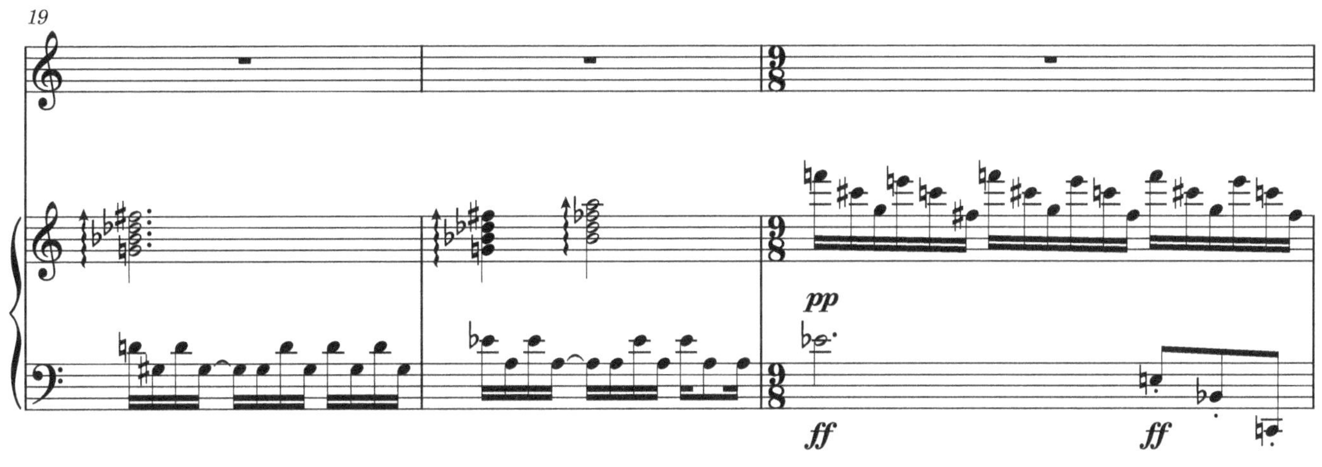
19
pp
ff
ff

22
pp
(ff)
8

24
fff
8
pp
fff

This page intentionally left blank to facilitate page turns

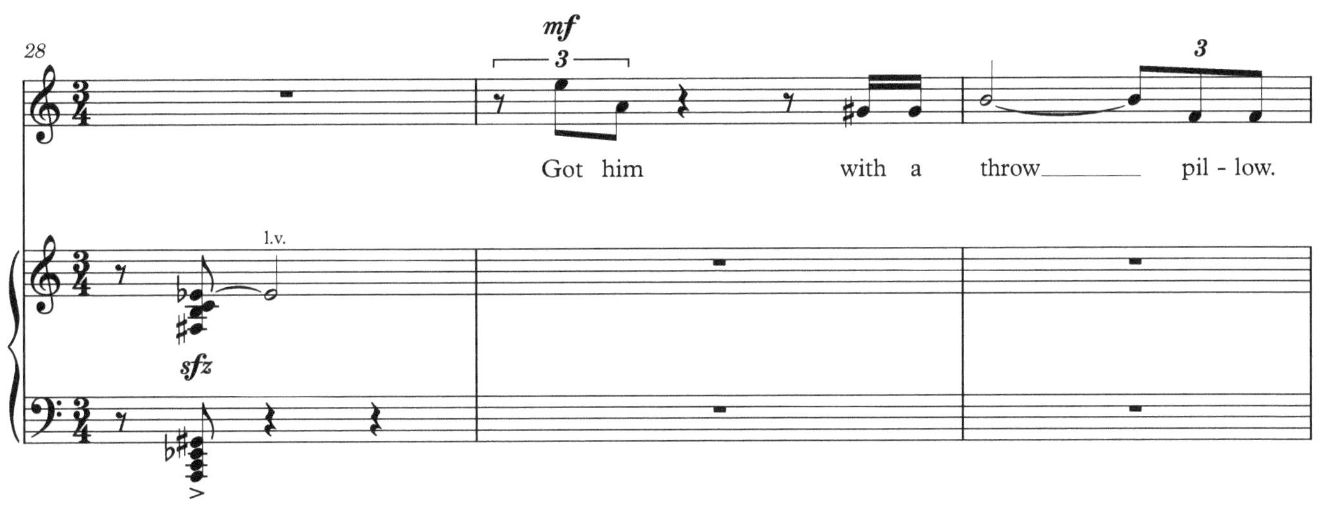
28
mf
3
3
Got him with a throw pil - low.
l.v.
sfz

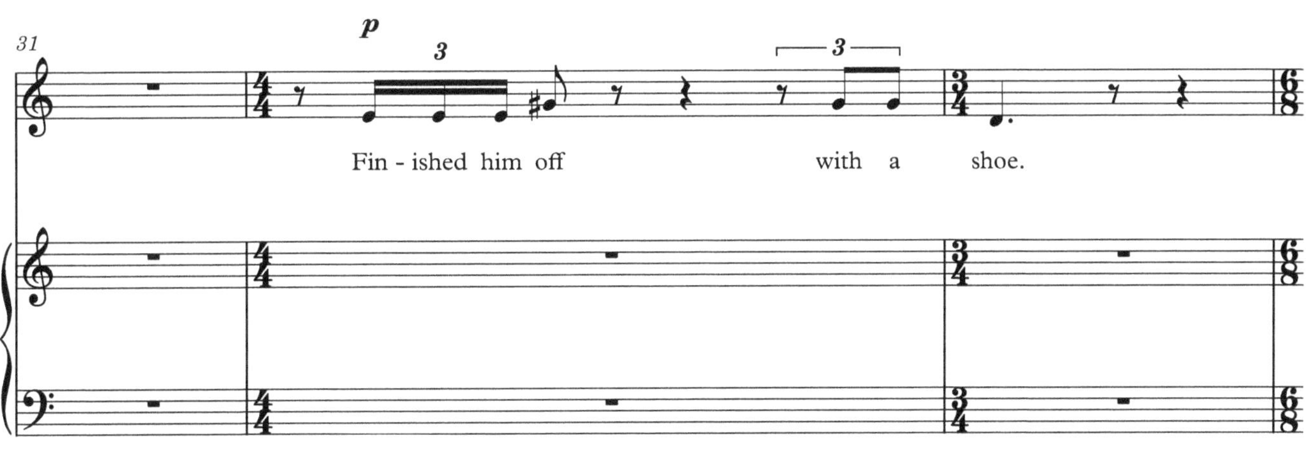
31
p
3
3
Fin - ished him off with a shoe.

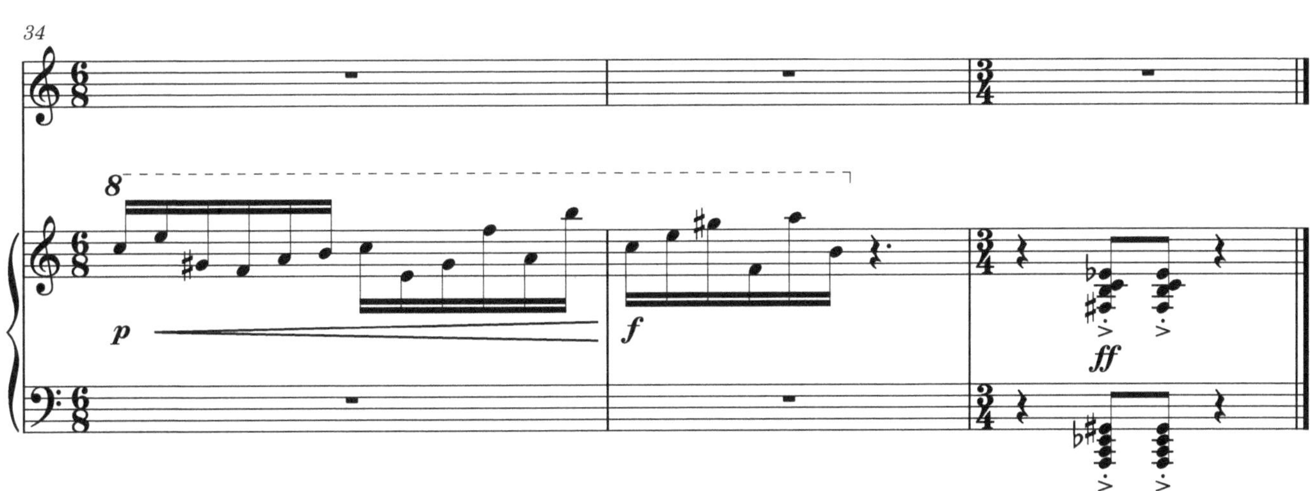
34
8
p
f
ff

for Kyle and Kateri
composed for songSLAM NYC II 2017

i carry your heart

E.E. Cummings

JASON WEISINGER
(2016)

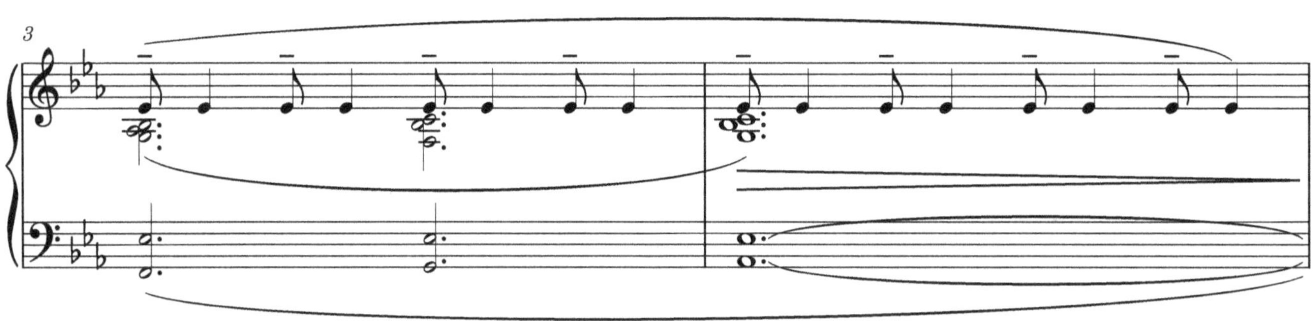

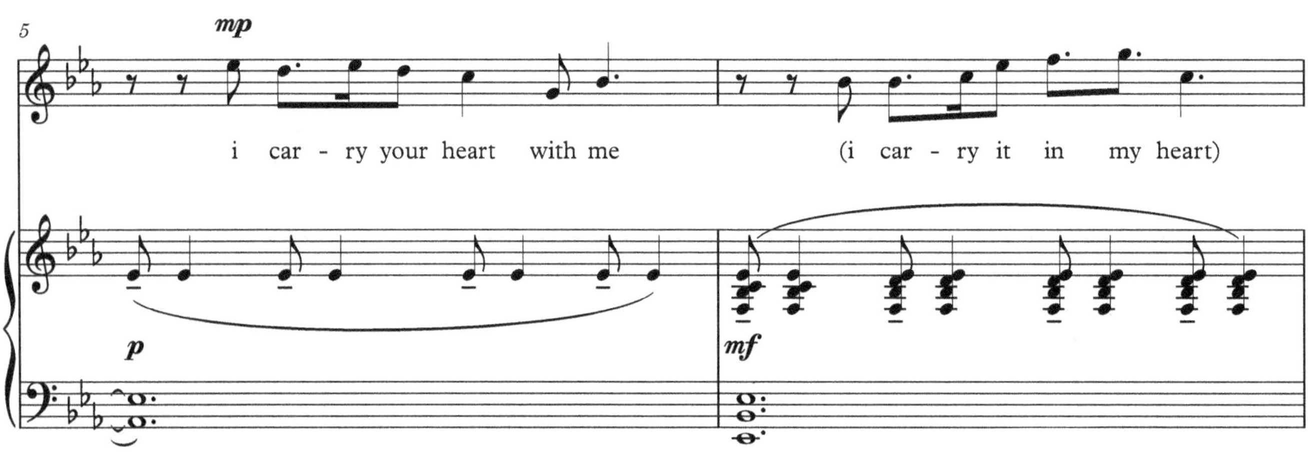

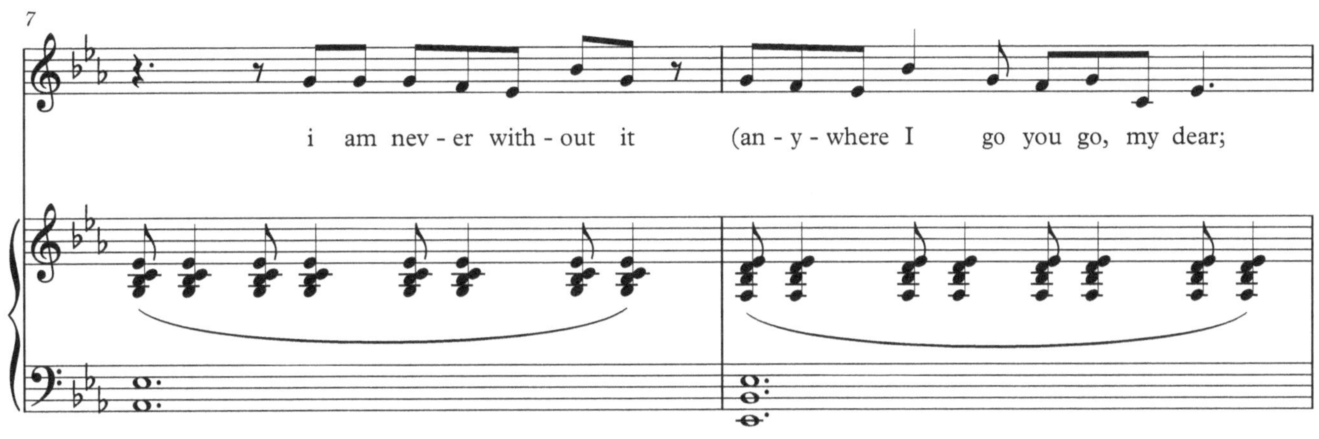
7
i am nev - er with - out it (an - y - where I go you go, my dear;

9
and what - ev - er is done by on - ly me is your do - ing, my dar - ling) i

11
fear no fate (for you are my
mf

12
fate, my sweet) i

13
want no world (for beau - ti - ful you are my

14
world, my true) and it's

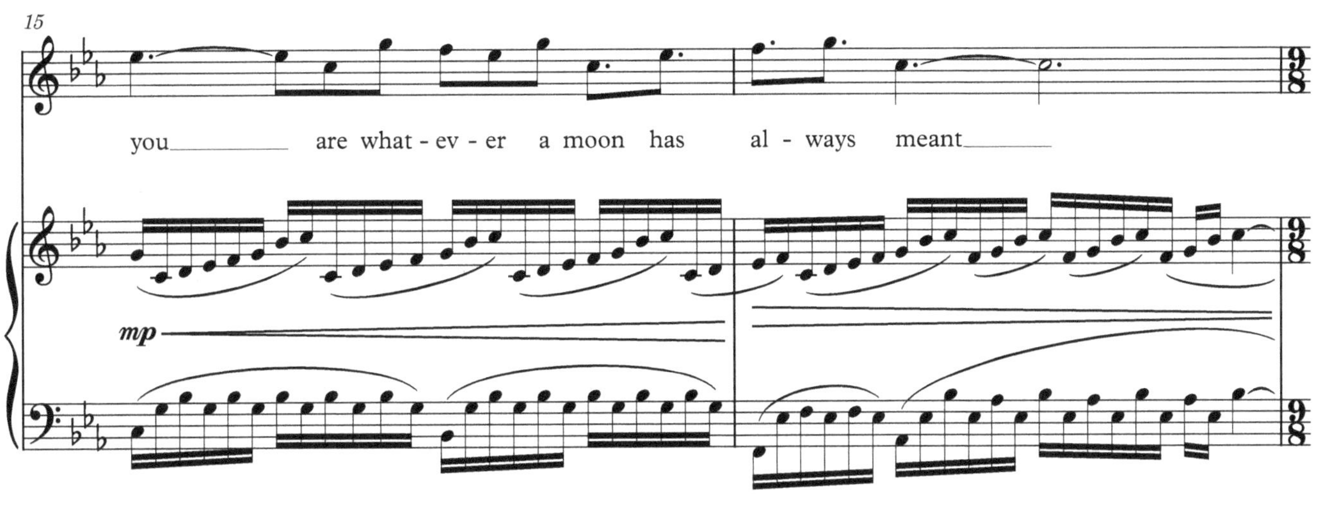
15
you are what - ev - er a moon has al - ways meant
mp

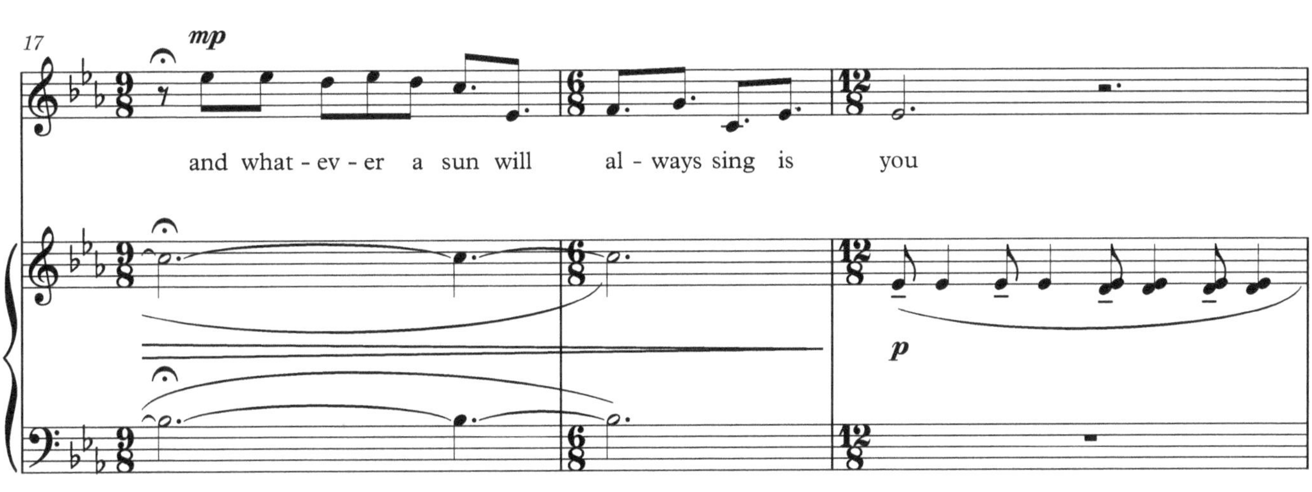
17
mp
and what - ev - er a sun will al - ways sing is you
p

20
here is the deep - est se - cret no - bod - y knows
mp

22
(here is the root of the root and the bud of the bud and the
mf

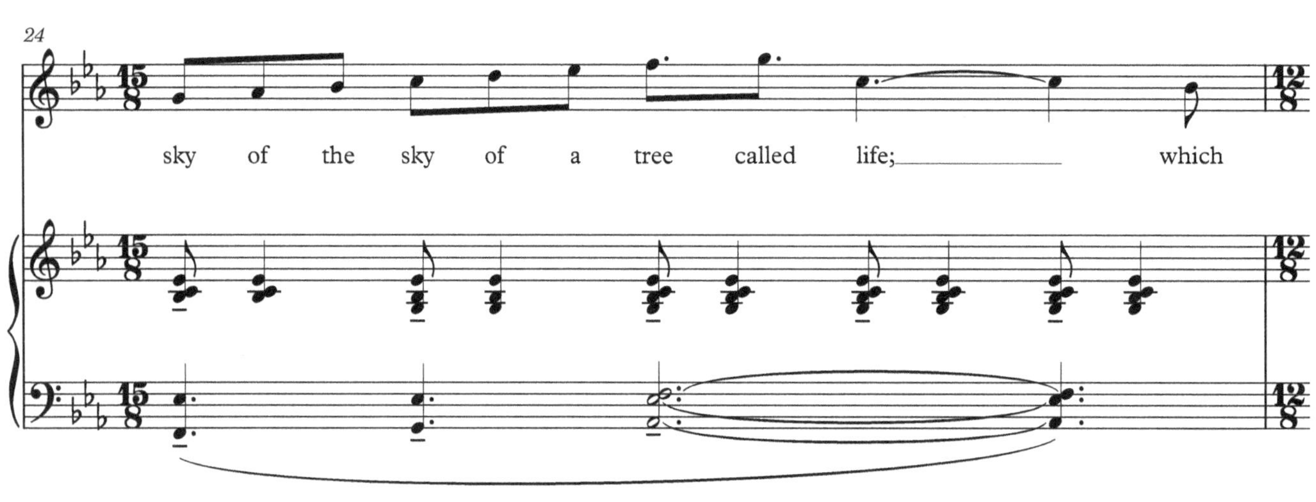
24
sky of the sky of a tree called life; which

25
grows high - er than soul can hope
f

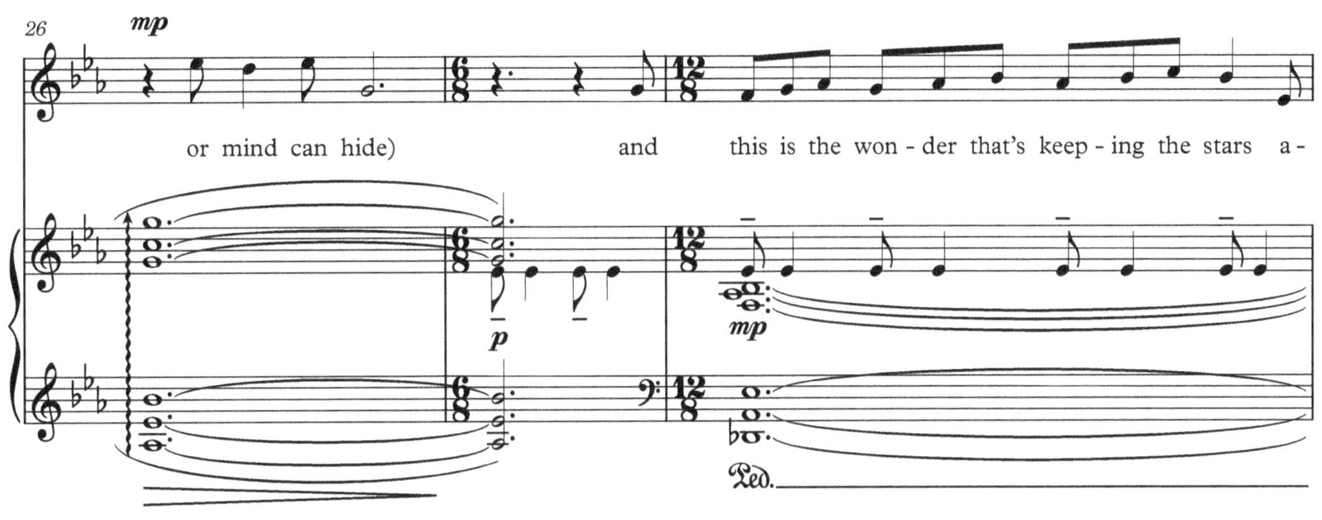

April 2016
Baldwin, NY

About the Curators

Martha Guth & Erika Switzer

www.marthaguth.com
www.erikaswitzer.com

Soprano Martha Guth and pianist Erika Switzer have been leading figures in the world of art song for over 20 years, delivering recitals around the world in places such as South Africa, Germany, Spain, France, England, and across North America. Guth and Switzer share a deep connection to the works of living composers: they have premiered dozens of new compositions, including works by Andrew Staniland, Tom Cipullo, and Juliana Hall, who have written new works for the duo.

Switzer and Guth are both accomplished artists on their own; Switzer has performed at New York's Weill Hall (Carnegie), the Kennedy Center, the Bard Music Festival, and the Spoleto Festival (Charleston, SC), among many other venues; while Guth has appeared regularly at London's Wigmore Hall, St. John's Smith Square, New York's Lincoln Center, and the Leeds Lieder Festival. Both have won numerous prizes and awards, and are prolific teachers: Guth is on the faculty of Ithaca College and SongFest, while Switzer is on the music faculty at Bard College and the Graduate Vocal Arts Program of the Bard College-Conservatory of Music.

Together, Guth and Switzer founded *Sparks & Wiry Cries*, a global platform dedicated to art song, spanning the publication, live performance, and commissioning of new works, in 2009.

About the Composers

Daniel Catellanos

b. 1995

dcastellanos725@gmail.com

Daniel Santiago Castellanos is a composer, singer, and pianist based in New Jersey. His first performed composition, *Eternal Light*, was labeled as “serene” and “attractively harmonized” by the *New York Times*. His most recent piece for mezzo-soprano and piano, *Death is nothing at all*, won first prize at the 2019 NYC songSLAM competition. Ensembles that have performed his music include the Semiosis Quartet, The Orchestra Now (TŌN), The Saint Thomas Choir of Men and Boys, and members of the Bard Conservatory Orchestra.

Soundcloud: https://soundcloud.com/dannycastellanos402633917

Abigail de Niverville (SOCAN)

b. 1993

abigail@adeniverville.com
www.adeniverville.com

Abigail de Niverville is an author, poet, and composer based in Toronto, Ontario. Born in Moncton, New Brunswick, Abigail draws inspiration from her experiences growing up on the East Coast in all her works. She holds a Master of Music from the University of Toronto, studying under Alexander Rapoport. Her debut novel *I Knew Him* was published by NineStar Press in 2019, and is available through most major book retailers. Recent musical works include *October 4th, 1993*, a one-woman mini-opera; *Letters*, for tenor and piano; and *Fragments*, for clarinet and piano.

Twitter: @adeniverville
Facebook: facebook.com/adeniverville

Natalie Draper (ASCAP)

b. 1985

drapernat@gmail.com
www.nataliedraper.net

Praised for her "individual and strong voice" (Colin Clarke, *Fanfare Magazine*), Natalie Draper explores character and evocative sound-worlds in her music. Her works have been performed at a variety of venues, including Roulette Intermedium, UC Davis, the Tanglewood Music Center, and the Canadian Opera Company. Her music has received honors and recognition--"Timelapse Variations" (2016) garnered positive reviews from Lydia Woolever in *Baltimore Magazine* ("dissonant melodies that build into a unified spiral"), Tim Smith in *The Baltimore Sun* (a "tense, darkly colorful churn"), and Mark Medwin in *Fanfare Magazine* ("... polyrhythm bolstering gorgeous pantonal harmonies and shards of chromatic counterpoint," while "...items burst forth, in a way that might make Mahler smile..."). In 2018, she remixed excerpts from "Timelapse Variations" for the background music of a short NASA film featuring the research of glaciologist Joe MacGregor. This video can be viewed in a variety of places, including Smithsonian Magazine. She has held residencies and fellowships at the Ucross Foundation (2010), the Tanglewood Music Center (2015), the I-Park Foundation (2018), and Yaddo (2019). She is an assistant professor in the music theory and composition department at the Setnor School of Music at Syracuse University.

Facebook: @drapernat
Twitter: @drapernat
Instagram: @drapernat13

Whitney George (ASCAP)

b. 1986

wegeorge@gmail.com
www.whitneygeorge.com

Whitney George's music traverses the affective terrain between tragedy and ecstasy, fragility and strength, bringing together romantically delicate intimacy and the spectacular darkness of the macabre. Her operas, staged multimedia works, and chamber music have had both international

and domestic premieres. George is the artistic director and conductor of The Curiosity Cabinet, a chamber orchestra formed in 2009. She holds an undergraduate degree from the California Institute of the Arts, a master's degree from Brooklyn College, and is currently a PhD candidate at the CUNY Graduate Center. In addition to her composing and conducting, George teaches at the Brooklyn College Conservatory of Music, works at the Hitchcock Institute of American Studies, and is on the composition faculty for Face the Music.

Instagram: @whitney.e.george
Twitter: @WhitTheCurious
Facebook: @WhitneyEGeorge

Wally Gunn (APRA/AMCOS)

b. 1971

wg@wallygunn.com
www.wallygunn.com

Wally Gunn is a composer whose work makes use of patterns and processes, and sometimes utilizes physical gesture and speech to heighten the theatricality of musical performance, creating music that is expressive and emotionally direct. His work often incorporates the extramusical themes of science and the natural world, as well as explorations of queer identity and experience. Hailing from rural Australia, Wally first played in rock bands, then attended Victorian College of the Arts in Melbourne, before moving to New York to study with Julia Wolfe at Manhattan School of Music, and then pursue a Ph.D. at Princeton University. Wally writes concert music and collaborates with theater makers and visual artists, and divides his time between New York, NY, USA and Castlemaine, VIC, Australia.

Instagram: @wallygunn
Facebook: @wallygunn

Meg Huskin (ASCAP)

b. 1995

meghuskin@gmail.com
www.meghuskin.com

Meg Huskin is a Chicago-based composer, vocalist, and writer. Her work embraces melody and the rhythms of language to tell stories that blur the boundary between modern and traditional themes. Recent performances of her work have taken place at the LunART Festival, Madison New Music Festival, and Chicago's inaugural songSLAM competition. She was commissioned by Lynx Project to create new work for their 2020 Autism Advocacy Series, a program which seeks to create music using poems written by young people with autism. She believes in the power of music and stories to create a more just and empathetic world, and much of her work aims to address issues of inequality and to magnify voices that have historically been underrepresented in classical music.

Meg graduated from the University of Wisconsin-Madison's Mead Witter School of Music where she majored in music composition, voice performance, and creative writing. As part of her senior thesis, she wrote a libretto based on an original story, *Fayaway*. She has studied with composers Gilda Lyons, Laura Schwendinger, Stephen Dembski, and others. She has participated in New Amsterdam Record's Composing Workshop, the Wintergreen Composer's Retreat and the From-Page-to-Stage Emerging Composers program. Her choral work "They Tore Down the Church" won the Mullins Sacred Music Prize in 2016.

Meg remains an active singer, having studied with soprano Mimmi Fulmer. Whenever she can, she supports Chicago's storefront opera community in ensemble roles, or technical support. As a writer, her articles have been published by I Care if You Listen.com and Lyric Opera of Chicago's program books.

Feliz Jarrar

b. 1995

fjarrar@marlboro.edu
www.felixjarrarmusic.com

Brooklyn-based Felix Jarrar is a composer and pianist with "(strong) dramatic instincts" (Lewis Spratlan, 2000 Pulitzer Prizewinner in Music). His works have been praised as "experimental and beautifully composed" (*Broadway World*) with "lush and memorable melodies" (*Operawire*). His list of accomplishments includes performances at diverse venues such as Symphony Space, (le) poisson rouge, Feinstein's/54 below, the BAM! Fisher Hillman Studio, Roulette Intermedium, and Carnegie Hall's Weill Recital Hall. His works have been performed internationally by members of the Metropolitan Opera Orchestra and Chorus, the Atlantic Music Festival Orchestra, and the duo Unassisted Fold. At the forefront of Jarrar's compositional output are his works for voice. Amongst his approximately 75 works, he has written over 50 art songs, five operas, and a cantata. Jarrar completed his Bachelor of Arts from Marlboro College with Highest Honors in Music Composition with Stanley Charkey and Matan Rubinstein and Piano Performance with Robert Merfeld and Luis Battle. He received his Master of Music degree from Brooklyn College with the Graduate Dean's Award in Music Composition on the Eleanor Kilcoyne, Cerf Music, and Chancey Memorial Scholarships. He primarily studied with Wang Jie, Tania León, and Jason Eckardt while holding the prestigious graduate fellowship for assisting ConTempo, Ursula Oppens' contemporary ensemble in the conservatory. He was mentored as a teenager by piano pedagogue Burton Hatheway.

Instagram: @the_original_fefe
Twitter: @FJComposer

Laurence Jobidon (SOCAN)

b. 1992

www.laurencejobidon.ca

Quebecois composer and organist, Laurence Jobidon studied at the Conservatoire de Musique de Québec and further trained in composition with Andrew P. MacDonald. Winner of the 2015 New Generation Orchestra Composition Competition for her piece « Le Harfang et Le Loup » and of the 2018 Prix Trois femmes - Mécénat Musica with Pascale St-Onge, librettist, for their chamber opera « L'hiver attend beaucoup de moi », Laurence has written for a variety of ensembles (solo, vocal, chamber, orchestral...). Her music has notably been performed at Opéra de Montréal, the Canadian Opera Company Noon-Concert Series, the SMCQ and the 28th International Review of Composers.

Isaac Lovdahl (ASCAP)

b. 1993

isaac@isaaclovdahl.com
www.isaaclovdahl.com

Isaac Lovdahl is a composer, conductor, educator, and vocalist currently based in Fargo, ND. After graduating with a B.M. in Vocal Music Education from Concordia College (Moorhead) in 2015, he spent four years directing high school, church, and community choirs across Minnesota. He is now pursuing a Master's of Music in Choral Conducting at North Dakota State University, and working as director of music at Lutheran Church of Christ the King in Moorhead, MN. His music has been performed in the United States, Germany, and Great Britain by high school, community, and professional ensembles and soloists. Lovdahl has sung as a chorus member and featured soloist with The Concordia Choir, The Singers - Minnesota Choral Artists, Minnesota Beethoven Festival Chorale, Oratory Bach Ensemble (Bach Roots Festival), Vox Nova Chorale, imPulse (MPLS), and Great River Chorale. His music can be found online through Santa Barbara Music Publishing, Graphite Publishing (VocalEssence Music Press), MusicSpoke, and his own website: isaaclovdahl.com. When not composing or busy with another musical engagement, he enjoys riding his bike, reading poetry, watching or playing a good game of basketball, and staying up too late.

Liam Moore (ASCAP)

b. 1989

liammusicmoore@gmail.com
www.liammusicmoore.com

Liam Moore is a composer, baritone and lover of language. He primarily writes chamber music, choral music and art song.

Liam took an early and earnest interest in music and as a child his parents signed him up for a local youth choir. This did nothing to cut down on the noise around the house, but certainly made his singing more tolerable. The music Liam writes can trace its roots to his mom's piano playing, his dad's record collection and countless hours of 16-bit video game music.

In addition to singing and composing, he generally plays stringed instruments well. Liam loves to learn, enjoys traveling and begrudgingly meets the minimum recommended amount of weekly physical activity.

Haley Olson

b. 1993

haleyolsoncomposer@gmail.com

Haley Olson is a composer, pianist and vocalist based in Minnesota. As a composer, she has written works that have been programmed and performed by ensembles and festivals such as the Occasional Symphony, the ECCE Ensemble the Space City New Music Festival, and the Sparks and Wiry Cries songSLAM. Haley holds degrees in composition from St. Olaf College, where she studied with Justin Merritt and Timothy Mahr, and the Peabody Institute, where she studied with Michael Hersch and Du Yun. As a performer, Haley has provided incidental music for improv and theatrical shows in Baltimore and the Twin Cities. She was the Composer-In-Residence for Brown Memorial Park Avenue Presbyterian Church in Baltimore from 2017 through 2019. An educator and advocate for teaching musical skills to students of all ages, she has worked with mentorship projects such as Baltimore's Junior Bach program and currently directs the children's choir and theory program at St. John the Evangelist Episcopal church in St. Paul.

Facebook: @h.elizabethmusic
Twitter: @theritenotes
Instagram: @theritenotes
Soundcloud: www.soundcloud.com/h-elizabeth-1

Nathan Scalise (BMI)

b. 1993

nathan.scalise@gmail.com
nathanscalise.squarespace.com

Nathan Scalise blends the rhythmic drive of rock, direct expression of folk, formal considerations of classical music, and ecstatic emotion of gospel into an accessible and individual compositional voice. Significant musical influences include the piano playing and singing of Nina Simone, and person-specific writing of Duke Ellington, as well as the soundworld of U2 and the song cycles of Schubert. His music has been awarded by NYC SongSLAM (2019 First Prize), Fifteen Minutes of Fame, and Dolce Suono Ensemble (2017 Steven Stucky Young Composers Competition), and performed professionally by artists including Contemporaneous, the Momenta Quartet, the Ajax Quartet, Hub New Music, 3G Percussion, Jacqueline Horner-Kwiatek (mezzo-soprano), Modern Medieval Trio, Jordan Bowman (soprano), Andrew Fuchs (tenor), Paul Neebe (trumpet), Ithaca New Music Collective, Opera Elect, and Orchestra 2001. He has also received performances by student orchestras, wind ensembles, chamber ensembles, vocal ensembles, and jazz ensembles at Swarthmore College and Binghamton University.

In addition to compositional activities, Nathan performs frequently as a trombonist, pianist/keyboardist, and drummer. He holds an M.M. in Composition from Binghamton University, where he studied composition with Daniel Thomas Davis and trombone with Don Robertson, as well as B.A.s in Music and Economics from Swarthmore College, where he studied composition with Gerald Levinson, trombone with Paul Arbogast, and piano with Hans Lüdemann. Raised in Brewster, Massachusetts, on Cape Cod, when not doing something musical, he is likely to be running, playing basketball, or cheering loudly for Boston sports teams.

Tilen Slakan (SAZAS)

b. 1993

tilen.slakan@gmail.com

Tilen SLAKAN is a Slovenian composer who started his musical path in the primary music school »Risto Savin« in Zalec where he played trumpet and piano. He continued playing the trumpet in the Artistic Music High School Velenje in the class of David Spec. At that time he also became very interested in composing and he got much help and encouragement from his teacher Slavko Suklar. He decided to continue his studies of trumpet and composition at the Academy of Music in Ljubljana, where he graduated in the class of Stanko Arnold. He finished his Master studies of theoretical-musical pedagogy and composition under Marko Mihevc. At the moment he is studying musical theory and composition for his PhD Degree under the supervision of Andrej Misson.

He regularly works with various orchestras (The Slovene Philharmonic String Chamber Orchestra, Slovene Philharmonic Symphony orchestra, Woodwinds Orchestra Zarja Šoštanj, Slovenian Police Orchestra, the Academy's Symphony Orchestra, String Chamber Orchestra "Camerata Laibach", Fran Korun Koželjski Velenje Symphony Orchestra, Risto Savin Žalec Symphony Orchestra, Brass Band Slovenia, Tambourine Orchestra "Tamburjaši", etc.), chamber groups (SToP – Slovenian Percussion Project, the Academy's Brass ensemble, Goodivas String Quartet, Dissonance String Quartet, RojoTango Orchestra, Piano Trio "Trio Liberte", the Academy's Trumpet ensemble and Percussion Studio, etc.), choirs (the Academy's Chamber Choir, Tone Tomšič Academic Choir, Mixed Choir Tabor, Women's Choir ČarniCe, Chamber Choir Orfej, etc.) and soloists (Stanko Arnold, Petra Vidmar, Nikola Pajanović, Jure Gradišnik, Sanja Zupanič, etc.).

Evan L. Snider (ASCAP)

b. 1991

tenorelsnyder@gmail.com
www.evanlsnyder.com

Throughout his body of work, Evan L. Snyder is unified in his dedication to storytelling. A winner of the 2017 Fort Worth Opera Frontiers Competition, his first opera, *A Capacity for Evil*, broke with conventional genres, telling a Holmesian detective tale on the operatic stage. The opera premiered fall 2018, with Detroit's Opera MODO and was enthusiastically received by the run's sold-out audiences. Evan's second operatic project, *The Clef of the Universe*, is a science fiction opera, following a group of archeologist crash-landed on an alien world. An aria excerpted from the new work was previewed at Constellation Chicago, during the 2019 Fresh Inc Festival.

Evan's interest in novel storytelling carries over to his work outside of opera as well. His musical portrait of a friend, *Theme Song for Dan Carty*, has received several performances, including as winner of the 2018 Detroit REVIVAL Project, as well as by the Fifth House Ensemble at the 2019 Red Note Festival. He has also received commissions from both Fifth House and the Lansing-based Contempus Initiative, including for his *Disappearing Landscapes*, a children's work exploring the impact of humanity on nature, which premiered on the 2018 Lansing Symphony's Family Series.

Storytelling a more well-trodden road, Evan has composed numerous songs, along with two full-length song cycles. His first cycle, *Ulysses*, a setting of Tennyson's dramatic monologue, was premiered in 2018 by Richard Fracker and Elden Little, and has also since been featured at the 2019 Source Song Festival. His second cycle, *Dynamic Roads*, is a work dealing with themes of moving and aging, which was created in collaboration with poet Peter Faziani. The work premiered May 2019, with bass-baritone Joseph Baunoch.

Dennis Tobenski (ASCAP)

b. 1982

dennis@dennistobenski.com
dennistobenski.com

Dennis Tobenski is a composer of acoustic new music, a vocalist, and a strong advocate for new music and the interests of living composers.

Dennis's *Only Air*, a 20-minute work for high voice and orchestra memorializing the gay teenagers who have taken their own lives in recent years, was commissioned by the Illinois State University Symphony Orchestra, and has been performed in a chamber version by The Secret Opera in New York and members of the Bay Area Rainbow Symphony in San Francisco.

In 2016 he released his debut album in collaboration with pianist Marc Peloquin: *And He'll Be Mine*, a disc of art songs by living American composers.

He is also the founder of NewMusicShelf, an online marketplace for independently-published composers to sell digital editions of their works. In 2018, he published the first four volumes of the *NewMusicShelf Anthologies of New Music*: four voice type-specific collections of art songs by living composers from around the world. The series has expanded to include current and upcoming volumes for flute, clarinet, alto saxophone, bassoon, horn, trumpet, tuba, piano, violin, and viola. The newly-launched *NewMusicShelf Signature Series* will include the *Sparks & Wiry Cries songSLAM Songbook, Vol. 1*, Jenny Lin's *Etudes Project, Vol. 1*, *The Lost Songs of the AIDS Quilt Songbook*, *The Lynx Project Songbook*, and Laura Strickling's *40@40 Art Song Project.*

Dennis received his B.Mus. in Vocal Performance and Music Theory & Composition from Illinois State University, and his M.A. in Music Composition from The City College of New York.

His principal teachers have included David Del Tredici, Chester Biscardi, and David Feurzeig. He is a member of the Board of Advisors for Composers Now, and the Board of Directors of New Music Recordings and the KeyedUp MusicProject. Dennis lives in New York City with his husband Darien Scott Shulman and their cat Pistachio.

Jason Weisinger (BMI)

b. 1988

jason.weisinger@gmail.com
www.jasonweisinger.com

Jason Weisinger is a GRAMMY-nominated multi-disciplinary artist based out of Brooklyn, NY. His music has been performed extensively throughout NYC in venues such as HERE Arts Center, The BMI Lehman Engel Musical Theater Workshop, Park Avenue Synagogue, The Duplex, and The DiMenna Center for Classical Music. In addition to composing, Jason has enjoyed success in a wide variety of repertoire as a vocalist. Highlights include a double bill of "Dido and Aeneas" (Sailor) & "Curlew River" (ensemble) with the Mark Morris Dance Group at the Brooklyn Academy of Music, a workshop of Ricky Ian Gordon's opera "Intimate Apparel" (Mr. Marks) with The Metropolitan Opera, and The Boston POPS revue "Simply Sondheim". He was a finalist in the 2016 Joy in Singing art song competition. As a choral artist, Jason has sung with ensembles such as GRAMMY-winning choir The Crossing, the GRAMMY-nominated Choir of Trinity Wall Street, the New York Philharmonic Orchestra, the American Symphony Orchestra, the American Classical Orchestra, and the Bard SummerScape Festival. Jason frequently serves as music director during the development and performance of many musicals including "The Ninth Hour" (MetLiveArts @ The Cloisters), "RUTH" (The Goodman Theatre), "Fora" (Eugene O'Neill Theater Center), and "The Cherry Orchard" (Jonathan Larson Foundation). Jason has studied and performed at the BMI Lehman Engel Musical Theater Advanced Workshop, Tanglewood Music Center, Fall Island Vocal Arts Seminar, Brevard Music Center, SongFest, New Music on the Point, Rocky Ridge Music Center, University of Cincinnati - College Conservatory of Music, SUNY Fredonia, and The New School for Jazz and Contemporary Music.

Instagram: @jasonweisinger
Soundcloud: JasonWeisinger

Supplementary Materials

Texts, program notes, composer biographies, and composer headshots can be found at:

https://newmusicshelf.com/anthologies/songslam-v1-info/

www.ingramcontent.com/pod-product-compliance
Lightning Source LLC
Chambersburg PA
CBHW081329090426
42737CB00017B/3060

9781949614077